Your prayers are changing the face of our ... for Jesus Christ,

I love Ya! Tom Sahma

Rom 12:11

Stories for a teen's Heart

book 3

Books in the Stories for the Heart Collection

Gift Books by Alice Gray

What teens are saying about this book

I love these stories! Each one has its own special way of helping me reflect on my life and faith. When I was in need of encouragement, this book really helped.

Monica Bethel, age 17

The stories are not only exciting and fun to read, but also heart touching and inspiring. No matter what type of mood I am in, I can pick up this book and get carried away by the stories. They dare me to experience the awesome presence of God's ultimate love and power.

Lauren Statton, age 15

This book has it all—from making me want to cry with joy to making me want to go help people. It is one of the best teen books out there.

Nathan Teeny, age 17

This book made me get more in touch with myself and everyone around me. I enjoyed it more than words can say.

Cherylyne Madsen, age 14

I'm not much of a reader, but this book is one I couldn't put down.

Eric Schwickerath, age 17

These stories are inspiring, and they've brought me closer to God. There's a story for every situation in our daily lives. I'd definitely recommend this book to all teens.

Heather Schwarzbury, age 17

These stories lifted my spirits when I was down, convicted my heart when I was wrong, and opened my eyes more to the ways in which God works. This book rocks!

Wil Hansen, age 16

I enjoyed reading these stories because they touched my life and helped me see things in a new perspective.

Aby Martin, age 14

This book speaks to the youth of this generation in a voice of honesty, creativity, and sincerity. I enjoyed the stories and would strongly encourage others to read them and find the happiness that I found in them.

Julia Flores, age 17

What teens are saying about other books in the stories for the Heart series

I started to read Stories for a Teen's Heart and just couldn't put it down!
It now ranks very high on my best-books-I've-ever-read scale.
Wendi

I really love the book and have already read it twice!
Tiffany

This book has made me laugh and cry and look at my relationship with God.
Jessica

These stories really made me think about my life in general and where it is now.
Andy

I have never read a better collection of "on fire" stories!
Each one touches and convicts your heart to the core!
Sarah

I like these stories. They're true and encouraging—some made me cry.
Lisa

What a great book! I have really enjoyed it!
I get closer to God every time I read another story.
Ann

The stories were so good. I have been through a lot of the same things.
Jami

I like the fact that the stories are about real people—they aren't fake.
They inspire me to live a better life for God.
Christy

They were very touching stories!
Rachel

Stories for the Extreme Teen's Heart is the best book I've ever read, and it has
had a big impact on me. I thank the people who wrote their stories to help teens.
Pete

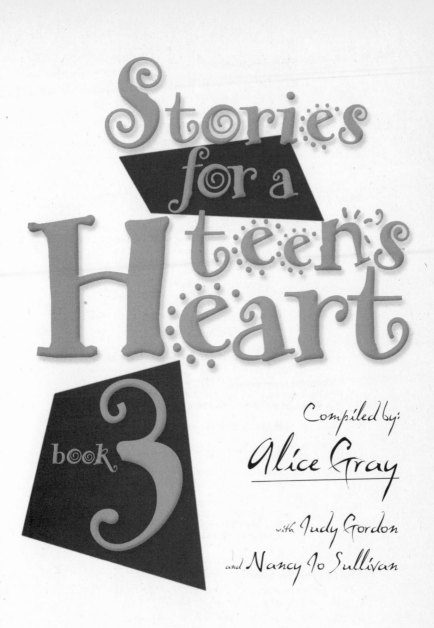

Stories for a teen's Heart

book 3

Compiled by:
Alice Gray

with Judy Gordon
and Nancy Jo Sullivan

Multnomah®Publishers *Sisters, Oregon*

STORIES FOR A TEEN'S HEART, BOOK 3
published by Multnomah Publishers, Inc.

© 2002 by Multnomah Publishers, Inc.
International Standard Book Number: 1-57673-974-0

Cover image by Digital Vision
Back cover image by Steve Gardner
Interior illustrations by Chaz Chapman
Interior icons by Elizabeth Haidle
Interior photos by PhotoDisc and Steve Gardner

Please see the acknowledgments at the back of the book for complete
attribution for material used in this book.

Unless otherwise indicated, Scripture quotations are from:
The Holy Bible, New International Version
© 1973, 1984 by International Bible Society,
used by permission of Zondervan Publishing House

Other Scripture quotations:
The Holy Bible, New King James Version (NKJV)
© 1984 by Thomas Nelson, Inc.
New American Standard Bible® (NASB) © 1960, 1977, 1995
by the Lockman Foundation. Used by permission.

Stories for the Heart is a trademark of Multnomah Publishers
and is registered in the U.S. Patent and Trademark Office.

Multnomah is a trademark of Multnomah Publishers, Inc.,
and is registered in the U.S. Patent and Trademark Office.
The colophon is a trademark of Multnomah Publishers, Inc.

Printed in the United States of America

ALL RIGHTS RESERVED
No part of this publication may be reproduced, stored in a retrieval system, or transmitted,
in any form or by any means—electronic, mechanical, photocopying, recording,
or otherwise—without prior written permission.

For information:
MULTNOMAH PUBLISHERS, INC.
POST OFFICE BOX 1720
SISTERS, OREGON 97759

Library of Congress Cataloging-in-Publication Data:
Stories for a teen's heart, book 3 / compiled by Alice Gray.
  p. cm.
  ISBN 1-57673-646-6 (alk. paper)
  ISBN 1-57673-797-7 (alk. paper)
  ISBN 1-57673-974-0
1. Teenagers—Religious life Anecdotes 2. Teenagers—Conduct of
life Anecdotes.   I. Gray, Alice, 1939–
BV4531.2.S83   1999
242'.63—dc21   99-40435
                                              CIP

02 03 04 05 06 07 08—10 9 8 7 6 5 4 3 2

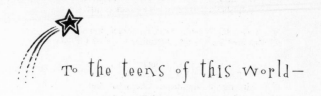

To the teens of this world—

Your light is brighter than you know.

You are a beacon of faith,

A lantern of love,

A candle of hope.

It's your time to shine!

A Special thank you to...

Ashley Blake
What a treasure you are! There are simply no words to express
our heartfelt gratitude for all your hard work.

The authors
You are the stars of this book.
The stories you have written are indescribably wonderful.

Jennifer Gates and Gayle Vickery
This book wouldn't have happened without your diligent
efforts in gathering permissions.

Doreen Button, Casandra Lindell, Erika Poston, and Lenette Stroebel
You are skilled treasure hunters. You sifted and sorted through stories,
and you unearthed the jewels.

Chaz Chapman
You have captured life in cartoon art. Thanks for making us smile!

Steve Gardner
You've done it again! Thank you for an extraordinary cover and interior design.

Cherylyne Macben, Heather Schwarzburg, Lauren Statton, Monica Bethel, Julia Flores, Wil Hansen, Aby Martin, Eric Schwickerath, Nathan Teeny
You chose stories that will speak to teens' hearts.
Because of you, this is not just an incredible book—it's a gift to your generation.

To our readers
We see the hurts and hopes of today's teens.
Your stories…your lives…your dreams…inspire us.

Contents

Yeah, You Make a Difference

Wanna Be Like You

Forever Friends

You Know What's Right

Hang in There

Love's All in the Family

With You All the Way

Another Chance

Worth Thinkin' About

It's a God Thing

Yeah, You Make a Difference

A Portrait of Me

Creative, sensitive.

Lover of

God, chocolate, and sunny days.

Who feels brave, scared, joyful.

Who needs friendship, encouragement, and acceptance.

Who gives notes, smiles, and bouquets of dandelions.

Who would like to see every orphan adopted

And every wrong righted.

LACEY BARNHOUSE, AGE 16

(Pictured here, Lacey was killed by a reckless driver on May 11, 2001.)

The Christmas I Got Rich

JACOB ANDREW SHEPHERD
AGE 13

When you live in a small town, shopping at a real mall can be a big deal, especially for my mom. When I was thirteen, my mom and I were in Portland at Christmastime. It was a Saturday, and the mall was packed with decorations and merchandise and people, and I loved it. My pockets were stuffed with cash—some of it I had earned, and some had come from distant relatives who thought that I would be better at picking out my gifts than they were. I had already done most of my Christmas shopping for my family and was looking forward to spending the whole wad on some cool clothes or maybe a video game.

My mom is the ultimate shopping partner. She was as excited as I was. She loves the holiday scents, the music, and, of course, the neat stuff you just don't find in our small town. Mostly, though, she loves people. She has a way of seeing past the clothing or makeup and seeing the real person. On this December trip to the mall, she saw Carla.

Carla was the type of girl that most people would look at out of the corner of their eye and then turn away. She had on old, worn-out clothes, black makeup, and no coat. She was only a teen, but the bitterness and pain etched on her face made her look much older.

Mom sat down right next to Carla. "Are you okay?"

"I'm fine," Carla mumbled without looking up.

Lots of times people answer like that, no matter how they feel. It didn't stop my mom. She lovingly persisted until Carla told her what was really wrong.

Tears began to stream down her face as Carla poured out her past. She knew nothing about her real parents and had been in and out of foster homes all her life. When she turned eighteen, her last set of foster parents kicked her out because they no longer received government money to keep her. She was homeless and without a coat—living under a bridge—venturing into the mall for warmth and discarded food scraps. Mom could sense that there was more and kept asking questions. Carla burst into tears and told how she had given up her newborn baby for adoption the day before. She couldn't afford to marry her boyfriend, let alone care for a baby.

About this time a young man walked up. Right away you could tell that he was with Carla. His clothes were tattered, and he was obviously not dressed for the Northwest winter. Rich shifted uncomfortably on his worn-out sneakers while Carla explained that he was also a foster kid who had been kicked out at age eighteen. Rich and Carla had been living under the bridge for quite some time.

I couldn't imagine what it must feel like not to have parents who love and care for you. I never had to worry if I was going to have a next meal or clothing to wear. My biggest problem was keeping all my clothes off the floor in my room.

As I listened to these unfortunate teenagers share through bitter and lonely tears, the pull that the mall had on me started to change. My heart sank, and my enthusiasm for more "stuff" sank with it. What could we do? Should we pray for Carla and Rich? Give them some encouragement and send them on their way?

What Mom and I did for the next two hours will always be burned in my memory. We went shopping all right, but we went with two new friends, Carla and Rich. You should have seen the look on their faces when Mom and I escorted them straight to Nordstrom Rack (where you can get last season's designer clothes for cheap). They gasped. "We've never been in a store like this!"

Mom grabbed Carla's hand and headed straight for the women's section, while Rich and I looked at men's clothing. "Those pants look great on you,"

I said, as Rich stepped out of the dressing room. "Are you sure that jacket's gonna be warm enough?"

After Rich and I picked out his jacket, pants, and a shirt, we joined Mom and watched Carla model her clothes. Her faced beamed as we rooted her on. Mom and I never had so much fun shopping!

We headed for the cash register, and my mom dug into her purse. I quietly stopped her, patting my pocket of cash. "Thanks, Mom, but I have it this time."

So, what did I get for Christmas that year? I'd say I got Rich…a friend named Rich.

To accomplish great things,
we must not only act,
but also dream;
not only plan,
but also believe.

ANATOLE FRANCE

In an Old, Battered Van

KATHERINE OPP

I was sprawled on my stomach on the church floor, concentrating on the picture forming beneath my hands. Should I add an extra tulip to the bouquet in my picture?

"What should I draw?" a young voice inquired. I leaned over to face six-year-old Adrianna beside me. With tiny fingers she pushed her brown bangs back from her eyes and smiled a smile that would have stolen the heart of the crabbiest old crone. Her eight-year-old sister, Holly, was nearby, busily scribbling on her paper. They were among the seven kids who had come for vacation Bible school that cloudy Monday morning.

"Why don't you draw your house?" I asked Adrianna. She looked at me in bewilderment. "We don't have a house," she said. "We live in a truck."

My close friend Erin and I exchanged puzzled glances. Was this just the wild imagination of a six-year-old, or was it true?

A little investigation proved Adrianna's claim. After talking with the church pianist, I discovered Adrianna and Holly's family had appeared in town two weeks ago. They lived with their parents and their two dogs in an old, battered van. The church was paying for them to stay in the trailer park across town while their father found work picking fruit in area orchards.

Now I knew why Adrianna's shoes were too small and why Holly wore only sandals even on chilly days. I could understand why their clothes were worn-out and shabby.

As I talked with them during the week, I discovered their mother was teaching them to read. Always on the go, the girls had never attended school and had never formed any long-lasting friendships with other children. That explained their timidity during playtime. Rather than joining in the games, they preferred to sit on the sidelines and watch.

But they did get very close to me. When our group went to the elementary school grounds to use the baseball field, the three of us would stay at the playground. I pushed Adrianna and Holly around and around on the tire swing until I was dizzy from watching them, yet they always pleaded for more pushes. They'd take turns sitting securely in my lap on the slide. I gave piggyback rides. We played hopscotch and "house."

Adrianna and Holly's version of "house" was sitting in the wooden playground Jeep suspended by springs. The game consisted of stopping at different places. The game said a lot about the life these girls lived. They knew nothing of having a bed, a bathroom, or kitchen.

When I'd read them Bible stories during our teaching time, I never knew how much of the stories they grasped. But both girls were quiet and happy when allowed to sit in a lap. One afternoon, Adrianna handed me a little plastic comb she had won earlier that day for answering a question. During the Bible story, Adrianna sat without moving a muscle as I patiently worked through the snarls in her long brown hair. For twenty minutes she absorbed each stroke as though she had never experienced such unhurried care.

On Friday night, the last evening of our vacation Bible school, I met Mr. and Mrs. Portz, Adrianna and Holly's parents. Mr. Portz was friendly enough, but Mrs. Portz seemed distant and withdrawn. She didn't talk much and sat in a corner with a plate of refreshments, eating as though it were her last meal. She laughed nervously and didn't meet my eyes once. At the end of the mealtime, Mr. Portz painstakingly saved some leftover cookies and cake in a plastic bag.

After the night's events, I walked with them over to their dirty, beat-up van. As I approached, a German shepherd stuck its head out the window and growled at me. Mr. Portz shouted a command and the animal disappeared. Before they drove off, Mr. Portz pressed a plastic bag into my hands.

"They're good plums," he told me. "I just got them this morning. Picked them myself. We'll get more soon."

The plums looked overripe and bruised, but I knew it was his way of saying, "Thank you for what you did this week. Thank you for loving my girls."

I boosted the girls into the back of the van as Mr. Portz tried to get it started. The motor groaned and coughed, then finally turned over. As they drove out of the gravel driveway, I saw Adrianna and Holly waving with all their might through the side of the window.

Tears stung my eyes. Tonight I would be warm and sleeping snugly while those girls would cook over a fire and sleep in a cold van. Perhaps tomorrow they would leave this town and head for another so their father could keep food in their mouths and clothes on their backs.

I think of those girls every day. I pray they will be warm and dry, that they will not be hungry, and that they will be able to go to school. I pray they will meet others who will show them the love of Jesus like we did that short week in July and that one day they will trust Jesus with their lives.

Standing Tall

JERRY B. JENKINS

When Ashley Maddox, a high school sophomore, complained he couldn't take the two-a-day summer football practices anymore, his father challenged him. "What's the matter?" Winston Maddox said. "Too tough for you? You tired?"

Practicing three hours in the morning and three hours in the evening was rough on everyone. But, no, Ashley said, the Arizona heat wasn't the problem.

"It's the language, Dad. The coaches swear all the time, profaning God and using 'Jesus Christ' as an expletive."

Winston called some Christian friends who had played football at several levels. "There's not much you can do about swearing," they told him. "That's just sports. All you can do is play hard and try to be a good example." That didn't satisfy father or son.

Winston didn't have a solution, but he told his son, "If you come up with an idea, I'll back you."

An hour later, Ashley returned. "I was reading in Ephesians about how important it is that we build up each other. I know my coaches don't claim to be Christians, but I'm sure they're trying to build us up rather than tear us down. But when they use God's name in vulgar ways, they tear me down."

Winston nodded. "And?"

"If you'll drop me off early tomorrow, I'm going to tell them that. And if they don't stop, I'm going to quit the team."

"I like your idea except for that last part," Winston said. "Your coach may take your ultimatum as a personal challenge and let you go. Why don't you just tell him how you feel, but don't give him an ultimatum?"

When Winston dropped Ashley off at school the next morning, the three worst offending coaches were having a meeting. Ashley asked if he could speak with them.

"I want to be a good football player," he said, "and I want us to have a great team. My Bible tells me how important it is to build each other up. You need to know that when you use language that profanes my God, you're tearing me down."

Ashley was met with silence. Finally the head coach spoke. "Most kids on the team use this kind of language all the time."

"I'm not talking about the kids," Ashley said.

More silence. Then finally, "Thanks for letting us know."

That day the coaches made it painfully obvious they weren't swearing by saying, "Golly gee!" or "Jiminy Cricket!"

Ashley told his father what happened. "It looks like I'm not going to get much playing time this year, but I don't care. All I want to do is set a good example and be a godly man."

Winston's eyes were moist. "I've never seen you stand taller."

Within a few days the coaches reverted to swearing, except for the line coach. He took Ashley aside. "I want you to know I respect you for what you said the other morning. I grew up in a home where that kind of language was not permitted. Now that I have a two-year-old, I try not to talk that way in front of him. If I can watch it there, I can watch it here."

Ashley was right about limited playing time. He caught a lot of grief, especially from the head coach. When discussing team leaders for the next year, the coach pointed at Ashley and said, "And I suppose you'd like to be our spiritual leader?"

"You bet," Ashley said. He was also the first to take on the team's biggest guy in one-on-one competition. He wanted to show that Christians weren't wimps.

During one game the starting fullback fumbled three times and was angry with himself. Ashley asked if he would like to pray about it. After they prayed, the fullback played a flawless second half. In a later game he fumbled and immediately asked Ashley to pray.

The next season the head coach had moved on. Ashley went to the August two-a-days under the same line coach but a new head coach.

After a few days the coaches announced, "We had a meeting to discuss Ashley Maddox. We don't know what happened to him in a year, but he's a whole new player. He's earned a starting job."

During the season, Ashley led three teammates to Christ and led a Fellowship of Christian Athletes huddle group.

One day he was twenty minutes late for weight training. "Where have you been?" the coach asked.

"Sorry, but I was talking to a guy about Jesus."

"All right then. Get to work."

What a difference a year made. What a difference courage made.

Just Listening

SUE RHODES DODD

I t was fall, and I was fresh out of college and happy with my big break in the working world: a junior reporter with a Midwest daily newspaper. I was awed by the excitement and chaos of the newsroom and thrilled to be working there even though I was more spectator than participant. As a young reporter lacking real-world experience, I was usually stuck reporting the more mundane: weather, calendar events, spelling bees, births, and deaths.

Secretly I dreamed of getting cloak-and-dagger back-alley news tips, scooping the competing daily with my investigative reports, and winning acclaim from my peers for writing compelling stories. But the reality for me was that most days were dull and uneventful, and I grew comfortable with the day-to-day routine.

One afternoon the phone at the obituary desk rang, and I was the only one nearby. I answered it. "Newsroom."

"Uh, yeah, hello . . . I . . . gotta report a death."

Sitting down and reaching for pencil and paper, I started taking down the usual information listed in the obit column: name of deceased, age, address, etc. I had been through the routine so many times I could do it in my sleep.

"Cause of death?"

"Carbon monoxide poisoning."

"Self-inflicted?"

"Yeah."

"Time of death?"

After a long silence, the caller answered. "Well…I'm not sure yet."

My mind snapped out of its boredom into full alert. I started listening intently to the caller as I quietly tried to catch the eye of the assistant editor sitting nearby. I tried my best to keep my voice calm and even.

My heart pounding, I asked the caller, "Do…you mean…the person hasn't…died yet?"

"Uh, yeah…but…dead…soon."

Finally I got the assistant editor's attention and waved him over. I scrawled a note: *Suicide caller*. The editor whispered, "I'll call the police. You keep 'em on the line."

Adrenaline pulsed through my veins, sharpening my focus and attention. Even though I was a lowly cub reporter, a life-and-death drama had just dropped into my lap. Hysterics would have been easy, but I had enough sense to go into my acting mode. And acting I was, as I *calmly* continued the conversation, using my most pleasant, soothing voice, "We're so glad you called us with this information. Could I ask you a few more questions?"

By now, the caller's words were beginning to slur, but he remained cooperative.

"You said the deceased's name is Joe, right?"

"Uh…yeah…Joe."

Gently I said, "That's *your* name, isn't it?"

I heard a nervous laugh. "Yes," he said.

I was rocked by the realization that someone would willingly take his own life—someone I was talking to, who was still very much alive at that moment. An emotional tug-of-war blurred my thinking. Part of me raged at the senselessness of suicide; part of me wanted to weep over this man's despair.

Finally I was able to summon enough strength to speak again, trying to keep my voice calm and even. "Joe, tell me about the carbon monoxide. Where is that coming from?"

"I turned on…all the…uh…burners on the stove…no…fire…. I'm feeling…s…s…sleepy."

"Oh now, Joe, don't go to sleep," I said. Fighting back panic, I hoped I could keep him on the line. Speaking with more serenity than I felt, I tried gently persuading him, "Joe, now, Joe, stay with me. I...I...like talking to you. Don't you like talking to me? Could you stay awake? Please...Joe...I'd like to talk to you some more."

"Yeah...sure. Th...that's n...n...nice."

The city desk became a frenzy of activity as the assistant editor called the police with the man's address. A group of reporters and editors gathered around to see what was going on. Sensing the drama, they fell silent and watched me as I spoke soothingly into the phone. I shut my eyes so I wouldn't be distracted by their stares. But there was no ignoring the banging of my own heart as I tried to keep Joe talking. Talking—talking about anything. Keeping the tone light, I chatted with him about his family, and I discovered that Joe had lost his job and his wife had left him.

"There's...j...j...just no reason...t...to...um...live."

Seconds ticked by like hours as we ventured into discussion of Joe's spiritual life. We talked about a church that he had attended recently. It was getting harder to understand what Joe was saying.

"Joe? Are you still there?"

"Yeah...h...h...hey...h...h...hold on."

Fighting panic, I pressed the phone against my ear. I strained to listen but couldn't decipher the sounds on the other end of the phone. What could be happening? Was Joe all right? All my pretended mental calm evaporated. Inside I screamed, *Joe! Live! Please, God, don't let him die!* Without realizing it, I had stood up, the phone still to my ear.

Then a different voice came across the phone. "Who is this?" the voice demanded.

After I identified myself, I summoned the courage to ask, "Is Joe all right?"

The voice responded. "There's gas everywhere. It's bad. I'm a police officer. We're all getting out of here. Thanks for calling us."

"Oh no, thank *you*," I said, quietly hanging up the phone as locked-up tears finally made their escape. The usually noisy newsroom had grown as silent as a morgue.

I looked up at the crowd of reporters and murmured, "They got there in time."

The newsroom erupted into cheers, but I felt numb. A crisis abated, my coworkers seemed to breathe a collective sigh of relief and went back to their own stories and phone calls and deadlines. I sank back down in my chair, still stunned by the whole ordeal.

I stared at the phone for a long time, a wild mixture of emotions rushing over me: relief, sadness, frustration, hope, anger, awe. Never had I been so close to something so hopeless, to someone so despondent. One of the city editors came over to my desk. With one hand she offered me the tissues I needed, and with the other, she clasped my hand in her own. She didn't say anything; she didn't have to. This usually detached editor was tending to tears of her own.

After a few minutes she left me to my own thoughts. I reached for the phone directory and looked up the name of the church Joe had mentioned. I told the pastor what had just happened. "If he lives through this, maybe you can help him," I said.

In the days that followed I checked on Joe's condition and learned that he did live. I hoped that the pastor and family and friends would help Joe with the problems that had driven him to attempt suicide. Out of respect for Joe's privacy, I never contacted him directly.

The following Friday our news staff held its regular meeting. Editors often presented special awards for reporters doing exemplary work. To my surprise, I was presented with an award for "keeping a cool head on the front lines." The crusty managing editor, who usually intimidated me with his gruff disposition and cynical perspective, actually smiled and winked at me during his presentation.

I was stunned; I couldn't believe it. Me? Getting noticed by all those ace reporters? Those tough editors?

One of the star investigative reporters said, "I'm just glad he called you and not me." At my puzzled look, he continued, "Because I probably would have hung up on the guy." He ducked his head and shuffled away.

One of the columnists who had never spoken to me before said, "He's right, you know. You're the only one in this newsroom who would have been so patient with the guy."

"But all I did was...just listen."

With a smile and a pat on my back, the columnist continued, "Someone willing to 'just listen' can be pretty hard to find."

As I drove home at twilight, I caught myself staring into the car waiting beside me. The man gripped his steering wheel and scowled straight ahead, lost in thoughts of his own. I wondered if he was frustrated or distressed about his own life. I wondered if his stern clenched jaw masked some deep heartache. I wondered if that man could be Joe or just someone else wrestling with the disillusionments of his own life. The driver behind me tooted his horn, and I eased out of my reverie.

I thought about the irony of finally receiving the acclaim I so craved. I wanted to be a star reporter, the envy of my peers. But I was no veteran reporter or a syndicated columnist impacting the world with my eloquent words. I was young and inexperienced and new on the job. I was plain old me, and all I did was listen. Just listen.

A single tear made its way down my cheek as I prayed, *Lord, help me never to squander Your opportunities. If You want me to do something—large or small—help me to pay attention and do it right...even if it's just listening.*

What Is Life?

What is life?
Life is a gift…accept it.
Life is an adventure…dare it.
Life is a mystery…unfold it.
Life is a game…play it.
Life is a struggle…face it.
Life is beauty…praise it.
Life is a puzzle…solve it.
Life is opportunity…take it.
Life is sorrowful…experience it.
Life is a song…sing it.
Life is a goal…achieve it.
Life is a mission…fulfill it.

DAVID MCNALLY

FROM *EVEN EAGLES NEED A PUSH*

clam chowder

DENISE JOLLY

When I was in high school, I dumped my first boyfriend and ran off with another guy.

It wasn't very long before I found myself pregnant and abandoned in Weed, California. I waited for the money that he said he'd wire, but it never came. So there I was: homeless, alone, and wanting to die. I had very little money, and I went to the store to buy razor blades to end my life. With the overdramatic emotionalism of my age, I could see no other alternative, though deep down I was hoping for some other answers.

The purchase left me with less than a dollar. I was hungry, so I went to the lunch counter in the back of the store hoping to find something on the menu for the little money I had. The only thing that I could afford was a small cup of clam chowder. I didn't like clam chowder, but I ordered it anyway. While I waited, I began to pray for some kind of sign to show me that I should stay alive.

I was interrupted when the waitress set a big steaming bowl of clam chowder in front of me. "But I only have enough money for the cup of chowder," I whispered to her.

She put down a big glass of milk beside the bowl of chowder and said, "That's all right, kid. You look like you need it!" Her hand briefly brushed mine.

I had to look back down quickly because my eyes were filling with tears. I knew that my prayer had been answered and that I had been shown that there was still kindness in the world. Somehow I would be able to go on.

I called my father, and he arranged for a bus ticket back home. Returning to school helped me cope with my pregnancy and the miscarriage that followed only a month later. It was several years after graduating that I renewed an acquaintance with a wonderful man, the very one I had dumped in high school. We eventually married and had two beautiful daughters.

The compassion of that waitress has stayed with me to this day. She could not have known the power of her actions, but she taught me that no kindness is ever wasted, no matter how small it might seem at the time. She might be pleased to know that I am now not only a mother and a grandmother, but also a woman who learned to love clam chowder.

The difference between ordinary and extraordinary is that little extra.

AUTHOR UNKNOWN

Twelve Teens and a Bag of Tricks

BRUCE WILKINSON
FROM *THE PRAYER OF JABEZ FOR TEENS*

When I was a youth pastor at a growing church in New Jersey, twelve high school kids proved to me that the hand of God is available to every believer who asks. Here's what happened:

After praying most of the school year about a summer ministry project, we decided to do six weeks of youth evangelism in the suburbs of Long Island, New York. How many kids total would we reach for Christ? We didn't know—we just knew it would be a lot!

We decided on a three-part strategy. We would begin with backyard Bible studies, switch to beach evangelism in the afternoon, and then wrap it up with an evening outreach in different churches. Sounds simple, but let me tell you, the team—youth pastor included—felt overwhelmed by the task.

We invited a specialist in children's ministry on Long Island to give our youth group some training. He told us that getting as many as thirteen or fourteen kids in a backyard club would be a smashing success. But while he was talking, I felt God was calling us to pray for a specific number of changed hearts—a number that would prove that only He could have done it.

After he left, I told the group, "If we don't have one hundred kids in each club by the end of the week, we should consider it a failure." Suddenly, all of us wanted to get down on our knees and pray!

I'll never forget those wonderful prayers. "Lord, please bless us!" and

"Lord, I know it's way over my head, but please, give me a hundred kids!" and "Lord, by Your Spirit, pull off something great for Your glory!"

Parents kept telling our team that our plan was impossible. And I'm sure they were right. But it started happening anyway. The first week, four of the six teams had more than a hundred children crammed into their meetings. By the end of the week we had shared the Good News with more than five hundred kids.

Then the beach phase of our mission to Long Island kicked in. I bought a beginner's magic kit—you know, "everything you need to amaze and impress your friends." Then I stayed up until 3 A.M. learning how to make an egg "disappear." By the next afternoon, we were unrolling our free show in the sand and pleading with God for His hand to be upon us.

We decided to ask the Lord for thirty decisions for salvation—by the end of the first day.

Our audience grew from a single row of squirming children to more than 150 onlookers. We rotated the entertainment from magic shows to story-telling to gospel presentations. Soon, adults began edging closer. Finally clusters of teenagers started joining the crowd. By the end of the afternoon we had reached a count of 250. And when we finally gave an invitation, thirty people accepted Jesus Christ as their Savior—right there on the beach.

Once we had established our beach ministry, we added an evening program for youth in local churches. God blessed our efforts beyond anyone's expectation—but right in line with the size of our Jabez prayer. By the end of our six-week outreach, we counted up to 1,200 new believers on Long Island.

Do you know what else happened? Twelve high school kids came back to their New Jersey neighborhoods convinced that *God can do anything*. And it wasn't too long before the whole congregation was touched by revival.

Impossible? Not at all. All because twelve students asked for blessings indeed, for more territory for God's glory, and for His hand of power to be upon them.

Jesus said, "The things which are impossible with men are possible with God" (Luke 18:27, NKJV).

Rookie Driver

CHARLES R. SWINDOLL
FROM *IMPROVING YOUR SERVE*

I'll call this young man Aaron, not his real name. Late one spring he was praying about having a significant ministry the following summer. He asked God for a position to open up on some church staff or Christian organization. Nothing happened. Summer arrived, still nothing. Days turned into weeks, and Aaron finally faced reality—he needed any job he could find. He checked the want ads, and the only thing that seemed to be a possibility was driving a bus in southside Chicago—nothing to brag about, but it would help with tuition in the fall. After learning the route, he was on his own—a rookie driver in a dangerous section of the city. It wasn't long before Aaron realized just how dangerous his job really was.

A small gang of tough kids spotted the young driver and began to take advantage of him. For several mornings in a row they got on, walked right past him without paying, ignored his warnings, and rode until they decided to get off…all the while making smart remarks to him and others on the bus. Finally, he decided it had gone on long enough.

The next morning, after the gang got on as usual, Aaron saw a policeman on the next corner, so he pulled over and reported the offense. The officer told them to pay or get off. They paid but, unfortunately, the policeman got off. And they stayed on. When the bus turned another corner or two, the gang assaulted the young driver.

When he came to, blood was all over his shirt, two teeth were missing, both eyes were swollen, his money was gone, and the bus was empty. After returning to the terminal and being given the weekend off, our friend went to his little apartment, sank onto his bed, and stared at the ceiling in disbelief. Resentful thoughts swarmed his mind. Confusion, anger, and disillusionment added fuel to the fire of his physical pain. He spent a fitful night wrestling with the Lord.

How can this be? Where's God in all of this? I genuinely want to serve Him. I prayed for a ministry. I was willing to serve Him anywhere, doing anything, and this is the thanks I get!

On Monday morning, Aaron decided to press charges. With the help of the officer who had encountered the gang and several who were willing to testify as witnesses against the thugs, most of them were rounded up and taken to the local county jail. Within a few days there was a hearing before the judge.

In walked Aaron and his attorney plus the angry gang members who glared across the room in his direction. Suddenly he was seized with a whole new series of thoughts. Not bitter ones, but compassionate ones! His heart went out to the guys who had attacked him. Under the Spirit's control, he no longer hated them—he pitied them. They needed help, not more hate. What could he do or say?

Suddenly, after there was a plea of guilty, Aaron (to the surprise of his attorney and everybody else in the courtroom) stood to his feet and requested permission to speak.

"Your Honor, I would like you to total up all the days of punishment against these men—all the time sentenced against them—and I request that you allow me to go to jail in their place."

The judge didn't know whether to spit or wind his watch. Both attorneys were stunned. As Aaron looked over at the gang members (whose mouths and eyes looked like saucers), he smiled and said quietly, "It's because I forgive you."

The dumbfounded judge, when he reached a level of composure, said rather firmly: "Young man, you're out of order. This sort of thing has never been done before!" To which the young man replied with genius insight:

"Oh yes, it has, your honor…yes, it has. It happened over nineteen centuries ago when a man from Galilee paid the penalty that all mankind deserved."

And then, for the next three or four minutes, without interruption, he explained how Jesus Christ died on our behalf, thereby proving God's love and forgiveness.

He was not granted his request, but the young man visited the gang members in jail, led most of them to faith in Christ, and began a significant ministry to many others in southside Chicago.

Only a life lived for others is a life worthwhile.

ALBERT EINSTEIN

Goodwill Shopping

MARY LOU CARNEY

I like shopping at Goodwill stores. Plundering through all that old stuff, looking for a cast-off cashmere sweater or a retro paisley skirt. I like pairing these finds with my "legit" clothes—jeans with the right labels and shirts with cool-at-the-moment logos.

But as I drove to my favorite Goodwill store that morning, I wasn't on my way to look for cool clothes. Instead, I was looking for anything that I could turn into a costume for our church's annual Christmas pageant.

I pushed open the door and, as always, was assaulted by the smells: dust and mothballs and Pine-Sol. Except for a clerk perched on a stool near the cash register, the store was empty. (Who else would be spending the Saturday after Thanksgiving *here?*) I sighed and began pawing through a pile of shirts, grabbing at anything even remotely colorful. *How did I ever get myself into this?* I wondered, and then immediately remembered how: My mom "volunteered" me.

A swoosh of cold air made me look up. A young woman and her little girl stepped through the open door. As the mother stamped her feet to shake off the snow, I noticed her ragged tennis shoes—the cloth kind I wear when I mow the yard. My eyes moved up to her wrinkled skirt and too-big sweater…and then to her face. She looked so young! Her face was round and innocent, like those angels hovering near the edges of gilded Christmas cards. She looked my way, and I lowered my eyes, embarrassed somehow. I suddenly became very interested in a silk disco shirt.

Later, as I was rummaging through a rack of lingerie, the young woman came up beside me. This time when I looked her way, her eyes held mine. *How old is she? Sixteen? Seventeen?*

"I need one of these," she said, fingering a peach-colored half slip. "When you have babies, it just ruins the elastic. I got seven kids."

I almost gasped, but the lump that was starting to form in my throat helped keep it in. I nodded, smiled, and moved on. *Seven kids!*

Her little girl glanced up as I came down the "home accessories" aisle. She was holding a piece of driftwood with obnoxious plastic flowers stuck in its top. "This here would be a nice Christmas gift for my mama." She touched the stiff petals gently. "Maybe I'll ask my grandpa will he buy it for her." She put it back on the cluttered shelf. Again I nodded and smiled, the lump in my throat growing bigger by the minute.

When I had finally found a few pieces I thought I could transform into something vaguely resembling the shepherd clothes and angelic robes, I headed for the register. The young woman and her little girl were there, ready to check out. I looked at the items she'd chosen: a plastic baby bottle with a clown face, a pair of little socks, a small sweater the color of faded roses. And the peach half slip.

"That'll be $2.85," the clerk said in between chomps on her gum.

The woman pulled a crumpled dollar bill and a handful of change from her pocket. She counted, then recounted. "Are you sure it's that much?"

The clerk snapped her gum. "Cash registers don't make mistakes."

"I'll...I'll have to put something back." Her hand hovered over the pile of purchases like a pale butterfly. Then it lighted on the half slip.

"No, wait!" I said, taking a dollar from my purse. She shrank from the bill. "I don't want charity. It's just something for me. It can wait...."

I looked at the garish garland hanging over the cash register. "It's not charity," I said, pressing the dollar into her hand. "It's a gift. Merry Christmas!"

She stared at the money and then looked up, a shy smile making her face almost radiant. "Why, then, thank you. Merry Christmas to *you!*"

I still like to shop at the Goodwill. But now I look beyond the thrill of the bargains, past the jokes my friends and I sometimes make about the clothes we find. Whenever I can, I look—really look—at the other people shopping there. Real people who need acceptance and friendship—and half slips.

We may not be able to do any great thing;
   but if each of us will do something,
however small it may be,
   a good deal will be accomplished for God.

DWIGHT L. MOODY

To Love the children

RACHEL V. NEET
AGE 15

Fifty of us teenagers eagerly flooded off the hot, sweaty bus. It had been a half-hour ride from our hotel in Oradea to this hotel in Felix, Romania, where we held Christian rallies every night. This was our last time coming here. We would shop and hold a park rally, then leave for Vienna the next morning.

Our group consisted of almost one hundred teens and leaders from Oregon. This was my first mission trip and my first time being in a different country. At the time I signed up, I had no idea how my heart would be broken by the things I saw there—especially the Gypsy children, the little ones we were destined to fall in love with.

Each day we handed out candy and performed dramas in a park during the humid afternoon, then headed back to our hotel for dinner. Following dinner we took a half-hour bus ride to Felix, a smaller resort town known for its hot springs. At Felix, our rallies included drama, music, face painting, clowning, and testimonies. This was where we met the Gypsy children the first night, and we saw them every night thereafter.

Out of all the lovable Gypsy children, our hearts were drawn to ten-year-olds Alina and Monica the most. They were our constant companions each evening and had their faces painted every chance they got. After only minutes of having the paint on, the girls brought us baby wipes to clean them off. At first, Jolie and I thought it was because they didn't like the designs, but later we realized they just loved having us touch, even scrub, their little brown faces. Starved for attention, Alina and Monica eagerly accepted all the love we gave them, hugging us back, giving us enthusiastic kisses.

Our little friends were the first to answer the altar calls each evening. As soon as we finished praying for them, they hurried to go pray for their friends and other people. Despite all the pain and suffering in their lives and the rejection from others because of their Gypsy heritage, the children showed us the meaning of faith and love.

So there we were, full of mixed emotions as we prepared for our last night in Romania. Alina ran to me as I entered the hotel courtyard. She limped badly and had several deep cuts that were infected, but she had one of the brightest smiles I've ever seen. She told me I was her "second mother" and begged me to bring her back to America with me.

I scooped her into my arms for a hug. The other Gypsy children also crowded around, eager for affection. With a huge grin, one little boy took my face in his hands, planting a kiss on each cheek.

"I wonder why Monica isn't here," I said a few minutes later to my friend, Jolie.

"I don't know," she replied as Alina sat nestled between us on the dead grass that sparsely covered the ground. The music from the portable speakers had begun playing, and it was time for the rally to start.

We didn't know much about either girl, but what we did know, Jolie and I learned through three-way conversations between the girls, the translators, and us. Monica's father was dead, and her mother worked as a hotel maid; she and her mother lived with Alina's family and several others in a run-down house. All these two girls asked for was our love, which we freely gave them.

That night, Monica completely avoided us until we were about to leave. Our translator later informed us that she thought we didn't love her because we tried to divide our attention equally among the children. Monica did eventually come, and in the sparse Romanian phrases we knew, we convinced her that we *did* love her and that Jesus loved her, too. She seemed to understand and kissed us good-bye with as much enthusiasm as the others did when we boarded the bus at dusk.

It's been several months now since I went to Europe. After leaving Romania, I saw cathedrals in Vienna, *The Sound of Music* tour at Salzburg, and the Dachau Concentration Camp in Germany. But the experience that most impacted and inspired me was being with the children. That's my favorite memory, and I now know that, wherever I go, my calling is to love the children.

Blessed are the happiness makers.

HENRY WARD BEECHER

Don't Forget to Shine

KIMBERLY SHUMATE

The sun was already warming the breeze by 9:30 A.M. as I walked down Santa Monica Boulevard on my way to school. Just another day in paradise, as every day of the week seemed to be in Southern California. Just a normal, bright, lovely morning when I happened upon a homeless woman and her overturned shopping cart. A soggy brown paper bag lay on the ground next to her. She sat beside it on the street corner, drunk and crying, as if mourning the loss of her best friend. As I knelt down slowly and gently touched her shoulder, I braced myself for her reaction. You never know how a person's going to react when you touch them. "Can I help you?" I asked softly.

"No," she sniffled, but I could scarcely believe her. Her cart was filled with dirty plastic bags stuffed with empty pop cans that were now scattered across the sidewalk. She had some personal items, but not many. She was filthy. Her hair, her fingernails, her clothes, and the white-and-turquoise beaded necklace she wore around her neck. The tiny detailing on the white beads was exaggerated by the dirt pressed deep into their pattern.

My mind skipped ahead to class and what my teacher would say if I were late again, but my senses returned swiftly as I gazed down and wondered what it must be like to live a day in her shoes. My life was so simple. Home, school, friends, family…. I had everything in the world to be thankful for, yet somehow I couldn't remember the last time I told my friends how special they were to me, or thought of how lucky I was to even be able to go to school, or said "I love you" to my mom and dad. Before I knew it, I found myself sitting on the ground beside her, our feet dangling in the gutter.

I gave her what little money I had, but it didn't seem to matter. She was inconsolable. Never had I seen someone so weary of life. Her breath smelled of whiskey and covered my face as she exhaled through her tears. The lines on her face were deep. Not wrinkles. Lines. The kind that you get from true despair. She frightened me a little. Her life frightened me and yet she was like a little child. She needed someone to take care of her. She needed love. *How helpless and alone she must feel*, I thought. The only love I had to give was the Lord's. I told her that God loved her, and she looked at me with a strange new expression, like she knew that it was true. Like most of us, she only needed to be reminded.

We stood to our feet and pulled her shopping cart onto its unstable wheels. One by one, the plastic bags, cans, and clothes were packed up. She then took my hand in hers, predicting my departure. "God bless you" is all she could say. She then gave me the only thing of value that she had. Carefully slipping the beaded necklace over her head, she placed it in my hand. "I want you to have this; it's all I have." As I embraced her, I pondered how long it had been since her last hug, and a lump formed in my throat.

As I left her there on that street corner, struggling with the burden of living another day, somehow her spirit seemed lighter by our exchange. Her tears had dried up and her eyes were brighter. It was then I realized that a little love goes a very long way. It's like a light that never fades. It just keeps shining, no matter where it goes or whom it touches. How fortunate, how blessed we are in so many ways, and how simple it is to shine.

Meaningful Touch

JOHN TRENT
FROM *LEAVING THE LIGHT ON*

The young GI stepped into line with the other teenagers to get his barbecued chicken. It's funny how some people can look eighteen—until you look at their eyes. I think it was his haunted look that caused me to notice him that evening. From the window of his eyes, he looked like a tired old man, not like the swarm of happy kids around him.

I was part of a work crew at Trail West, Young Life's beautiful camp high in the Colorado Rockies. It was my job that night to stand at the head of the line and hand out the best smelling, best tasting barbecued chicken I'd ever eaten—before or since.

We had our huge grill fired up in the middle of a large, grassy meadow, rimmed by massive, solemn pines that stood like a majestic fence around us. The sun was sliding behind the surrounding mountain peaks as the fragrant smoke from our barbecue drifted across the clearing.

It was 1969, the summer of my junior year of high school. It didn't occur to me then, but while the laughing, noisy high schoolers waited for their meal that evening, a number of their dads, friends, schoolmates, and older brothers were fighting and dying in the rice paddies and jungles of Southeast Asia.

It was easy to spot the young Nam vet in our midst. In an era of sideburns and shaggy haircuts, his government-issue "buzz cut" drew plenty of sidelong glances. He had actually graduated from high school a couple of years before, but his parents had gotten special permission for him to attend the camp.

That's the kind of crazy war it was: Two weeks before, he'd been fighting for his life, watching buddies drop all around him. Then suddenly his tour was up; he was airlifted out of a fierce firefight to Saigon, got on a commercial airliner, and headed home. Just like that.

Now he was on leave, standing in line in a Rocky Mountain meadow with a bunch of kids who didn't seem to have a care in the world.

I first noticed him when he was about the fourth person from the front of the line. His face was extremely pale and he was visibly trembling. I remember thinking, *Something's wrong with this guy. He must be getting sick.*

As he got closer to the grill, he began shaking even harder. I picked up a piece of chicken with my tongs and was just about to serve him when he suddenly dropped his plate, spilling beans and salad on the ground and on the person in front of him. With a choked cry, he took off on a dead run for the forest.

Everyone stopped talking and just stared. We all wondered, *What in the world's wrong with him?*

Our Young Life leader headed off after the young soldier, and after they both disappeared into the trees, the dinner line resumed its onward march.

Doug found him hiding in the trees, shaking like a leaf. The older man, a burly ex-football player, towered nearly a foot above the soldier and probably outweighed him by a hundred pounds. But without saying a word, he gently put his arms around the trembling camper and held him tight.

The young soldier buried his face in our leader's chest and sobbed uncontrollably. They stood together in the twilight for nearly twenty minutes. The young man sobbing, the older man holding him, saying nothing.

When he finally was able to compose himself, they sat on a log together and the vet tried to explain what was going on.

"Over in Nam," he said, "if you were out in open country like that, with so many people milling around, you could expect the mortar rounds to start coming in." He had just seen his sergeant killed, right in front of him, by an incoming shell. And no matter how hard he tried, he couldn't keep the sights and sounds from coming back.

Just before he reached the head of the line, it was as if he could hear the whistle of artillery fire and the screams of "Incoming! Incoming!" He couldn't take it any longer and ran to find cover.

That was day two of the camp, of what would become the most important week of this young man's life. Before the week was over, the soldier surrendered his life to a new commander, Jesus Christ. But not for the reason you may think.

On the final night of camp, as we all sat around a big bonfire, campers were encouraged to stand up and make public their confession of faith if they had come to know Christ that week.

Many young men and women responded to the opportunity, citing talks by the speaker, the encouragement of a close friend from home, and other causes as reasons for coming to know Jesus personally. The young soldier was one of the last to stand.

His story was much different from the rest. He began by telling how skeptical he had been about coming to camp. In fact, the only reason he'd agreed to come was that his parents promised to buy him a used car. The thought of his own wheels pushed him over the edge, and he came reluctantly to camp.

While everyone had been "real nice" to him, it wasn't a special friendship that had shaped his decision. And even though he thought the speaker had some good words to say, and made the gospel clear, it wasn't because of him either that he was responding to Christ.

What had really broken through to him was "that big guy," Doug, who had been willing to stand there in the trees with him and hold him until a piece of nightmare loosened its grip. In short, God used a hug—not a lecture, not a long walk through the trees, not a testimony—to win the bigger spiritual battle he was fighting.

Wanna Be Like You

Tribute

You never talked to me about how to treat people,
but every act of kindness
I have ever shown another person
was because I was trying to imitate you.

PAMELA MCGREW

The Silent Flute

FELIX MAYERHOFER

One of the things I enjoyed as band director was recruiting new members. I'd enter a class at the beginning of a school year and ask, "Who wants to join the band?" Every hand would shoot up! Each student had an idea what he or she wanted to play: some the trombone or clarinet, others the flute, drums, or trumpet.

It took about two weeks for the kids and their parents to decide what instruments they wanted to buy or rent. When the day of their first lesson arrived, I could hear the commotion as the flute students scurried toward the band room. When I opened the door, they whizzed by me, found a seat, and anxiously waited with great expectation for me to make them instant players.

I showed them how to blow into the hole of the top section of the flute. Going down the line, each student made a sound for me, until I came to a pretty but fragile girl. Her name was Jennifer. Even though she tried with the biggest breath she could muster, nothing came out.

"Don't worry," I assured her. "You'll soon be able to play." I had the students put the three parts of the flute together, then taught them how and where to place their fingers. At the end of the rehearsal, the kids left the band room as excitedly as they had entered, with the trumpets scrambling in next.

Besides their individual group instructions, the entire band got together once a week. As the beginning band improved, Jennifer was always there, but looking frailer as the weeks passed. She still couldn't get a sound, but her friends continued to encourage her. Jennifer knew the fingerings and did everything correctly, so I knew she'd been practicing. She was a sweet and patient girl. Since she'd made the effort to learn, I didn't pressure her.

After a rehearsal, I asked Jennifer to stay. "Jennifer," I said, "you don't seem to have enough energy to play the flute. Is anything wrong?"

With maturity beyond her years, she looked up at me with her big blue eyes and said, "I have cystic fibrosis and I'm going to die."

As tears clouded my eyes and a lump came to my throat, I asked with difficulty, "What is cystic fibrosis?"

"It's an inherited disease," she explained, "with a thick sticky mucous that clogs my lungs and airways, making it hard for me to breathe. My older brother died two years ago of the same disease, but luckily my younger sister doesn't have it."

"Why did you take up the flute since you have trouble breathing?" I asked.

In a small but determined voice, she responded, "I've always wanted to play the flute and love it, even though I can't make a sound."

I wanted to hug her as if she were my own child, and when she left, I sat down heavy hearted, having trouble holding back the tears.

As the weeks passed, Jennifer coughed and choked more, and during one of our rehearsals, her seat was vacant. I was told she had had a serious breathing attack and would be out for a few days.

When she returned to band, Jennifer tried playing her flute like she had never been ill. I began teaching the flute players three new notes. Each student played them for me to make sure they knew the fingerings. When I came to Jennifer, I decided to jump to the next player because the notes were higher and more difficult.

"I want to try it, too," Jennifer said softly. Lifting the flute with her delicate hands, she put the instrument to her lips, and out came three beautiful notes. I never saw a broader smile on a child's face, like she'd been touched by an angel. There was stunned silence, then the band broke out in cheers and loud applause, and yelled, "All right, Jennifer!" It was a moment to be remembered.

We never heard her play again. The principal came into the band room the following rehearsal and informed us that Jennifer had died quietly in her sleep. There wasn't a dry eye in the band.

She left all of us with wonderful memories of her courage and what it was to never give up.... Jennifer's silent flute will be forever missed.

You Got Another One, Joey!

BOB PERKS

y tire had a staple in it. Of all times for this to happen…a flat tire. But when is a good time for a flat tire? Not when you are wearing a suit and you have been traveling for nearly five hours, and, adding to this bleak picture, nightfall is approaching. Wait. Did I mention that I was on a country road? Okay, now you have the picture.

There was only one thing to do: call AAA. Yeah, right. The cell phone that I had brought for moments like this wasn't in range to call anyone. "No Service," it said. No kidding!

I sat moaning and complaining for a few minutes. It's a male thing. Then I began emptying my trunk so that I could get the tire and the tools needed to get the job done. I always carry a large plastic container filled with what I call my "just-in-case stuff." I hate leaving anything home so I bring everything—just in case. Cars buzzed by me and a few beeped sarcastically. I could almost hear the horns saying, "Ha, ha!"

"You'll get yours!" I retorted.

Darkness began to settle in. Thankfully the flat tire was on the passenger side, away from all the traffic, but I didn't have the benefit of the headlights of passing cars. Suddenly a car pulled off the road behind me. In the blinding light I saw a male figure approaching me.

"Hey, do you need any help?"

"Well, it certainly isn't easy doing this with a white dress shirt and suit on," I said.

Then he stepped out into the light. I literally was frightened. This young guy was dressed in black and nearly everything imaginable was pierced and tattooed. His hair was cropped and poorly cut. He had spiked leather bracelets on each wrist.

"How about I give you a hand?" he said.

"Well, I don't know…. I think I can…"

"Come on, it will only take a few minutes."

He took right over. While watching him, I happened to look back at his car and notice someone sitting in the passenger seat. I suddenly felt outnumbered. Thoughts of carjackings and robberies flashed through my mind. I just wanted to get this over with and survive it.

Then, without warning, it began to pour. The night sky had hidden the approaching clouds. It hit like a waterfall and made it impossible to finish the tire change.

"Look, my friend, just stop what you're doing. I appreciate all your help. You better get going. I'll finish after the rain stops," I said.

"Let me help you put your stuff back in the trunk. It will get ruined," he insisted. "Then get in my car. We'll wait with you."

"No, really. I'll take care of everything," I said.

"You can't get in your car with the jack up like that. It will fall. Come on, get in," he said as he grabbed my arm and pulled me toward the car.

Crack! Boom! Lightning flashed and thunder roared like a freight train. I jumped into his car.

Oh, God, protect me!

Wet and tired, I settled into the backseat. Suddenly a small, frail voice came from the front seat of the car.

"Are you all right?" She turned around to face me.

"Yes, I am." I sighed with relief when I saw the old woman. It must be his mother.

"My name is Beatrice, and this is my neighbor, Joey," she said. "He insisted on stopping when he saw you struggling with the tire."

"I am grateful for his help," I said.

"Me, too!" she said with a laugh. "Joey takes me to visit my husband. We had to place him in a nursing home, and it's about thirty minutes away from where I live. So every Monday, Wednesday, and Friday, Joey and I have a date." She laughed and shook her head.

"We're the remake of *The Odd Couple*," Joey said as he joined in with the laughter.

"Joey, that's incredible what you do for her. I would never have guessed, well, ah, you know I…" I stumbled with my words.

"I know. People who look like me don't do nice things," he said.

Silence. I felt really uncomfortable. I never believed that I judged people by the way they dressed. I was angry with myself for being so stupid.

"Joey is a great kid. I'm not the only one he helps. He's a volunteer at our church. He also works with the kids in the learning center at the low-income housing unit in our town," said Beatrice.

"I'm a tutor," Joey said quietly as he stared at my car.

Silence again. This time, however, it was a moment of reflection rather than the uncomfortable feeling that I had insulted someone. He was right. What he wore on the outside was a reflection of the world as he saw it. What he wore on the inside was the spirit of giving, caring, and loving—the world he wanted to see.

The rain stopped, and Joey and I changed the tire. I tried to offer him money and, of course, he refused it. He walked to his car, and as they drove off, Beatrice smiled and waved as she began to laugh again.

I could almost hear her saying, "You got another one, Joey. You got another one."

TWo Shirts

FROM *MORE RANDOM ACTS OF KINDNESS*

A friend who was working in the Dominican Republic with Habitat for Humanity had befriended a small boy named Etin. He noticed that when Etin wore a shirt at all, it was always the same dirty, tattered one. A box of used clothes had been left at the camp, and my friend found two shirts in it that were in reasonably good shape and about Etin's size, so he gave them to the grateful boy. A few days later he saw another boy wearing one of the shirts. When he next met up with Etin, he explained that the shirts were meant for him. Etin just looked at him and said, "But you gave me two!"

Head of the class

=◎=

BEN JACKSON
AS TOLD TO GINNY WILLIAMS DYE

My junior year began the way the rest of my high school years had begun—with me wishing the teacher would keep the door to the Special Ed classroom closed. I hated that room. As soon as I walked through the door, I was branded as someone different. Someone not as smart. Someone to look down on.

There were more than two thousand kids at my school. When the bell rang at the beginning of the day, they would stroll into their "normal" classes. Me? I would wait till the halls were almost empty and then duck into my seat in the Special Ed room. I always sat at the back of the class—hoping no one I knew would glance into the room and see me there.

I hated being labeled as dyslexic. Dyslexia is a learning disorder that affects my ability to read. Because of my dyslexia, I'd pretty much given up on trying to be a leader in my school.

That is, until my junior year—the year I became a Christian.

I'd already been doing other things—like being in clubs and singing in the choir. But when I became a Christian, my feelings changed. Because of my newfound faith, I discovered a new courage and boldness. Even with my disability, I suddenly felt God wanted to use me to make a big difference in my high school. After praying and talking to friends, I made my decision: I would run for senior class president.

I can still remember the day I decided. My friends were gathered around me, talking excitedly about my chances. I was a jumble of emotions—excited, that I was about to actually declare my candidacy; nervous, that I would dare try such a thing; and fearful, that I would make a fool of myself.

My friends and I plastered the school with flyers and posters. I went out of my way to talk to everyone I could. Thankfully, most of the students in my high school didn't know I was a "Special Ed" kid. The school was big, and most people were so involved in their own worlds they didn't know what was going on in mine. They simply knew I was the guy who was running for president.

Election day came. All the candidates were required to give a speech. I was so nervous that day as I waited on the platform in front of the entire senior class. As I stared out into the crowd, I wanted to jump up and run from the auditorium. What made me think I could be president? What made me think I could stand up in front of all those people and talk? All I could do was pray silently and ask God for courage.

Gradually, my heart quit beating quite so fast, and I felt like I could breathe again. I was even able to listen as the other presidential hopefuls gave their speeches.

They all started the same. "Hello, my name is…. I am running to be the senior class president." Then they rambled on about what they were going to do.

When my turn came, I took a deep breath and walked unsteadily to the podium. Taking a tight grip on the podium, I delivered my prepared speech. "Hello. You all know who I am. And you know why I'm up here. If you don't, then I haven't campaigned very well up to now, and you're not going to vote for me anyway." I can remember surprised laughter rippling toward me. "I'm here to offer you change…." And with that, my speech was off and rolling.

My speech lasted less than a minute. There was a long silence when I turned and walked from the podium. And then the place erupted in cheers. By the end of the day, it was announced over the intercom that I was the new senior class president!

The rest of my junior year and the summer flew by. In no time, it was September. Classes were starting, and I was beginning my term as president.

Everything went smoothly for the first two weeks. Then my worst fears were realized.

It happened in biology class. By now, most of the school knew me as president, but there were still many who didn't know about my struggle with dyslexia. That day in biology, when test time came, I went, as usual, into a separate room to take the test. (Dyslexic students sometimes need to take tests privately, away from all distractions.) The bell had already rung when I walked back into the biology room and laid the test on the teacher's desk.

"Been to the Special Ed room, have you?" someone blurted out. "Well, what do we have? A dumbo for a president?"

Someone else joined in.

"Yeah! What makes him so special is that he gets special attention. I guess that's what makes him 'Special Ed'!"

"Just what this school needs—a dumbo dyslexic president!"

I just stood there and stared at the three smirking guys who were laughing in my face. When they'd left, my teacher came up behind me and put his arm around my shoulder. I shrugged it off and walked out of the room.

My mind started to race. Those guys were right. What had made me think I could be the senior class president? I was nothing but a "dumbo dyslexic."

My feelings hadn't changed the next morning when I drove to school. As president, I had my own parking spot that was reserved for me. As I prepared to wheel my Honda Civic between its lines, I screeched to a halt and stared in disbelief. On the pavement, painted in huge, red letters, were the words: DUMBO DYSLEXIC PRESIDENT! Swallowing hard, I pulled my car over the offensive words and just sat there. Bowing my head on the steering wheel, I let feelings of defeat wash over me.

I don't know how long I sat there before I remembered God. I started pouring out my pain and confusion to Him. Gradually, I calmed down enough to think things over. Just because three guys thought I was a loser didn't mean I was. It had taken a lot of votes to get me into office. A lot of people believed in me. And I knew I could do the job. I might not be a great reader and test taker, but I knew I was a good leader, and I knew I had some great ideas.

The school bell had already rung by the time I got out of the car. As I walked toward class, I felt determined: Whether everyone thought I should be president or not, I *was* president. I was going to do the very best job I could. The results would have to speak for themselves. I had asked God to help me forgive the three guys responsible for this. I didn't want their hate to create hate in my own heart. It would only hurt me.

Later that morning, I walked to the principal's office and requested the words be cleaned from my parking spot. By the time the afternoon bell rang, they were gone.

I worked hard that year and did the best I could to live up to my campaign promises. Many people told me I was one of the best presidents the senior class ever had. The opinion that mattered most, though, came in the last week of school.

I had never said anything about the offensive words painted on my parking spot to the three guys in my biology class. There had been a few more remarks, but I had ignored them every time. On this particular day, I had just finished my biology exam and was leaving the classroom. The three were waiting for me. I tensed, unsure of what they wanted.

"Hey, man, I just wanted to say I'm sorry about what happened at the beginning of the year. You've done a great job."

"Yeah. I guess we were the ones who were pretty dumb. I'm really sorry, man."

"You showed us there's a lot more to you than just being dyslexic. I'm really sorry I was such a jerk."

Once again I was speechless as I stared at them. Finally, I just reached out and we all shook hands.

It was good to hear those guys say those things, but what was even more important was how God felt about me.

No matter what anyone else thought, I knew God had made me to be someone special, and I knew I was much more than just dyslexic. I was determined to be all that God had created me to be.

Nothing Quite as Wonderful

There is nothing like warm clothes just out of the dryer
or true love or first love or secret admirers.
There is nothing like best friends, a child's giggle, or a good cry.
There is nothing like letters written to you or a sad good-bye.
There is nothing like puppy kisses,
and there is nothing like the morning sun.
There is nothing like summer vacation or reflecting on a job well done.
There is nothing quite as great as this life we live,
and there is nothing quite as special as the love we give.
But most importantly, there will never be anything as beautiful as You,
for You are my God who loves me through and through.

ANONYMOUS

A Promise

Teena M. Stewart

Gaby stood in the restaurant lobby with a mass of squirming, chattering teens and wondered if her meager three dollars would cover the dessert she had decided to order instead of dinner. Finances were tight at her house, and it was all her mother could scrape up. She had felt guilty even asking her for anything. She fingered the bills in her purse nervously as she bantered wisecracks back and forth with several of her friends. Creekside Church's youth group, to which Gaby belonged, had planned to go out for treats after the conclusion of their usual Wednesday night meeting. Now over forty kids chattered animatedly in the restaurant's lobby as they waited for the waiters and waitresses to clear enough tables for the noisy, giggling mass of humanity.

Finally they signaled that the tables were ready, and the troupe walked over to the area that was prepared. Gaby slid into a seat next to her friend and buried her face in the dessert menu. It took a while for everyone to make a selection and even longer for the waiters to take each individual order, but the kids didn't mind. They enjoyed each other's company as they waited for their food. Shortly after the food arrived, but before they could plunge in, Bubba, one of the youth group helpers, patiently held up his hand and sshhed everyone. He launched into a brief prayer thanking God for their food. At the word "Amen," the pack attacked their meals like starved beasts.

When it came time to pay, Brett, the youth pastor, asked for the check.

It would be no easy task to divide up such a large sum among so many. He was surprised when instead of handing him a bill, the manager grinned and handed him a note.

Brett looked perplexed. "What's this?" he asked.

"The entire bill and tip for the group has already been taken care of by a gentleman who left a short while ago."

Brett looked around.

"He wishes to remain anonymous," the manager added.

The youth group's noise quieted. Teens and youth pastor looked at each other in stunned disbelief. Then the manager read the note aloud to the group.

"Young people," he read, "I promised the Lord that if He would show me anyone who would pray before their meal in a public restaurant, I would buy their meal. Not only are you the first ones I've seen pray in public, but you're a whole group!

"Well, I'm keeping my promise to God as He has always kept His promises to me. God's blessings to all of you. Don't thank me. Just remember me in your prayers."

It was signed, "The Lord's Servant."

Many lives were touched that night, but one in particular, the one who was concerned about paying for her meal, realized that God provided above and beyond her needs. The entire group was blanketed with His love. But more importantly, He showed them the value of having a servant's heart. It was a lesson none of them would soon forget.

Danny's Gift

SANDRA P. KLAUS

It had been a crazy day. Everything had gone wrong. It was roasting outside, and I had spent my whole day doing things for everyone else. I wasn't sure which level was higher, the heat or my frustration.

Now, on top of it all, I had to play the piano at a nursing home.

The residents straggled in. The afternoon church service was about to begin. While gray-haired men and hunchbacked women shuffled to their chairs, leaning on walkers and canes, I greeted each one, faking a smile. "How are you…? You look wonderful…. Is that a new dress?" I would ask as the wrinkled residents passed by.

Deep inside, I felt resentful. *Life isn't fair. I have to work all week at my job. Then I have to work on Sundays. I'm so tired….*

I sat restlessly at the piano and wondered how I could lead these people in joyful song. A nurse wheeled a young man past me. "Hi, Danny!" I called out. I had seen Danny at the home many times before. I knew that he was in his early twenties and had been severely injured in a car accident some years back. His days were now spent in an adult high chair with wheels.

I stood and took Danny's chair from the nurse and pushed it to his usual spot in the back row. "There you go, Danny," I said, looking into his eyes. "Good to see you. How are you?" His answer was garbled, as usual. Smiling,

I nodded and started to walk away, then stopped. I felt drawn to Danny, feeling God wanted me to listen to this young man.

Not today, Lord, I thought. *We're already running late.*

But I sensed God pleading with me to stay, so I pulled up a chair. "I'm sorry, Danny. I couldn't understand what you said. Try it again."

Struggling to form the words correctly, Danny forced out something that sounded like, "Icanoco."

"Try it again," I coaxed.

"Icanoco."

Over and over, Danny tried to say something, but to no avail.

"Let's do one word at a time," I suggested, determined to see this through.

Danny started with, "I."

I repeated, "I."

"Ca..."

After numerous wrong answers, I said, "Can. I can."

This brought a smile.

"Now what, Danny?"

Danny emitted an *n* sound, which I quickly interpreted as "not." "Okay. I cannot," I said. "You cannot what, Danny?"

Danny labored, then, almost intelligibly, he said, "Come."

"I cannot come?" I asked.

Danny nodded.

"Of course you can, Danny," I assured him. "Look, you're already here. What do you mean you can't come? To the service?"

Danny's head waggled from side to side. "No," he said, "Icanocompla—"

"Come play? You cannot come play?" I asked, groping for understanding. No, that wasn't it either.

Suddenly it hit me. Danny was merely answering my question of "How are you?" His answer was a simple one: "I cannot complain."

I stared at him while the words replayed through my mind: *I cannot complain.* Now I understood why God had nudged me to listen to Danny. *Lord, forgive me for complaining about trivial things, when all the while I am rich beyond words. Danny's words should have been mine. Thank you for using Danny to show me that.*

I smiled all the way back to the piano bench, and this time I led the residents in joyful song with a truly thankful heart.

Love must be active, as light must shine.

DWIGHT L. MOODY

Spring in New York

CHARLOTTE WECHSLER
FROM *SMALL MIRACLES*

That year, winter in New York City lingered lazily into late April. Living alone and legally blind, I had tended to remain indoors much of the time.

Finally, one day the chill was gone and spring stepped forth, filling the air with a penetrating and exhilarating fragrance. Outside my backyard window, a merry little bird kept chirping persistently, beckoning me, it seemed, outdoors.

Aware of the capriciousness of April, I clung to my winter coat, but as a concession to the change in temperature, discarded my woolen scarf, hat, and gloves. Taking my three-pronged cane, I stepped out cheerfully onto my open porch leading directly to the sidewalk. Lifting my face to the sun, I gave it a welcoming smile in acknowledgment of its warmth and promise.

As I walked down my quiet dead-end street, my next door neighbor called out a musical "Hello" and asked if I wanted a lift to where I was going. "No, thank you," I called back in return. "These legs of mine have been resting all winter, and my joints are badly in need of an outing, so I think I'll walk."

Reaching the corner, I waited, as was my habit, for someone to come along who would let me walk across with them when the light turned green. It seemed to take somewhat longer than usual for the sound of traffic to cease, yet I had no offers. As I stood there patiently, I began to hum a tune that returned to me from somewhere in the back of my head. It was a "welcome to spring" song I had learned in school as a child.

Suddenly a strong, well-modulated masculine voice spoke up. "You sound like a very cheerful human being," it said. "May I have the pleasure of your company across the street?" Flattered by such chivalry, I nodded, smiling, whispering a barely audible "Yes."

Gently he tucked his hand around my upper arm, and together we stepped off the curb. As we slowly made our way across, we talked of the most obvious topic—the weather—and about how good it was to be alive on such a day. As we kept in step together, it was difficult to determine who was the guide and who was the one being led.

We had barely reached the other side of the crossing when horns impatiently began blasting forth again at what was assuredly a change in the light. We walked on a few more paces to get away from the curb. Turning to him, I opened my mouth to thank him for his assistance and company. Before a single word had left my lips, he spoke up. "I don't know if you realize," he said, "how gratifying it is to find someone as cheerful as you to accompany a blind person like me across the street."

That spring day has stayed with me forever.

Four Quarters of Love

NANCY JO SULLIVAN
FROM *MOMENTS OF GRACE*

That morning, the school gym had been transformed into a fair for the day. Underneath the basketball hoops, long tables were packed with videos and colorful brochures. Tall bookshelves held collectible children's classics: *The Berenstein Bears, Arthur Goes to Camp*, and *The Babysitter's Club*.

I had volunteered to work at the fair as the checkout lady, a last minute favor for my daughter. My assignment was to run a cash register at a central table. Just minutes before the book fair began, I scribbled out a to-do list on a scrap of paper. My house was a mess, I had deadlines at work, and the car needed repair.

"I'm so busy," I told the other parent volunteers. I wanted everyone to know what a sacrifice I was making.

All morning long the children came in to browse, one class per half hour. I watched young students page through paperbacks and hardbound books covered with glossy paper jackets. One by one, I tallied totals on a calculator, the children handing me checks their parents had written out—checks for ten, twenty, and sometimes even thirty dollars.

Around lunchtime, a classroom of sixth graders arrived. One boy from the class drew near a table adjacent to mine, the bargain table. It was packed with erasers and stickers and pencil boxes, all marked one dollar.

Blue-eyed and freckled, the boy picked up a poster of a race car, a fuchsia-colored Ferrari set against a metallic black background.

"Wow," he whispered, his eyes wide. For several minutes, he studied the glossy print, admiring every detail.

"It only costs a dollar," I said with a smile.

The boy dug in his pockets, pulling out four quarters. "It's my lunch money," he said. He had no check from his parents.

A bell rang. Though it was time for him to return to his classroom, the boy lingered on, trying to decide if he should buy the poster. Meanwhile, a group of first graders began filtering through the fair.

Soon a tiny boy wearing a Johnny name tag made his way to the bargain table. Standing on his tiptoes, the child caught a glimpse of the poster held by his older classmate.

"Wow," Johnny whispered loudly.

"It's only a dollar," the boy said as he lowered the poster so Johnny could see.

"I don't have any money," said the little boy.

Without hesitation, the older child handed me his four quarters, exact payment for the race car print.

With a grin, he placed the poster in Johnny's hands, rushing off to join his waiting class.

I remembered my morning resentments, how I had begrudged my gift of time, how I had wanted someone to notice my "good deed."

I saw that the most honorable "gifts of goodness" are given in secret and flow from a humble heart.

A heart that has no need to be recognized.

A heart that sacrifices without a hint of resentment.

A heart that joyfully shares what is hardest to share.

I spent the rest of the day happily performing my checkout lady duties.

I smiled as I tallied totals, talking and joking and reading with the kids. I even bought a bunch of stickers, secretly tucking them into newly bought books.

I forgot about the messy house, the work deadlines, the unrepaired car.

I had better things to do.

The Secret Act

DONALD E. AND VESTA W. MANSELL
FROM *SURE AS THE DAWN*

Sir Ernest Shackleton, famous British explorer of the Antarctic, was once asked what was the most terrible moment he experienced on the frozen continent. One might think he would tell about some horrendous polar blizzard, but he didn't. Instead, he said his most terrible moment came one night when he and his men were huddled together in an emergency hut and the last rations had been passed out.

After his men were snoring soundly, Shackleton remained awake, his eyes half-closed. Suddenly he noticed a surreptitious movement by one of his men. Squinting in the man's direction, he saw him stealthily reach over one of the other men and remove his biscuit bag from his pack.

Shackleton was shocked! Up to that moment he would have trusted his life to this man. Now he had his doubts.

But then, as he watched, he saw the man open his own biscuit bag, take out his last morsel of food, quietly put it in the other man's bag, and replace it in his pack.

As Shackleton related the story, he said, "I dare not tell you the man's name. I feel his act was a secret between himself and God."

carrying the Torch

MELISSA MARIN
AGE 17

My Aunt Kristy has always been a positive influence on my life. She is very strong in her faith, she runs three miles every day, and she can make the grouchiest person laugh. Several times she has opened her door to foster children, and the number one thing in her life is family. All who know my Aunt Kristy hold a special place for her in their hearts.

One evening, after arriving home from basketball practice, there was a message on the answering machine. "Hi, Melissa, this is Aunt Kristy. Give me a call when you get home." Her voice was cheery as always.

The phone rang twice. "Hello," she answered.

"Hi, it's me. I'm returning your phone call."

"Hi, Liss. I called because I was going to see if you would house-sit for me this weekend, but it doesn't look like I'm going out of town after all." She sounded tired.

"Why not?"

"Well," she hesitated. "I went to the doctor today and things didn't go too well."

"What's wrong?"

"The doctor diagnosed me with MS."

Multiple sclerosis! That doesn't sound good, I thought. There was a long silence over the phone. Neither of us knew what to say.

She tried to reassure me. "Everything is going to be okay. It's not as bad as it sounds."

We chatted for a little while longer, trying to keep the conversation away from MS. When all the small talk ran out, we ended the conversation with "I love you" and said good-bye.

Once the whole family heard the news, nobody knew what to say or how to act. We all wanted to ignore the fact that Aunt Kristy was ill—everybody except Aunt Kristy.

One afternoon we all decided to go and keep her company. When we got to her house, there was a pile of books about MS lying by her chair. Aunt Kristy wanted to educate us. At first, none of us wanted to hear it, but once we heard the confidence in her voice, we knew she was going to be okay. She told us how doctors hope to have a cure in the next ten years and how the medicine she is taking will slow the stages of MS.

Grandma abruptly changed the subject. "It looks like it's going to start snowing. I'd better get home before Grandpa starts worrying."

"I'll walk you to the door," Aunt Kristy said.

When she got up, she pushed the blanket off her lap and underneath was her Bible. That's when I realized that even though my aunt had been diagnosed with an awful illness, she did not lose her faith in God. Her faith is what gave her the power to look MS in the face and say, "You don't scare me!"

It has been almost a year since my aunt was diagnosed, and new surprises keep coming into her life. In June of 2001, my aunt found out that she had been nominated and chosen to be one of the people who carry the Olympic torch in the 2002 Winter Olympics.

God has a plan for everybody, and even though His plans may not seem clear, He will never leave our side. Seeing Aunt Kristy's example and strength, I have learned that even in the darkest of times, God is always there holding our hand.

When the World Fell Silent

PHILIP D. YANCEY
FROM *WHAT'S SO AMAZING ABOUT GRACE?*

Bill Moyers' documentary film on the hymn "Amazing Grace" includes a scene filmed in Wembley Stadium in London. Various musical groups, mostly rock bands, had gathered together in celebration of the changes in South Africa, and for some reason the promoters scheduled an opera singer, Jessye Norman, as the closing act.

The film cuts back and forth between scenes of the unruly crowd in the stadium and Jessye Norman being interviewed. For twelve hours groups like Guns N' Roses have blasted the crowd through banks of speakers, riling up fans already high on booze and dope. The crowd yells for more curtain calls, and the rock groups oblige. Meanwhile, Jessye Norman sits in her dressing room discussing "Amazing Grace" with Moyers....

Finally, the time comes for her to sing. A single circle of light follows Norman, a majestic African-American woman wearing a flowing African dashiki, as she strolls on stage. No backup band, no musical instruments, just Jessye.

The crowd stirs, restless. Few recognize the opera diva. A voice yells for more Guns N' Roses. Others take up the cry. The scene is getting ugly. Alone, *a cappella*, Jessye Norman begins to sing, very slowly:

Amazing grace, how sweet the sound.
    That saved a wretch like me!
I once was lost but now am found
    Was blind, but now I see.

A remarkable thing happens in Wembley Stadium that night. Seventy thousand raucous fans fall silent before her aria of grace. By the time Norman reaches the second verse, "'Twas grace that taught my heart to fear, And grace my fears relieved…," the soprano has the crowd in her hands. By the time she reaches the third verse, "'Tis grace has brought me safe this far, And grace will lead me home," several thousand fans are singing along, digging far back in nearly lost memories for words they heard long ago.

When we've been there ten thousand years,
    Bright shining as the sun,
We've no less days to sing God's praise
    Than when we first begun.

Jessye Norman later confessed she had no idea what power descended on Wembley Stadium that night. I think I know. The world thirsts for grace. When grace descends, the world falls silent before it.

Forever Friends

The glory of friendship
is not in the outstretched hand,
nor the kindly smile,
nor the joy of companionship;
it is in the spiritual inspiration that comes to one
when he discovers
that someone else believes in him
and is willing to trust him.

RALPH WALDO EMERSON

The Real Me

CYNTHIA M. HAMOND

At fourteen, I was the new girl at a rural school in an apple orchard valley. My class had twenty-eight students equally divided between boys and girls. It was the tightly knit group of twelve girls that kept me an outsider. They teased me about my bright red hair, my height, my clothes, my shoe size, my accent, and anything else they could think of. I cried myself to sleep every night after my parents' pep talk. They said all the right things like "give it time" and "once they get to know you they'll love you." I wanted to believe them, but the evidence proved otherwise.

Then, a few months into the school year, my parents' predictions came true. I was playing out in left field for the girls' baseball team when a ball rocketed right at me. I put my mitt up as a shield and the ball packed itself right into my glove. That play saved the game, and we beat the boys' team for the first time. After that, the girls couldn't just exclude me from the victory party. It turned out that they liked my sense of humor, and a few actually said that they wished they had my mass of auburn hair.

Suddenly, I was in! Friendships grew, and soon I was included in the overnights and birthday parties.

Spring break came and went, and we returned to a school of freshly waxed floors, redone bulletin boards, and one new girl. Rosa was petite and quiet. Her family had come to work in the apple orchards.

I knew how she felt, so I smiled at her and helped her find her way around. The final weeks of school passed and we came to our last day and the traditional eighth grade graduation dance.

I decided it would be a nice gesture to invite Rosa over to help her get ready for the dance, so I graciously bestowed my favor upon her.

"Leave it to Cindy to go the extra mile," my friends all said.

I played the fairy godmother and she was the Cinderella. I waved my wand and the magic happened. She was transformed! Her hair, her makeup, her nails, even a new dress from my closet. Rosa was ready for her ball.

We stood side by side in front of the mirror.

"Oh, thank you, Cindy!" We smiled at each other's reflection.

"I only wish my friend Tracie could see me now. I wished she would come to the dance. She said she's never gone to one. She made me promise to have the best time ever and to remember every moment so I could tell her all about it tomorrow. She was so excited for me."

Tracie! I had never even thought of her. And that's the moment I saw the real me in the mirror, and believe me, it was not a pretty sight.

Tracie was one of the fourteen girls in our class. I was so happy when the twelve welcomed me into their inner circle that I never looked back or looked around. I especially never looked at Tracie, the one who stood alone until Rosa became her friend.

Even in my most self-serving moment, when I had deemed Rosa worthy and reached down to pull her up to my standard, I had not even thought of Tracie. She wasn't one of us—she had never been. That was a given long before I showed up.

By my action, I proved to Tracie once again that she somehow fell short of the rest of us. Yet, instead of being bitter, she wished for her friend only the best.

That night at the dance, Rosa was a hit. Yet I couldn't stop thinking about Tracie. This was the first time that I was aware of her absence. This time, however, I hurt inside because I knew why.

I never did redeem myself. School was out, Tracie's family didn't have a phone, and we lived fifteen miles from each other—all good excuses not to face her. In the fall, we moved on to different high schools.

But the girl I never considered, the one I was blind to, she was the one who helped me see more of the truth about compassion than the twelve who were my friends.

Tracie taught me to really see the people around me, that no one should go unnoticed. She taught me to be happy for others when their dreams come true, even if it's something you wanted first but could never have. She taught me that sometimes the mark of a true friend is in the letting go. And she taught me that a good heart grows through the day-to-day acts of kindness—not just the grand gestures.

Tracie, I thank you. I pray that God is illuminating your chosen path. I hope for you all the good things. And, Tracie, to this very day I am sorry.

I breathed a song into the air;
    it fell to the earth I know not where.
And the song, from beginning to end,
    I found again in the heart of a friend.

HENRY WADSWORTH LONGFELLOW

Scribblings in My Yearbook

TERESA J. CLEARY

I opened my yearbook with anticipation as it finally landed back on
my desk after making the rounds
in English class. It seemed like it had taken forever to get those few messages
written—but then, of course, everyone who was going to write something
had to read what had already been written.

I smiled as I saw the scribbled message in the top corner of the page. It
was from my best friend, Jenny.

> Teresa, looks like we made it! Ah! Finally seniors! Although we may
> lose touch with everyone else after this year, it's comforting to know
> you will always be near in mind and heart. Thank you so much for
> being my friend.
> Love, Jenny

Next, I read the message from my friend Josh, who had hated school
and life in general when I first met him. Josh was the wildest friend I had.
He could drink and party like no one else, though he said his life had really
calmed down since he met me.

> Teresa, I can't tell you how much your friendship has changed my
> attitude about school and mostly about people, and how much I

appreciate it. Always remember that there's no problem you can't conquer with the help of your friends.

Love, Josh

I then read a lot of messages that contained the standard fare for signing someone else's yearbook. *You've got a great personality. You're so cute and sweet. Hope you never change. RMA! (Remember Me Always!)*

And then I saw the neat handwriting in all capital letters that could only belong to Bill. Bill and I had become friends last year in study hall. Instead of doing our work, we would either pass notes or get permission to go next door to the library where we'd talk about school, our lives, and a lot of times, our faith. Like me, Bill was a Christian, and I think that's why we were able to share with each other not only what was on our minds, but also what was in our hearts. Yet when others sat with us, I would steer our conversation to more standard topics like teachers, after-school jobs, and what we were doing over the weekend.

This year, Bill and I only had English class together, and we'd lost touch. His message began:

I could begin by telling you the usual stuff. You've got a great personality. Never change. RMA. How's that? The trouble is, you DO have a great personality, and the only thing I hope never changes is your true concern for people, especially your friends. I'm very proud to have been one of them. (By the way, who's the other one? Ha ha.)

I can't say how much it meant to me to have you to talk to in study hall last year. I miss talking like we used to. I hope you feel that you can come to me if you have a problem or just need to talk to someone. If nothing else, I'm a great listener.

The love of Christ, Bill

I smiled and then looked again at how Bill had ended the note—"The love of Christ." I wished I had the nerve to sign my yearbook entries to my friends that way, but I was too caught up in what other people thought of me to do anything so—well—radical. After all, my friends might think I'd gone over the deep end with religion, or I might get a reputation as some kind of Jesus freak. In one way I admired what Bill had done, yet in another way I thought it was a bad move. Why ruin things for yourself senior year? I'd just keep Jesus tucked away in my heart.

In the days to come, I did hear kids teasing Bill about how he'd signed their yearbooks. "Hey, Bill! What in the world is 'the love of Christ'? What are you, some kind of religious fanatic?"

Bill would just smile and take the opportunity to quickly tell the others how he'd accepted Jesus as his Savior and how that decision had changed his life. While most people walked away before Bill got very far, I did see a few of them staying to listen and ask questions. I even heard one guy ask Bill to meet him at lunch. I saw them later huddled in a corner of the cafeteria in deep discussion.

Curiosity got the better of me. I stopped Bill in the hallway between classes that afternoon and asked how his meeting went. "Good!" Bill said enthusiastically. "Steve has a lot of problems in his life that aren't going to be solved overnight, but I think he understands how Jesus can help him with them. I was hoping what I wrote in everyone's yearbook would give me the chance to talk to them about Jesus. I really think it was a smart decision."

"But don't you hate all the teasing you've gotten?" I asked. "Not to mention your new nickname, 'The Preacher.'"

Bill laughed. "I knew there would be a cost for my actions, but it seems like a small price to pay." The bell rang, and we both raced for class.

I dropped into my seat and looked around the classroom. I smiled at Jenny who was in the next row and waved at Josh who was sitting across the room. He waved back and held up his yearbook—he had finally brought it. His yearbook landed with a thud on my desk.

I opened the front cover of the book and began reading the many scribbled messages that covered the first two pages. Many of the notes were from Josh's old friends and contained advice like, "Party hearty!" and had marijuana leaves drawn all over them. This was a crowd I really didn't come into contact with. I turned to the back cover and read the messages there. More of the same.

Well, Lord, what should I say? I prayed as I picked up my pen. Josh had said our friendship had already had a major impact on his life. Yet I knew there was part of myself I hadn't shared with my friend. I'd never told him about Jesus. Maybe I would get teased by my friends. Maybe I'd be called "The Preacher" or even worse. But then, maybe Josh's life would be changed more than it already had been.

I whispered a silent prayer, bent my head over the yearbook, and began to write.

Dear Josh,

I've enjoyed our friendship more than I could ever say. But there's a part of my life that I've never talked with you about, and I'd like to share it with you sometime....

What is a friend?
I will tell you.
It is a person with whom
you dare to be yourself.

FRANK CRANE

Stray No More

JANE KISE

I kind of thought of Melissa as a stray puppy—skinny, straggly hair, socially awkward. When we met in fifth grade, I must have been a head taller and light years more mature. Luckily for Melissa, I'd been taught to look out for strays, so I included her in our recess four-square and jump rope games.

In seventh grade, Melissa embarrassed me sometimes. If someone asked, "How'd you like the new Aerosmith song?" she waited for me to speak and then gave the same answer. In cooking class, she asked my advice before doing so much as unwrapping a stick of butter. I had a sneaking suspicion that if I'd asked her to put salt in our teacher's coffee, she would have done it.

By high school, I felt kind of responsible for Melissa. For school parties, I invited her to hang out with my crowd so she'd be asked to dance. We were both in band and on the swim team. When Melissa said that she wanted to host an end-of-season team banquet, I quickly offered to help in order to save her from doing something stupid.

I shouldn't have been surprised when Melissa chose the same college that I did. For one thing, we each wanted a small school that had both a swimming team and a good science program. And for another, she'd followed me everywhere for eight years.

Being on the swim team made us instant friends with some of the most popular students on campus. The captains planned touch football or capture the flag games for every Friday afternoon. And every Saturday night, someone on the team hosted a party. For the first time in her life, Melissa was part of the "in" crowd.

After chemistry one morning, as we walked together to our post office boxes, Melissa said, "I asked my mom if I could host the team at my house in January. It'll be too cold for football by then, and I've got some ideas for indoor games—or maybe an outdoor treasure hunt."

"A what?" I asked. I hadn't been on a treasure hunt since my ninth birthday. What was Melissa thinking?

"We'll need about three or four drivers for the hunt. And could you maybe help with food?" I found myself agreeing to head home the afternoon before the party to bake brownies and pop popcorn.

Inside, though, I wondered, *What am I getting into? Will anyone actually come?* The team never partied without beer, even though Melissa and I politely turned it down. There'd be no alcohol at Melissa's house, any more than there would have been at mine. After this party we'd be labeled the babies of the team. But I'd given my word.

In the weeks leading up to the party, I racked my brain for other activities in case Melissa's plans bombed. I also arranged to purchase several pizzas at a price I could afford. I just didn't want Melissa hurt.

The day of the party, temperatures plunged to twenty below zero. No one would want to go mucking about in the snow for clues.

Melissa called me in the afternoon. "Glad you got those pizzas," she said. "We'll just stay at my house instead of doing the treasure hunt." Great. Now we had at least five hours to kill in her basement. That is, if the more sophisticated team members even showed up.

But they did. Melissa lived about four miles from campus, and the whole group made it by around seven o'clock. After passing out pop and pizza, Melissa stood on a chair to get everyone's attention. "Okay, we're going to break into teams, just as if we were heading out on the treasure hunt. I've written out clues, and once you solve the first one, come get the next one from me so the other teams will have a sense of who's in the lead."

She had us number off, grade-school style. Some of the junior and senior guys snickered, trading places so that they were teamed with their girlfriends, but soon the groups were huddled around the clues Melissa distributed.

"Hey, it's a code we have to break," someone said. I looked at our first paper, thinking Melissa must have copied it from a book. But, no, it was her handwriting.

Gwen, a psychology major, quickly found the pattern. Our first stop would have been the local McDonald's where the manager had instructions to give us the next clue when we all ordered hot chocolate.

The next sheet held a series of riddles. The solution? A gas station where Melissa's brother worked. We then worked our way through the next clues: a page that required a mirror to solve, an unbelievably clever map puzzle, and an acrostic where the answers were the names of swimmers.

If the weather had cooperated, the "treasure" of chocolate coins would have been around the neck of a concrete frog in the city park's lily pond. Melissa handed the coins to the winning team and quipped, "Wasn't this easier than wading through the snow to get them?"

A bunch of the swimmers actually applauded. "Melissa, this was so clever!"

"How'd you come up with this?"

"We vote to make this an annual event!"

The rest of the evening flew by with songs around Melissa's player piano, a novelty to all of us. The guys fought to operate the pedals. Then we played round after round of a dictionary game until we ran out of slips of paper and the pencils were too dull to use.

As our teammates said good-bye, one of the juniors said, "You know, this was way more fun than usual. I didn't know you could have such a good time without being half drunk, if you know what I mean. Thanks."

Melissa just beamed while we cleaned up. She said, "I never could have done it without you."

"You take that back," I said. "*You* just hosted the best party ever, not me." I took a good look at her, perhaps for the first time since fifth grade. Still short, but graceful now—straggly hair and nervous hands long gone—a stray no more. That is, if she'd ever really been a stray.

With that last thought, I vowed to be as loyal a friend to Melissa as she had been to me.

chocolate chip cookies Taste Better as Dough

DANAE JACOBSON
AGE 17
FROM *THINGS I'VE LEARNED LATELY*

There's something about chocolate chip cookies that is special. Almost anyone can make them, whether or not you know much about baking. And if you don't burn the cookies or use two cups of baking soda instead of flour, they usually turn out pretty good.

Even better than the cookies, though, is the cookie dough. Sometimes my friends and I will get together to watch movies or listen to music while we make cookie dough instead of cookies. Forget the baking sheet—we dig right in with our spoons. And despite repeated warnings, none of us has ever gotten salmonella from the uncooked eggs.

Maybe it's because I usually eat dough with a bunch of friends while talking, laughing, and singing. Maybe it's because we grew up being told by Mom, "Don't eat the dough!" But whatever the reason, my friends and I agree that chocolate chip cookies definitely taste better as dough.

And you know what? I've learned that that's true about a lot of things in life. It's so easy to look ahead and imagine how wonderful life will be "when I get to college" or "when I turn twenty-one" or "when I get married." But today is all we are guaranteed. What if today *is* the best part? If we're always waiting for and dreaming about the finished product, we can miss out on what is really the best! So my advice and philosophy is to live in the now. Take a big bite of the cookie dough, and share it with someone you love.

Sweeter Than Chocolate

=◎=

JANET LYNN MITCHELL

I officially celebrated my fiftieth day in the hospital—nineteen years old and three thousand miles away from any family member or friend. Little did I know that only about a third of my stay was over. It seemed that lately God had asked me to face challenges I would have rather turned my back on. I had but two choices: I could keep on trying or give up the hope of ever walking again.

But, God, I am tired—tired of being in pain and tired of hospital life, I cried while peering out the window of my room. In the middle of my discussion with God, I sensed I wasn't alone. Turning my wheelchair, I saw a nurse standing in the doorway. I tried to figure out if I had seen her before, but I didn't recognize her. As if she were conducting a survey, she spoke. "Janet, my name is Sharon. I'm wondering if you'd tell me what your favorite candy is?"

For a second I wondered, too. I wondered if she actually thought that candy could make things better. But I answered her respectfully. "I love light milk chocolate with chewy caramels in the middle. Just thinking about them makes me hungry."

That evening an older couple knocked on my door. Never expecting company other than the folks I had met in the hospital, I wasn't prepared for guests. I had spent the last hour consumed with "what ifs," wondering if this tenth surgery was going to do the job. I had planned on spending the evening alone, trying to rally my emotions, giving myself a pep talk. Biting back my tears, I reluctantly invited them in.

"Hey. Are you the Janet from California?"

"That would be me," I replied.

The gentleman walked toward my wheelchair. Demonstrating his Southern warmth, he reached toward me and took my hand. For a moment, he embraced it, holding it, offering me the touch of another human being. *How did you know that I longed for my father's touch?*

Sitting down next to me, the gentleman spoke. "Hi, I'm Joe Posey, and this is my wife, Evelyn. We brought you a box of light milk chocolate caramels." Pausing, he chuckled. "I suppose that the caramel is in the middle. I didn't try 'em," he added with a grin.

"Would you like to?" I offered. "It's much more fun eating chocolate caramels with a friend."

Helping herself to a chocolate nugget, Evelyn began to explain the facts surrounding their surprise visit. "Janet," she said, "one of the surgical nurses here told our church about you. She's been with you in your last few surgeries and knows about your situation. She asked our church members to pray for you while you were here alone in Georgia."

"And you know," Joe piped up, "Evelyn and I have been prayin', and tonight we thought that we'd come by and find out just who we've been prayin' for."

Wow, was I stunned! A surgical nurse, whom I had never spoken to, cared enough to tell her church about me.

Glancing at my steel leg braces and my Buster Brown shoes, Joe curiously quizzed me. "What kind of mileage do you get with those?"

"None yet," I said with a smile. "I'm still working on the parallel bars."

"I bet if I'd come by and oil 'em good, you'd be the slickest gal in therapy!" Mr. Posey joked.

That night was the beginning of a wonderful friendship. The Poseys returned to visit me every few days. Daily, Evelyn called to check on my progress and my spirits. With each visit, Evelyn took my laundry, washed it, and returned it neatly folded in a bag. And if I was lucky, I'd find a piece or two of light milk chocolate caramels on my nightstand. The Poseys were just the medicine I needed for my troubled heart.

During my hospital stay, the Poseys taught me to look and listen for ways in which I could be a blessing to another. "Dare to crawl out of your comfort zone and extend your hand to a stranger," Joe said. "For strangers are just friends waiting to happen!"

Five months passed, and the day finally came—I was going home. Throughout my prolonged stay, God had been perfectly faithful to me. He had stood by my side and cheered me on as I learned to walk again. And through the Poseys, He had provided for my deepest needs of love and friendship, even adding the sweetness of light milk chocolates with chewy caramel inside.

One of the most beautiful qualities of true friendship is to understand and be understood.

AUTHOR UNKNOWN

Your Life Will Be Richer—If

Your life will be richer if on this day
You will make an effort to:
Mend a quarrel.
Search for a forgotten friend.
Dismiss a suspicion and replace it with trust.
Write a letter to someone who misses you.
Encourage someone who has lost faith.
Keep a promise.
Forget an old grudge.
Examine your demands on others and vow to reduce them.
Fight for a principle.
Express your gratitude.
Overcome an old fear.
Take two minutes to appreciate the beauty of nature.
Tell someone you love them.
Tell them again.
And again.
And again.

AUTHOR UNKNOWN

Missing the Dance

MICHELE WALLACE CAMPANELLI

Would you like to be my date for the winter dance?" asked Rick.

I couldn't believe he was asking me. My two best friends had gotten dates weeks ago, so I had given up hope of anyone asking me. Rick was the coolest guy in the senior class! And he wanted to go with me? "Are you serious?"

"I've already taken care of the tickets, and my parents will let me use their car," he responded.

How could I ask for more—Prince Charming driving me to the ball in a chariot. My mouth worded, "Yes," as my heart leaped with joy. I had never been to a formal dance before, and now was my chance. This would be the best night of my life!

The moment I got home I told my mom about Rick's invitation. Immediately she took me shopping to find the perfect dress. We decided on how to fix my hair and what color of nail polish to wear. This was going to be a special evening.

Before I knew it, days had passed. I couldn't sleep at all. Butterflies fluttered in my stomach, and my head was throbbing. Friday morning I woke up, and the whole world seemed to spin. I tried to lift my head off the pillow, but I couldn't move.

"Honey, you're going to be late for school…. Are you okay?" My mom came into the bedroom. Her hand flew to my forehead. "Oh no! You've got a fever."

I didn't feel hot; I felt cold, so very cold.

My mother helped me dress, and she drove me to the doctor. I had been there only a few minutes before my doctor called an ambulance. I couldn't understand what he was telling me. All I could hear was a muffled, "One-hundred-four-degree fever."

The hospital looked so blindingly bright as a nurse with long, dark hair stuck two IVs in my arm. I didn't remember seeing her come into my room, only the blanket being thrown on top of me. "Cold, very cold," I responded.

"It's filled with ice," she explained. "You have a bad infection. Your doctor ordered fluids and antibiotics for you. Just rest."

I closed my eyes.

It seemed only a few minutes later when I heard my doctor's voice. "Good morning. I'm glad you slept through the night. Luckily, we've brought your temperature down. You are one special little girl. You have a very serious ear, nose, and throat infection, but it seems we now have it under control."

"Mom?" I gasped. "Dad?"

"We're right here." My mother grabbed my hand.

I looked up at them.

"Did I miss the dance?"

My mom smiled. "I called Rick. I got his number out of your address book and let him know that you were in the hospital."

"Oh no," I cried.

"There will be other dances," said my doctor. "Be thankful you'll be alive to see them."

Days passed, and I got increasingly stronger and no longer had a fever. The medical staff discovered that I had developed a bad strep infection, which my doctor treated with antibiotics.

I hadn't heard from Rick at all. That bothered me. I worried that he was angry. Not only had I missed the dance, but I had let him down. Who could blame him if he never spoke to me again?

The same nurse who had given me my IVs came into my room holding a hospital robe. "Put this on," she said.

"Why do I need to do that? Aren't I going home today? I have a gown on already."

She just smiled and left, shutting the door behind her. I didn't feel like putting on the robe, but I did what she asked. Maybe there was another X ray or test my doctor needed before I could be released.

Suddenly the door swung open and standing before me were my parents holding balloons and a CD player, my two best friends in formals, and their dates and Rick in tuxedos.

"Would you care for a dance?" Rick asked. "Just because you missed the winter dance doesn't mean we can't have our own right here, right now."

Tears came to my eyes. "Sure," I stammered.

The nurse closed the curtains and left only the bathroom light on. My friends coupled together as Rick wrapped his arms around me and began to sway to the music.

"I'm so glad you are okay," he said. "I called your parents every night to check up on you."

"They didn't tell me." I pulled at my hair so it wouldn't look unbrushed.

"Don't worry." He smiled. "You look beautiful."

My friends and I danced for what seemed like hours. We didn't mind the people watching from the hall or my parents dancing beside us. My hospital robe was less than formal, but I didn't care. When the CD was over, Rick helped me into a wheelchair and took me downstairs to his parents' car, which was waiting to take me home.

I will never forget that afternoon for as long as I live. I didn't have my hair fancily done or even a pretty dress, but I felt truly beautiful, truly loved.

More Than a Crown

ANITA HIGMAN

A grin crept across the teacher's face. She raised her eyebrows. "So, who is going to be our new Annual King and Queen this year? As you know, it is up to each of you. All you have to do to win this honor is to sell the most yearbooks."

My heart pounded hard like a bass drum in band class. I knew that this was my only chance. A chance at winning the one thing I had always wanted: to be crowned Annual Queen at my school.

My mind raced. If I started my quest right after the classroom bell, I just might make it. After all, the only thing I had to do was sell the most yearbooks. Yeah, right. That was about as likely to happen as my winning a one-thousand-dollar shopping spree at the mall.

But still, I wanted this prize so badly that I could almost taste it. It would make me feel like I really fit in somehow. I knew that this was my only chance to be a school queen of any kind. Ever. All the other chances to be queen would never be mine, because they were voted on. That meant only the popular girls would be queens. So this was it—my chance of a lifetime.

I sighed. This would take grit and determination. I decided that right when the bell rang, I would become a selling machine. I would work harder than anyone else.

The bell blared. I jumped like a frightened bird. My stomach felt like I had swallowed a marble...maybe a whole bagful! Where was my grit now?

Who was I kidding? I might not even sell one yearbook. I couldn't think of anything else to do in my panic but talk to God about it.

Oh, Lord, I prayed. *I hear that You care about the small things here on earth. I want to be crowned Annual Queen. Maybe it really isn't all that important. But it seems to matter a lot to me right now. And I would really like wearing an awesome dress up on stage when I'm crowned. That is, if it is okay with You. And if all of that isn't possible, then please help me to just do my best. Amen.*

Lightning didn't strike or anything like that after I said my prayer, but I wasn't afraid anymore. I just got up out of my chair and proceeded to ask every human being that I met if they would like to buy a yearbook from me. First, I ran up to Mrs. Fairfield. "Would you like to buy a yearbook from me?" She answered an amazing yes, and so I was on my way with a smile—for a change! Over the next several days I asked teachers, people in our town, and anybody and everybody who would listen. I kept asking and selling until the other classmates could not believe my never-give-up attitude. I *had* to sell the most. And I *did* sell the most.

One morning I walked into class and received the most awesome surprise. Some of the girls in my class, one by one, began to give me their tickets. Smiling, they each came around and handed me their sales orders to add to mine. They had been so impressed with my determination that they gave them to me as a gesture of friendship.

I cried. Not then, but later, when the rest of the world had fallen asleep. I was awake for a long time and grateful for what had happened…that God had known what I really needed and had given it to me.

Yes, I worked hard to win, and it was a special honor to be Annual Queen, but it was the acts of kindness to me that day and the offerings of friendship that meant more to me than any crown.

New in Hicksville

CATHY M. ELLIOTT

We can't really be leaving, I thought as my father locked the front door. All my pouting, whining, and digging in my heels had done no good. My best complaints were wasted on deaf ears. The movers had finished packing our possessions and now we were off to our new home in the Northwest—like it or not.

I didn't like it. Because my father was in the military, our family often moved from place to place. It was unusual for us to stay at one tour of duty for longer than a couple of years. But this place had been the exception to the rule, and we had lived on the naval base for more than five.

My roots were planted deep. This was home, and it had hurt my heart to say good-bye to dear friends, to know I wouldn't graduate from high school with my class. How could I adjust to a tiny school of four hundred when I'd been a part of a major sophomoric strength in a school of four thousand?

Our Buick rolled quietly along the highway, and orange groves zipped past as quickly as pictures on a spinning top. The landscape changed with the miles, but my attitude did not. I sulked on my side of the backseat and wished myself home again. My father's retirement was the end of my existence—of that I was sure. So what if we had our first new home? I had no friends in this town. It helped only a little that my uncle, aunt, and cousins also lived in the destination I silently referred to as "Hicksville."

The car crested the last mountain, and we descended into a green forested valley. We approached the lumber mill, and I looked out through the glass to see logs stacked halfway to the clouds. The air was heavy with a woodsy scent—like the inside of a pencil sharpener. It took only moments to travel the tiny main street and pull into the driveway of our new home. I uttered an inaudible prayer. *Please, God, help me to belong. I don't know anyone here and no one knows me. I'm scared to be the new girl.*

My new room had a window that framed a lush view of pine, fir, and cedar trees that reminded me of our family trip to Yellowstone National Park—except this was my own backyard. Not bad. As I unpacked my belongings, Mother called, "Come outside, honey. You have company." *She must be kidding. Who do I know here?*

Four teenage girls, chatting and giggling, awaited me on the porch. One held out her hand and said, "Welcome. We heard there was going to be a new girl in school this year, and we wanted to say 'hi.' So, what grade are you in?" Soon we were engrossed in conversation, exchanging phone numbers, and planning when to get together. I liked them. They didn't seem like hicks at all.

That summer, the girls and I spent countless hours poring over school yearbooks as they introduced me to my future classmates through pictures. The faces of every student, teacher, bus driver, and administrator were familiar by the first day of class. It took me by surprise when I walked into the high school foyer, surrounded by new friends, and recognized buddies-to-be from their portraits. Somehow, a miracle had occurred. I was already a part of it all. I belonged. Maybe my best high school days were yet to be.

It took a while for me to realize that my heavenly Father had more than answered my prayer. He had prepared the way for His selfish child long before we moved, granting grace and mercy where none was deserved.

Those final two years of high school were very unlike the first. Opportunities waited at my new school that had once been the pale flicker of an unattainable dream in my old school where gobs of students vied for one slot on the cheerleading squad. I met families who lived in that one place for decades, pouring their hearts into the community year after year. And there, in beloved "Hicksville," I made friends that would last a lifetime.

Mailbox Friend

ASHLEY BLAKE
AGE 18

I t was two days before my thir-
teenth birthday, and my family was
moving to a new town nestled in
the heart of Central Oregon. I was actually excited about the move, yet there
was still that anxiety that often comes with change. New school, new church,
new people—ugh! My view of the future ranged from exciting to terrifying,
depending on my mood and attitude.

Somewhere between unpacking and tackling loads of homework, I
decided to sign up for a pen pal through *Brio* magazine. It was the perfect
opportunity to make a new friend, and I also thought it would be fun to meet
someone from a different place. My self-addressed envelope was promptly
returned with a girl's name and address enclosed on a note card. "Rachel
Oliver," it declared in confident handwriting. She was my age—in fact, just
seven hours older—and lived in Greencastle, Pennsylvania.

Rachel and I quickly discovered that we had a number of mutual interests: animals, sports, music, and most importantly, a passion to serve God.
Though I didn't realize at the time how much it would affect my life, having
Rachel as my friend has completely rocked my world. I know that God's
hand was right there when our names were matched.

Rachel and I were honest with each other from the start, and we committed to being accountable in our walks with God. Throughout our years
of correspondence we have contemplated, discussed, and analyzed just

about every topic in our lives: parents, homework, guys, spiritual struggles, siblings, the future, and countless other subjects. It is such a blessing to get an objective opinion about what's going on in my life, along with the encouragement to keep seeking God and His will.

There's something about receiving real, physical letters. Many times when I needed uplifting words, a letter would arrive at just the right time. Or on days when terms weren't the best with my parents or the world didn't seem to be cooperating with me, I would pick up an old letter and reread it. Not only did Rachel's words bring a smile to my face and dissipate my gloomy spirits, but also they encouraged me to keep my priorities straight and focus on God.

Rachel came to visit me the summer of 1999, exactly three years after our first letters were exchanged. We packed all that we could into that week: snowboarding, attending youth group, horseback riding, hanging out with friends, and so much more. Being together added another dimension to our friendship.

The following year I visited her world in Pennsylvania. That also was a jam-packed week! Rachel introduced me to all her friends (I finally got to put faces to all those names), and we explored her little town, went to Hershey Park, visited Baltimore, played guitar together, and simply enjoyed each other's company.

Rachel has been such an example and encouragement to me—her desire to serve God absolutely blows me away. After a trip to New York, Rachel was ecstatic. "New York City is incredible," she wrote. "Eight million people, Ash! And God knows every one of them, right down to their favorite flavors of gum, or if they hate gum, or whatever…you know what I mean." Talk about a heart for lives! Rachel has this amazing charisma that draws people to her. You know what it is? It's her heart for God—Jesus shines through and affects her entire countenance. She has inspired me so much to go beyond mediocre Christianity and to step out boldly in my faith.

In recent years, Rachel and I had hoped to go on a mission trip together, but God had something different in mind. We went on mission trips at different times, but to the same country: Panama. What an experience! That was the most incredible, intense thing I have ever done, and it impacted my life forever. It not only drew me closer to God, but also enhanced my friendship with Rachel.

After nearly six years of correspondence, Rachel and I continue to communicate primarily by "snail mail," with sporadic e-mails and telephone calls in between. It amazes me how much one person can enrich and change a life. But when I think about it, I realize that's why we're here—to touch and bless other people's lives, leaving the hope of Jesus in our wake. My pen pal has been the prime example of that approach toward life, and I thank God every day for sending me Rachel, my "mailbox friend."

Editor's note: If any of you girl readers would enjoy having a pen pal experience like Rachel and Ashley's, that opportunity is still available to *Brio* subscribers. *Brio* is a magazine for teenage girls published by Focus on the Family. For subscription information, contact:

Brio Magazine
Focus on the Family
PO Box 35500
Colorado Springs, CO 80995-3550

You Know What's Right

Do all the good you can,

By all the means you can,

In all the ways you can,

In all the places you can,

At all the times you can,

To all the people you can,

As long as ever...

...you can!

JOHN WESLEY

The Interview

MICHELE WALLACE CAMPANELLI

The job of a lifetime, that's what it was, secretary for the district attorney. I couldn't wait for my interview tomorrow afternoon. This kind of position is what I've dreamed of, what all those years of college and entry level positions were for.

That night I spent two hours going through my closet to pick out just the right outfit. What would I say? I curled up into my pillowy bed and stared at the ceiling, unable to sleep. How should I act? Nervous, I shut my eyes and tried to get some rest, but I kept tossing and turning.

Finally, the alarm clock woke me. I tried to open my eyes, but something was wrong. My face felt stiff, strange. My hands flew to my cheeks.

"No!" My lips were unable to open all the way.

I ran to the bathroom and looked at myself in the bathroom mirror, horrified. My face was contorted like a stroke victim's. My eyes were misaligned. I couldn't move the right side of my face. I barely recognized myself. What was happening to me? What nightmare did I wake up to?

My mother came into the room. "What's wrong?" Her eyes bulged as she withdrew in terror.

"What's happening to me?" I slurred to her.

"I'll take you to the emergency room," she finally gasped.

When Mom and I arrived, we were immediately rushed in. The nurse took one look at me and called in a specialist. There, under the blazing white lights, my mother and I waited.

After several hours of tests, the doctor finally explained. "You have Bell's palsy. It is a condition in which your face muscles tighten because of stress. You need to get plenty of sleep, and in a few days your face will return to normal."

"But I have a job interview this afternoon," I said. Sadness washed over me.

"I'm sorry," the doctor said. "You should reschedule, maybe for later in the week."

During the long car ride home, all I could think about was how bad it would look to reschedule. Certainly that would dampen my chances. Nobody reschedules with the district attorney. All the other applicants would have the advantage then, I concluded.

I looked at my watch and made the decision. "Mom, drop me off on Jacob Street. I'm going to the interview."

"Honey, I don't think you should. You look...strange," she said ever so gently.

I knew she was right. He probably would take one look at me and judge me by my appearance rather than by my experience and talent. I probably shouldn't go. But if I didn't, I'd always wonder if I could have gotten my dream job.

"No, Mom, take me there."

Reluctantly, she took me. I walked right into the formidable office with the mahogany furniture and pillars of white marble, not letting my own self-consciousness or any disease stop me. Not now, not when I had worked so hard for so long to be given this opportunity.

I went to the woman sitting behind the front desk and said, as well as I could, "Nicole Jenkins to see Mr. Robertson."

She stared at my face. "He's expecting you. Go right in."

I entered the room and saw a gray-haired man sitting behind a large desk reading a file.

Suddenly my nerves got the best of me and I had to sit. I took the chair in front of him.

"Hello," he said. "Miss Jenkins?"

"Yes. Please excuse me. I'm having a Bell's palsy attack. My doctor explained to me that it would last a few days. I came right from the hospital."

He paused. "You're very dedicated to come when you're not feeling up to speed."

"Yes, Sir."

He spent a few minutes looking over my application. "Is everything on here correct?" He held it out to me.

I glanced over the paper. "Yes, but I failed to mention that I type seventy-five words per minute."

"Wonderful," he smiled. "Out of one hundred points, you had our highest score on the application test. You scored well above average on grammar and computer programs."

"It comes easy for me," I honestly replied.

"Well, you are certainly qualified. When are you available?"

"In two weeks."

He gazed at his desk calendar. "The twentieth then. Be here at 9 A.M."

I gasped. "You're hiring me?"

"Yes, you're perfect for the position."

I stood. "Thank you for believing in me. I won't let you down."

"I know." He smiled and rose from his desk to shake my hand. "Not only have you got the skills I'm looking for, you also have the character."

No Turning Back

CYNTHIA TOBIAS
FROM *DO YOU KNOW WHAT I LIKE ABOUT YOU?*

Kelli, a quiet, conscientious fourteen-year-old, attended a public high school in the middle of a very liberal city. Her greatest struggle in ninth grade was not academic, but spiritual. When she learned about a "Meet Me at the Flagpole" event for teens to honor the National Day of Prayer, it was something she felt she should do. Although several other kids in her church youth group had expressed interest in participating, most of her classmates had never even heard of the event. When she mentioned it to them, their reaction was swift and abrupt: "What a dumb idea!" they told her. "If you show up at the flagpole and pray, everybody in school will think you're strange. You'll get stuck with everybody calling you 'weird' for the rest of your life. Just pray by yourself at home!"

The night before the "Meet Me at the Flagpole" event, Kelli's dad could sense she was really struggling. "Kelli, is everything okay?" She looked up at him and made a valiant effort to hold back her tears.

"Dad, I really want to do the right thing. I feel that praying at the flag-pole is something I should do tomorrow, but I don't know one other person who will be there. What if I get there and no one else shows up? What if my friends find out and think I'm just weird?"

Kelli's dad reached out and put his arm around her shoulders. "Kelli, I have always been so proud of you and your stand for Christ. This may be one of the hardest tests you've had so far, and I know you'll make the right decision. I'll take you to school tomorrow, and whatever you decide to do about the flagpole prayer is all right with me."

It was barely dawn when Kelli woke her dad. "Dad," she whispered, "will you take me to school now? I'm going to pray at the flagpole—even if I'm the only one there."

Her father's heart ached as he watched his precious girl grip the car's armrest all the way to school. Her face was pale but determined as she smiled at him. "It's okay, Dad. I prayed about this, and all night long I kept hearing the same song in my head: 'Though none go with me, I'll follow Jesus; no turning back, no turning back.' I guess being considered weird wouldn't be the worst thing that could happen to me."

As the car rounded the corner in front of the school, Kelli noticed quite a crowd had gathered—but not to pray. She recognized many of her friends and lots of other kids who were considered "popular" huddled near the flag-pole. They were giggling and pointing at two students standing near the flag-pole with their heads bowed in prayer. Momentary panic flashed across Kelli's face as she opened the car door.

Her dad reached over and took her hand. "Kelli, just remember, I love you no matter which of those two groups out there you join." Kelli smiled and nodded as she left the safety of the car and headed across the street. Her dad felt tears stinging his eyes as he watched his daughter bravely walk over toward the flagpole. How he wished he could go along, holding her hand for support. For a long, torturous minute, he watched her join the two students at the flagpole and bow her head in front of some of the most influential kids in the school. He was so proud that she had the courage to stand up for her convictions.

Suddenly, several teens broke loose from the watching crowd. Together they moved over to the flagpole and stood by Kelli. She lifted her head long enough to smile at them before continuing her prayer. As her dad watched, the number of students in the two groups began to shift. Before he finally drove away, the largest group by far was made up of those bowing their heads at the flagpole. He eagerly looked forward to talking with Kelli. He already knew exactly what he was going to say: "Kelli, I think you made the difference. I think those kids were waiting for *you*."

Attacked!

GREG O'LEARY
FROM *SMALL MIRACLES*

I was walking down a dimly lit street late one evening when I heard muffled screams coming from behind a clump of bushes. Alarmed, I slowed down to listen and panicked when I realized that what I was hearing were the unmistakable sounds of a struggle: heavy grunting, frantic scuffling, the tearing of fabric. Only yards from where I stood, a woman was being attacked.

Should I get involved? I was frightened for my own safety and cursed myself for having suddenly decided to take a new route home that night. What if I became another statistic? Shouldn't I just run to the nearest phone and call the police?

Although it seemed like an eternity, the deliberations in my head had taken only seconds, but already the girl's cries were growing weaker. I knew I had to act fast. How could I walk away from this? No, I finally resolved, I could not turn my back on the fate of this unknown woman, even if it meant risking my own life.

I am not a brave man, nor am I athletic. I don't know where I found the moral courage and physical strength—but once I had finally resolved to help the girl, I became strangely transformed. I ran behind the bushes and pulled the assailant off the woman. Grappling, we fell to the ground, where we wrestled for a few minutes until the attacker jumped up and escaped. Panting hard, I scrambled upright and approached the girl, who was crouched behind a tree, sobbing. In the darkness, I could barely see her outline, but I could certainly sense her trembling shock.

Not wanting to frighten her further, I at first spoke to her from a distance. "It's okay," I said soothingly. "The man ran away. You're safe now."

There was a long pause and then I heard her words, uttered in wonder, in amazement.

"Dad, is that you?"

And then, from behind the tree, stepped my youngest daughter, Katherine.

A person's true character is revealed
by what he does when no one is watching.

AUTHOR UNKNOWN

A Date to Remember

LORI SALIERNO
FROM *DESIGNED FOR EXCELLENCE*

When I was in my first year of college, I had a running partner. He was kind of cute and I liked him so it made exercising fun. After one of our workouts he said, "Lori, uh, how would you like to go out on Saturday?"

I thought, *Wow! A date. Seize this moment.* So I said, "Yeah, I'll go out. That'll be great."

He suggested we eat and see a movie.

Saturday came and we went out to dinner and talked about our running styles and our dreams to be world-class runners. Then we went to a movie.

During the first ten minutes of the movie, I began to sweat behind my ears because of what was happening on the screen. I got fidgety as I watched things start coming off of people—things being clothes. When the clothes came off, the people would come together, and I got more nervous.

The guy said, "Wow! What do you think?"

"I don't think I like it."

"Keep watching. It gets better." I watched, but it didn't get better.

I said, "Lord, what do I do?"

God said, "Lori, if I were sitting next to you in the flesh, what would you do?"

"I'd ask you for a ride home."

"Then you need to leave."

I cleared my throat two or three times, and finally the words squeaked out. "I have to go."

"Bathrooms are out back," he said.

"No, I have to leave. I can't watch this movie."

"Why not?"

"Because I'm a Sunday school teacher." We argued, and I tried to explain I wouldn't watch the kind of movie I told my students not to watch. Finally, I got up and started toward the door. He stomped out after me.

We were arguing when we got to the foyer. The guy behind the popcorn stand said, "Well, check out the fight tonight."

The guy was fighting mad all the way back to my dorm. Neither of us spoke a word. When we arrived, he stopped the car and said, "Please get out. I want you to know, Lori Marvel, I will never take you out on another date. I spent good money on you, and you can't handle a mature movie. Now get out!"

I went to my room, threw myself on my bed, and started to cry. I said, "Lord, You know I don't get that many dates. When I do, being a Christian with convictions isn't much fun."

We didn't run together anymore. The guy wouldn't even talk to me in the cafeteria. A few months later I was at work when he approached me. "Lori, may I ask you a question?"

"Yeah," I said. I knew he didn't want a date!

"Have you ever been in a locker room after practice with about twenty-five naked men?"

"Now, let me think," I said. "Ummm, no, I don't believe I've been in that situation."

"Let me tell you what it's like." He told me the favorite topic of the guys is young women. He said they discuss their body parts in detail and how much they can get from certain women. "Today your name came up in the locker room," he said.

One of the guys had said, "Hey, has anyone ever dated the Marvel chick?" Everyone got quiet.

The guy who ridiculed my standards and convictions said, "I have. And I want you to know you'll not get anything from her. If you bring up her name again this way, I'll deal with you personally. Lori Marvel is a lady."

Resolved: Never do anything which I should be afraid to do if it were the last hour of my life. A choice is made in one moment but lasts an eternity.

AUTHOR UNKNOWN

The Greatest Reward

LIEZL WEST

AGE 15, CAPE TOWN, SOUTH AFRICA

It was one of those open house parties—teens smoking and getting drunk. Being a Christian, I knew I probably shouldn't be there. I had a little voice at the back of my head telling me to get out of there, and fast, but I stayed anyway.

It wasn't long before I was offered alcohol. Suddenly the voice inside my head became much louder, and I simply said, "No thanks."

"Oh, don't be such a baby, Melissa," said Rachel, my best friend. "Just have a little; it won't kill you."

"Yeah, Melissa, you chicken," said someone in the crowd of people.

It hurt me to hear my best friend trying to make me feel so small and trying to make me do things that were totally against my beliefs. I thought they were against her beliefs, too.

"Rachel, I said no thanks!" I was trying hard to stop myself from crying.

Just then from the back of the room I heard someone start to chant, "Chicken, chicken, chicken," and then the whole room sort of caught on and everyone started chanting. I so badly wanted the floor to swallow me up and the chanting to stop.

"Come on, Melissa," Rachel said. "Just take a little; it's that easy."

It's that easy. Hey, I thought, *well maybe it is for you and the rest of the people in this room, but not for me.*

"Melissa, why don't you just take a drink?"

"Well, because…because…" I hesitated. "Because I'm a Christian!" I blurted out the words before I could stop myself. Then I burst into tears.

The whole room was silent, and all of a sudden they started laughing at me. I didn't know what to do, and I was crying uncontrollably. I ran out of that house as fast as I could, barely seeing where I was going. I wanted to run far, far away and never come back.

I suddenly felt very angry. *How could you let this happen to me, God? There I was standing up for You and what I believe in, and this is what I get in return. I think You must have made some mistake here.*

After a very long Monday of feeling sorry for myself, I was walking through the now empty school hallway when a girl came up to me and said, "Hi." I was quite surprised, since I remembered she was at the party and witnessed the whole thing.

"I've been looking for you the whole day," she said.

"Really?" I asked. "Why?"

"Well, I know that what happened to you at the party on Saturday night is not something you want to talk about again, but I'm not here to laugh at you, but simply to tell you how much I respect you for what you did. You were such an inspiration to me. I never could have done what you did. You stood up for what you believed and never gave in to temptation, no matter what price you had to pay for it. You, Melissa, are a true Christian, and I hope we can become better friends."

I remember that day as if it were yesterday. Sarah and I have been close friends ever since. I wouldn't have wanted that night to happen any other way. Even if this wasn't the reward I had wanted from God in the beginning, this is the only reward I want now. Making a difference in somebody else's life is the greatest reward you could ever ask for.

Sacrifice

LAFCADIO HEARN

In a Japanese seashore village over a hundred years ago, an earthquake startled the villagers one autumn evening. But, being accustomed to earthquakes, they soon went back to their activities. Above the village on a high plain, an old farmer was watching from his house. He looked at the sea, and the water appeared dark and acted strangely, moving against the wind, running away from the land. The old man knew what it meant. His one thought was to warn the people in the village.

He called to his grandson, "Bring me a torch! Make haste!" In the fields behind him lay his great crop of rice. Piled in stacks ready for the market, it was worth a fortune. The old man hurried out with his torch. In a moment the dry stalks were blazing. Then the big bell pealed from the temple below: Fire!

Back from the beach, away from the strange sea, up the steep side of the cliff came the people of the village. They were coming to try to save the crops of their rich neighbor. "He's mad!" they said.

As they reached the plain, the old man shouted back at the top of his voice, "Look!" At the edge of the horizon they saw a long, lean, dim line—a line that thickened as they gazed. That line was the sea, rising like a high wall and coming more swiftly than a kite flies. Then came a shock, heavier than thunder. The great swell struck the shore with a weight that sent a shudder through the hills and tore their homes to matchsticks. It drew back, roaring. Then it struck again, and again, and yet again. Once more it struck and ebbed; then it returned to its place.

On the plain no word was spoken. Then the voice of the old man was heard, saying gently, "That is why I set fire to the rice." He stood among them almost as poor as the poorest, for his wealth was gone—but he had saved four hundred lives by the sacrifice.

If I take care of my character my reputation will take care of itself.

DWIGHT L. MOODY

It's up to you

One step *must start each journey;*
One word *must start each prayer;*
One hope *will raise our spirits;*
One touch *can show you care.*
One voice *can speak with wisdom;*
One heart *can know what's true;*
One life *can make the difference.*
It's up to you.

AUTHOR UNKNOWN

What Would Jesus Do?

KATRINA CASSEL

Long before WWJD became a fad, my friend Rhonda and I had our own "what would Jesus do?" experience. It began when I found the book *In His Steps* in my mom's bookcase. It was a really old, worn book with small print, but for some reason, I decided to read it. It was about some people who decided to ask "what would Jesus do?" before doing anything for a whole year. Even though the book was old, the message still caught my attention, and I gave the book to my friend Rhonda to read.

After we had both read the book, we began to talk about what it would mean to ask ourselves, "What would Jesus do?" in every situation. We made an agreement to try it for two weeks. Those were two of the hardest weeks that I had ever lived through!

The first major test came at lunchtime of day one. A student named Deb entered the lunchroom, hair in disarray, wearing dark blue kneesocks with a pink skirt and an amusement park T-shirt. She was looking for a place to sit. Since she usually dominated any conversation and sprayed people with her food while she ate, she wasn't a popular lunch companion. I tried not to look at her, but her eye caught mine. *What would Jesus do?* I silently asked myself. *I don't want to do what Jesus would do,* I argued.

"Would you like to sit here?" I forced myself to say. I'd like to say that I discovered some hidden charm and talents in Deb and we became friends, but that wasn't the case. Rhonda was much more gracious than I was, steering the conversation to include Deb and giving me a kick under the table that let me know that Jesus would be a little more welcoming than I was being.

Day two of the "what would Jesus do?" quest presented a new challenge. My biology test was returned with a 94 percent written on the top. A quick glance through the test revealed that the teacher had miscalculated and I should have only gotten an 84 percent. *This is a teacher error. Jesus wouldn't expect me to tell the teacher about it, would He?* Reluctantly I approached the teacher hoping that he would say, "Don't worry about it, my mistake; we'll just leave the 94 percent in the grade book." No such luck. He quickly erased the 94 percent and replaced it with an 84 percent.

"But don't you feel honest?" Rhonda asked. "Isn't your integrity worth more than 10 percent?"

"Don't ask me that on report card day," I growled. "That 94 percent would have helped make up for mutilating that frog's brain in lab last week."

Situations confronted me each day requiring me to act in ways that I wouldn't normally and do things I really didn't want to do. Sometimes it meant taking a stand against something that was wrong; other times it meant making the time to read my Bible even when I didn't feel like it or was super busy. Trying to do what Jesus would was hard, but I grew through it. I spent more time thinking about Jesus and my lifestyle. I took more care with my schoolwork, and I became more sensitive to the people and situations around me. Even with the growth I experienced, it was a hard two weeks.

At the end of each day I put a large *X* over the calendar square. At the end of the two weeks I breathed a sigh of relief. "I'm glad that's over," I said, getting my schoolbooks from my locker.

"Are you kidding?" Rhonda said. "It was great! After all, that's really what the Christian life is all about—living the way Jesus would. I've been thinking…we should continue this for the rest of the school year—after all, *that's what Jesus would do!*"

A New Way of Seeing

=◎=

KIMA JUDE

C risp autumn weather urged us into the outdoors. My three college roommates and I decided to take a break from studying to toss a Frisbee, sit in the grass, and watch people. As I waited in the car for my friends, I turned my face toward the sun and smiled.

Nearby, a man in an overcoat caught my eye. He had a full head of gray hair yet was clearly in robust health. Except for his vision.

He wore dark glasses and swept a white cane across the ground in front of him. He was walking in a peculiar pattern, his stride purposeful and at the same time somewhat aimless. It seemed that he had strayed from the sidewalk onto a dirt knoll covered with fallen leaves. The area was just broad enough that the full arc of his cane did not reach the sidewalk for which he was searching.

I watched as he moved from one end of the knoll to the other, walking in circles, getting nowhere. I couldn't see his eyes behind the dark glasses, but his frustration was obvious. I marveled at the desire for independence that seemed to drive men like this, solitary and sightless, into the world.

Just then my friends returned, oblivious to the man a few yards from the car. As we drove away, I shared the poignant scene and how moved I was by his courage.

"But why didn't you help him?" one friend asked.

An obvious question, even at the time, and it startled me. *Why didn't I help him?* That question nagged at me for several days. What was missing in me that I was content to sit there and observe this man's struggle without even asking if I could help? Maybe I'd spent too much time in classes studying and taking notes. Maybe I'd become too much a student of life instead of a participant in it. I tried to convince myself that I was respecting a man's choice for independence. But the detached way I watched through glass was disquieting.

Some weeks later, while walking at a brisk pace to class, I passed a man out walking his dog. When I got to the corner, I quickly scanned the road to make sure there was no traffic. When the *Walk* signal appeared, I stepped into the street.

Behind me, the dog barked. I glanced over my shoulder and stopped short, right in the middle of the intersection. The dog wore a harness—a trained seeing eye dog—and he was straining to lead this blind man across the street. The young man, unsure of the traffic condition, tried to restrain his four-legged guide.

This time, I recognized the opportunity. I had learned something about compassion, I think—wisdom to know when help was needed and when to stand back.

"It's okay," I called to the young man, waiting to see if he'd accept my help.

After a brief moment, the man gave his dog the lead and stepped out into the street. The dog calmed down and joyfully led his master ahead. Deliberately, I shortened my stride and allowed them to pass me.

We reached the other side; he went his way and I went mine. I took the time to help this young man without offending him or taking away his independence, and that felt good. I still made it to class on time, this time without lingering regret or nagging questions. Once in class I took notes and made observations about life, just as before—but this time I thought about how lessons are really learned. Some of the most important ones cannot be taught in a laboratory or by lecture. Instead, our wise and gentle God sends them into our very paths.

And when there is a lesson to learn, He gently pushes us again and again until we begin to understand. The lessons He sends always apply, often in ways we don't expect. Two strangers crossed my path, and I began to learn sensitivity for the needs of other people—the need for help versus the need for independence. All along, God knew what lessons were needed.

You see, a short time later my younger sister lost most of her eyesight to diabetes. Fleeting disquiet once moved me to godly change, and that change now moves me to reach out with compassion in a very personal way.

Always do right – this will gratify some and astonish the rest.

MARK TWAIN

True to Me

SUE RHODES DODD

I was in love with Ethan. He was smart and popular—and best of all, he liked me, too. He was attentive and complimentary; I felt like a princess.

"I'm the luckiest guy in the world!" he'd say.

He'd brag to his friends: "Hey, guys, back off. She's with me!"

He always sat beside me, whether at a party or game or movie. We had fun together, and he usually called me every night. I thought he was the dream boyfriend. Until he started pressuring me.

Ethan had seemed at first to be the perfect gentleman. He held my hand a few times or slipped his arm around me, but he didn't try to kiss me until we had been seeing each other for a few weeks.

One afternoon at a neighborhood park, Ethan made his move. I turned my face so that his nose bumped my cheek. Without missing a beat, I blurted out the first thing that popped into my mind. "Have you ever seen so many pinecones on a tree before?" I asked, pointing to the huge trees hanging above us. I even reached down and picked up a prickly cone and showed it to him.

"Ouch, these are sharp," I said, "but aren't they pretty?"

Ethan sighed. "You're not very good at changing the subject, are you?"

I studied the pinecone as though it were the most fascinating wonder of all creation. Crisis abated, I sighed with relief. I was sure that Ethan assumed

I had not kissed anyone before. But in reality, I had, which was why I was avoiding kissing Ethan.

About a year earlier, Jason had kissed me. I had felt used because once Jason had kissed me, he dropped me and moved on to another girlfriend. I decided that next time, I'd be more cautious.

I thought I was safe with Ethan. He was certainly better than Jason, who was a player with a reputation for taking whatever he wanted.

At the park, Ethan tolerated my examination of pinecones for about ten minutes before he tried the direct approach.

"I want to kiss you," he said.

"I don't want to."

"But I want to show you that I love you."

"I'm not ready."

Turning on all of his charm, Ethan smiled and coaxed, "C'mon, it's just a little kiss."

"Please don't pressure me.... I don't want to."

Annoyed, Ethan stood and suggested we walk home.

"Ethan, if you really care about me, you'll respect me," I said. "I like you very much, but I don't want to kiss you. Not yet."

Ethan nodded, saying he understood, and we walked home, hand in hand.

It was spring. I was in love with a wonderful guy, and he was in love with me. Ethan sent me flowers and asked me to his prom. We went to different high schools, so that meant two different proms. I was so excited that I couldn't stand it. I bought a beautiful shimmery blue dress, and we started making plans for the big night.

Neither of us had a driver's license yet, so my parents offered to drive. Ethan declined, and I assumed his parents were driving. I was wrong. He wanted a taxi to take us. Alarms went off in my head. Why that expense when our parents were happy to pick us up?

"Because it's a special night," Ethan said, "and I want to be alone with you."

"That's really sweet, but I'm more comfortable with our parents taking us."

Again Ethan nodded, and I assumed all was fine. I was wrong again. Our discussion about the taxi was on Tuesday night, and his prom was on Saturday. He didn't call on Wednesday or Thursday, so I left him a phone message on Friday. He didn't call back, and I got stood up for the prom. Both of them.

I was devastated.

Raging emotions sent me into a tailspin. I kept asking God, "Why?" I kissed Jason, and he dumped me. I didn't kiss Ethan, and he dumped me. I was furious at boys in general and even at myself for liking someone who in the end treated me so badly. I cried myself to sleep for a week. I never heard from Ethan again.

Thinking through the relationship, I noticed that Ethan had been possessive of my time and attention. That's not necessarily a bad thing, but he always wanted to do things his way or no way at all. He seldom asked what I wanted to do. I was too easygoing to notice that Ethan took advantage of me.

I realized that I needed the kind of guy who would love and respect me no matter what. Everybody deserves that. There were other boyfriends, and I had a lot of practice setting boundaries, communicating, negotiating, messing up, starting over, and of course I had a lot of fun, too. But I tried to remain true to myself, to keep the choices I had made regarding things like kissing.

Years later, I fell in love with Jerry and married him. For the first time, I was with someone who loved me so much that he was willing to respect boundaries with me. He cared how I felt. About everything. Even if he didn't always agree with me, my feelings mattered to him.

For all of Ethan's *talk* about love, that relationship was more about his selfishness. Jerry loves me enough to honor my needs above his own, and I do that for him. Our relationship is not about him or me; it's about loving God and one another enough to do the right thing.

Respect and trust are part of true love. Not a day goes by that I don't thank the Lord for Jerry. We have more fun together than all our past relationships added together! Guess what? He was worth the wait.

Goody Two-Shoes

DEBRA WHITE SMITH

D id you do your algebra home-
work?"
"Of course not."
"You?"
"No. Do you think we could get Denise Booker to give us the answers?
She's always right."
"Are you kidding? That Goody Two-Shoes? She wouldn't give the
answers to her own grandmother!"

Suppressing a moan, I rested my head against the stall door in the girls
rest room and listened as Stephanie Fisher and Emily Ramos headed into the
hallway. I sure didn't *want* to overhear that conversation, but it seemed I was
always in hearing distance when someone called me "Goody Two-Shoes."

Ever since ninth grade, when all my friends started "going wild" as my
mother called it, I had felt like an outcast. Only a few other kids and I had
started tenth grade without drinking, smoking, cursing, or losing our vir-
ginity. As for the rest of my classmates, by tenth grade they were anything *but*
Goody Two-Shoes.

Sighing, I left the stall and stared at myself in the mirror, suddenly disgusted with my wide-eyed innocence. *I even look like a Goody Two-Shoes,* I
thought. Blond ponytail, blue eyes, freckles, only a trace of makeup, and
braces.

Gritting my teeth in sudden rebellion, I plundered through my backpack for the dark lipstick I'd purchased on a whim only last week. Deftly, I coated my lips in the reddish cream, rubbed them together, and stood back to examine the effect. *Not bad.* Next, with a flick of my wrist, I released my hair from the ponytail I put up earlier that morning and let it fall around my shoulders in a blond cloud.

The transformation was amazing. I stared into the mirror, hardly recognizing myself…or the gleam in my eyes. For once, I, Denise Booker, was going to fit in with my classmates.

"No more Goody Two-Shoes," I muttered to the stranger in the mirror. "From now on, you're just like everybody else."

But that isn't so easy when you're a Christian. Gritting my teeth, I shoved that disturbing voice to the back of my mind, grabbed my books, and raced to algebra. *Maybe if I hurry I can "help" Stephanie and Emily with their homework. Becoming their friend oughta help eliminate my flawless image.*

By last period, which was study hall, I had "helped" several classmates with homework, accepted an invitation to a big party that weekend, and had even managed to say a couple of curse words when I spilled my soda at lunch. Reflecting over my accomplishments, I propped my chin on my hand and stared out the window. *Not a bad day for someone who woke up this morning as a Goody Two-Shoes.*

While I was thinking of what I'd wear to school the next day, I heard someone shout, "Hey, Denise! I hear you're gonna be at the bash this weekend!"

Trying to hide my gasp, I looked up into the jaunty smile of Travis Jacobs, senior class president. Before today, he'd never even looked at me. My pulse was racing. *How does he know my name?*

"Yeah," I managed to get out of my mouth, while in my mind I was trying to figure out exactly how it would all happen. *I have no idea how I'm going to get past my parents. Or God.* Concentrating on Travis's sparkling brown eyes and shiny black hair, I desperately tried to escape that quiet voice in my head. It had been tormenting me all day.

"Well, save a dance for me." With a flirting wink, Travis took his seat across the room.

A hot rush flooded my stomach. Then surged to my face in flames of expectation. *Travis Jacobs likes me!* This day seemed too good to be true!

"Hey," a voice whispered from behind me. "Are you gonna explain biology to me?"

Still smiling from ear to ear, I turned to face Emily Ramos. I'd sat with her and Stephanie at lunch and had promised I'd explain the difference between viruses and bacteria to her during study hall. "Sure."

"I'd be careful if I were you," Emily said, casting a cautious glance toward Travis.

"What?" I blinked, not certain of Emily's insinuation.

"Travis…Travis isn't as nice as he might seem."

"He's not?" I croaked, feeling as if I were in a foreign country, speaking a foreign language. "What do you mean?"

"I mean…" Emily's eyes filled with tears. "I mean you just better watch out."

My eyes widened in astonishment. I never expected to see tough Emily Ramos cry. "It's okay," I muttered, wanting to give her a hug, but not sure how she'd accept it.

With a hard bite on her lip, Emily brushed away the tears and looked deeply into my eyes, a trace of disappointment marring her gaze. "When did you change?"

"What? What do you mean?" My gaze faltered and I stared at the tops of my perfectly white sneakers.

"You know what I mean."

"I…"

As I searched for something—anything—to say, Emily's words hung between us to cast a glaring light upon my recent "change." Then the day flashed before me in the shape of a nightmare. In just a few hours, I'd yielded to the temptation to throw away all I stood for. I'd gone against the Bible, against my parents, against God—and all for one dumb reason. I was tired of being called "Goody Two-Shoes."

"I always kinda admired you, I guess," Emily continued.

"Admired me?"

"Yeah. Seems you were the only one left with any guts, if you know what I mean." Then as the tardy bell rang, Emily made her way across the room and crammed her head into a magazine, the biology completely forgotten.

Stunned, I asked for permission to go to the rest room, only to lock myself into a stall and lean against the door. With one gulp and then another of the antiseptic-smelling air, hot, accusing tears flooded my eyes and stained my cheeks.

Forgive me, I prayed as my thoughts spun in a confused jumble. *Sometimes the temptation almost seems to be too much.*

After what seemed like an eternity, my tears ended. I splashed my face with cold water, grabbed a paper towel, and stared into the mirror—into the clear blue eyes of the person I again recognized. Goody Two-Shoes was back. But I knew there was much more to it than just being good or having guts. *Perhaps I could explain it all to Emily.*

Hang in There

In the Storm

When life whirls

rattles

bumps

and

roars,

GOD IS

peace

calm

and

hope

in the eye of the storm.

JUDY GORDON

Curt's Tears

KAY MARSHALL STROM

Green and gold balloons, brightly colored streamers, hot dog and popcorn stands—the high school parking lot looked more like a carnival than a school day. I glanced at the posted list of workshops the students had to choose from for their first annual "Faire Day":

50 FUN DATE IDEAS
HOW TO FIND A GREAT SUMMER JOB
PLANNING A PROM YOU'LL NEVER FORGET
THE BEST OF THE BEST NEW VIDEO GAMES

And, at the bottom of the list, the one I was scheduled to present:

A CRY FOR HELP FROM SUICIDAL TEENS

From the very beginning I'd had my doubts about that workshop. It seemed like an awfully depressing topic for something billed as a fun event.

In my room, I put twelve chairs into a circle and stacked up all the rest. No sense making it look like I'd expected a crowd in case no one showed up.

By the time I finished, a couple of kids had wandered in. I got out the basket of folded slips of paper I'd prepared, each with a role-playing situation typed on it, and set it out. Several more kids came in. Soon all the chairs in the circle were filled, and a couple of the guys were putting out the ones I had stacked away.

"Get together in groups of three or four," I told the kids.

I took the basket around so that each group could draw a slip. I told the kids to quickly lay out a general plan for a skit demonstrating the situation they'd drawn, then when they came up front they could ad lib their parts. We would all discuss solution options when they were finished.

As quickly as one group was set up and working, enough kids had come in to form another group. To my amazement, the room was almost full.

"Our group's ready!" a girl called out. "Can we start?"

"Sure," I said.

The girl played a passive mother who stood by as her husband berated their son. "Your grades are lousy!" the guy who played the father yelled. "All you do is pound those drums and shoot hoops!"

The boy tried to explain that he *loved* basketball and playing his drums.

"It's a waste of time! We're getting rid of all that junk today!" The "dad" spit out his words. "You make me sick! You're a loser, and a loser is all you'll ever be!"

When the group finished, a boy in the back of the room said, "I feel sorry for that kid. I mean, if even your own parents think you're a loser…"

A girl, her eyes flashing, snapped, "So he just sits by and accepts somebody else's opinion of him? Why?"

"Yeah!" said another. "We aren't little kids anymore! When are we going to start believing in ourselves?"

I had to cut off the discussion so the other groups would have time to give their presentations. One by one, each group acted out their assigned situation.

Your parents are getting a divorce. You are certain you're to blame….

You were arrested for shoplifting. Your parents are angry and embarrassed….

You are constantly being picked on by school bullies….

After each presentation, there was heated discussion that sometimes flamed into red-hot arguments. It didn't take me long to realize that those kids had wisdom and insight far greater than mine. Their words didn't come from research and theory and outside observation. No, they sprang from painful, personal experiences. They reacted because they *felt* the pain and frustration and fear.

Finally, with only a few minutes left, we were ready for the last group's performance. Curt, an overweight sophomore with a blotchy complexion, approached the others in his group who were sitting together talking. He quietly made his way over to Kristy, a pretty junior with long auburn hair. Curt stammered out, "So, uh…would you go to the Fall Masquerade Dance with me?"

Kristy looked him up and down, then burst out laughing. The others stopped talking.

"What's so funny?" one asked.

"This…this…*geek!*" she managed between peals of laughter. "He asked me to the Fall Masquerade Dance! Can't you just see it? Me and…*him?*"

Kristy practically split her sides laughing, and her friends joined right in.

"Well, at least he wouldn't need a costume!" another said, and everyone roared.

Poor Curt! Such humiliation! Tears filled his eyes, and he sank into a corner where he covered his face and sobbed.

"Great presentation!" I said. "You guys are real actors! Especially you, Curt!"

I waited for the kids to take their seats so we could spend the final minutes discussing possible ways to deal with such a devastating event. Kristy and the others did, taking dramatic bows on the way. But not Curt. He stayed slumped in the corner.

"Great acting, Curt," I repeated. "You can go ahead and sit down now."

He didn't move.

"Curt?" I said hesitantly.

Finally he looked up at us. His eyes were red and his face was streaked with tears. "I wasn't acting," he said in a flat voice. "I was just being me."

All movement and chatter halted. We stared, shocked into silence.

"I've never had a date," Curt continued. "I've tried, but this is what always happens. My friends say I shouldn't aim so high.… I should just ask loser girls. I did, but even *they* laughed at me." Then, looking straight at Kristy, he said, "So tell me, is it really worth living through another two and a half years of you and your friends treating me like dirt?"

Curt's words hung heavy in the silent air. Kristy, embarrassed, stared down at her polished nails.

It was a tall, skinny guy who was the first to move. He went up and put his hand on Curt's shoulder. "Yeah, it's worth it, man," he said. "There's more of us than there are of them." As he helped Curt to his feet, other kids went up. They touched him, patted his back, even hugged him. Kristy joined those gathered around him. "I'm sorry, Curt," she said softly. "I really am. I never meant to hurt you. I guess I didn't understand.… I didn't think about your feelings."

To my amazement, every single kid in the classroom joined the group that rallied around Curt. Some talked, others didn't. But they all encouraged with their support. And when they left the room together, Curt's tears were beginning to dry.

Plum Purple City Lights

JANET LYNN MITCHELL

M om, I've found exactly what I want for Christmas! It will look great in my room!"

Wanting to buy her what she truly wanted, I hurried off to buy Jenna's Christmas present—a thirteen-foot wallpaper mural of Manhattan's skyline. In just weeks, my sixteen-year-old daughter's bedroom took on a new look. The night lights of the Manhattan Bridge, Empire State Building, and Twin Towers stretched across her walls. Curtains, a bedspread, and a lamp were the added touches to convert Jenna's California hideaway into the glittering lights of New York City.

Truthfully, I did not share Jenna's taste in interior design. We had spent hours together shopping and contemplating different ways in which she could redecorate her room. I'd shown her flowers in pinks and yellows, and she again escorted me back to the store to take "one more look" at lower Manhattan at dusk, fashioned in plum purple and blues.

"It's cool, Mom. I love it! Can't you see? The city is alive, and its lights reflect off the water a silhouette of New York. Look, there are even two American flags flying proudly!"

I saw them. The two American flags were the size of small safety pins. And to me, the mural reflected a busy city, full of action and little peace. But, nevertheless, this was for Jenna's room. Thus I quickly resolved that any "flowers" Jenna may ever display would be in a vase!

Like many moms, each night since she was born I've eased my way into my daughter's room to ask Jenna about her day and listen to her dreams of the future. Often we've sat studying the skyline, talking about the different places we someday want to visit. Night after night, Jenna and I have pointed to different buildings and skyscrapers, pondering what their occupants might have done that day. Night after night I'd point to the Towers, sometimes even laying my hand across them saying, "Let's pray for the people who work here."

To which Jenna responded, "Mom, I pray for them every night!"

It's now one year later. Life in New York City has drastically changed due to September 11, 2001, and so has the view of the skyline. But Jenna's room remains unchanged. The Twin Towers still stand tall, adhered to Jenna's walls. Those two little flags the size of safety pins remain—untouched—declaring freedom.

I now see what wasn't clear a year ago. It's more than okay for moms and daughters to differ in their likes. For it is God who gave Jenna her taste of "interior design." And for an entire year, Jenna had prayed for people she didn't know and for a city she has never seen. How grateful I am that I quickly gave in. Putting my dreams of flowers to bed, I allowed Jenna the freedom to follow her heart.

I still find my way to Jenna's room each night. We talk about her day and her plans for tomorrow. Yet just before I kiss her good-night, a lump forms in my throat. I try to speak as I point toward Jenna's wall mural. "I know, Mom," she whispers while gazing at her walls. "I'm still praying."

He's My Brother

MAX LUCADO
FROM *TRAVELING LIGHT*

Eric Hill had everything you'd need for a bright future. He was twenty-eight years old and a recent college grad with an athletic frame and a soft smile. His family loved him, girls took notice of him, and companies had contacted him about working for them. Although Eric appeared composed without, he was tormented within. Tormented by voices he could not still. Bothered by images he could not avoid. So, hoping to get away from them all, he got away from it all. On a gray rainy day in February 1982, Eric Hill walked out the back door of his Florida home and never came back.

His sister Debbie remembers seeing him leave, his tall frame ambling down the interstate. She assumed he would return. He didn't. She hoped he would call. He didn't. She thought she could find him. She couldn't. Where Eric journeyed, only God and Eric know, and neither of them has chosen to tell. What we do know is Eric heard a voice. And in that voice was an "assignment." And that assignment was to pick up garbage along a roadside in San Antonio, Texas.

To the commuters on Interstate 10, his lanky form and bearded face became a familiar sight. He made a home out of a hole in a vacant lot. He made a wardrobe out of split trousers and a torn sweatshirt. An old hat deferred the summer sun. A plastic bag on his shoulders softened the winter chill. His weathered skin and stooped shoulders made him look twice his forty-four years. But then, sixteen years on the side of the road would do that to you.

That's how long it had been since Debbie had seen her brother. She might never have seen him again had it not been for two events. The first was the construction of a car dealership on Eric's vacant lot. The second was a severe pain in his abdomen. The dealership took his home. The pain nearly took his life.

EMS found him curled in a ball on the side of the road, clutching his stomach. The hospital ran some tests and found that Eric had cancer. Terminal cancer. Another few months and he would be dead. And with no known family or relatives, he would die alone.

His court-appointed attorney couldn't handle this thought. "Surely someone is looking for Eric," he reasoned. So the lawyer scoured the Internet for anyone in search of a brown-haired, adult male with the last name Hill. That's how he met Debbie.

His description seemed to match her memory, but she had to know for sure.

So Debbie came to Texas. She and her husband and two children rented a hotel room and set out to find Eric. By now he'd been released from the hospital, but the chaplain knew where he was. They found him sitting against a building not far from the interstate. As they approached, he stood. They offered fruit; he refused. They offered juice; he declined. He was polite but unimpressed with this family who claimed to be his own.

His interest perked, however, when Debbie offered him a pin to wear, an angel pin. He said yes. Her first time to touch her brother in sixteen years was the moment he allowed her to pin the angel on his shirt.

Debbie intended to spend a week. But a week passed, and she stayed. Her husband returned home, and she stayed. Spring became summer, and Eric improved, and still she stayed. Debbie rented an apartment and began homeschooling her kids and reaching out to her brother.

It wasn't easy. He didn't recognize her. He didn't know her. One day he cursed her. He didn't want to sleep in her apartment. He didn't want her food. He didn't want to talk. He wanted his vacant lot. He wanted his "job." Who was this woman anyway?

But Debbie didn't give up on Eric. She understood that he didn't understand. So she stayed.

I met her one Sunday when she visited our congregation. When she shared her story, I asked what you might want to ask. "How do you keep from giving up?"

"Simple," she said. "He's my brother."

...As Debbie followed Eric, God follows us. He pursues us until we finally see Him as our Father, even if it takes all the days of our lives.

Courage is not the absence of fear,
but the conquest of it.
Courage is knowing what is right
and doing it.

RITA ROBINSON

I ASKed

I asked God for health, that I might do greater things;
I was given infirmity, that I might do better things.

I asked for strength, that I might achieve;
I was made weak, that I might learn to obey.

I asked for riches, that I might be happy;
I was given poverty, that I might be wise.

I asked for power, that I might have the praise of men;
I was given weakness, that I might feel the need of God.

I asked for all things, that I might enjoy life;
I was given real life, that I might enjoy all things.

I got nothing I asked for, but everything I had hoped for;
Almost despite myself, my unspoken prayers were answered.

I am, among all men, most richly blessed.

A PRAYER FOUND IN THE POCKET OF A YOUNG, UNKNOWN CONFEDERATE
SOLDIER WHO MET HIS DEATH ON A CIVIL WAR BATTLEFIELD.

They Want Me for One Reason

DAVE DRAVECKY
FROM *WHEN YOU CAN'T COME BACK*

E ver since that backyard game of catch with my dad, baseball had become my life. It's what I watched on TV when I was indoors. It's what I played when I went outdoors. It's what I read about when I sprawled on the living room floor and spread out the Sunday paper.

My life was wrapped up in baseball. And my life as a ballplayer was wrapped up in my arm. It wasn't long before that arm gained the attention of the neighborhood. When they chose up sides for sandlot ball, I was the one they all wanted on their team.

They wanted me for one reason—my arm.

It wasn't long before that arm caught the attention of the entire school, when, as a teenager, I pitched my first no-hitter. My name started showing up on the sports page. Before long it made the headlines.

All because of my arm.

That arm attracted the attention of major league scouts, and the part of me that was my boyhood became my livelihood. My ability to provide for my family was not based on how good of a personality I had, how smart I was, or how hard I worked. It was based solely on what my arm could do on game day. The more strikes that arm could throw, the more I was worth. The more games that arm won, the more people wanted me on their team.

When people talked with me, it was the center of conversation. "How's the arm today, Dave?" "Is your arm ready for tonight?" "Better get some ice on that arm; don't want it to swell."

My arm was to me what hands are to a concert pianist, what legs are to a ballerina, what feet are to a marathon runner. It's what people cheered me for, what they paid their hard-earned money to see. It's what made me valuable, what gave me worth, at least in the eyes of the world.

Then suddenly my arm was gone.

How much of me went with it? How much of what people thought of me went with it?

I felt apprehensive. I wondered how my son would react when he saw me. Would he be afraid? Would he feel sorry for me? Would he keep his distance? And what about my daughter? Would she be embarrassed when we went out to eat? How would she feel when people stared? How would my wife feel? What would she think about a man who couldn't tie his own shoes? Would she still find me attractive, or would she be repulsed to see me in my nakedness with my carved-up body?

When I came home from the hospital, I realized that all Jonathan wanted was to wrestle with me and play football on the lawn. All Tiffany wanted was to hug me. All Jan wanted was to have her husband back.

They didn't care whether I had an arm or not.

As important as it had been to my boyhood, as important as it had been to my livelihood, my arm meant nothing to the people in my life who mattered the most. It was enough that I was alive and that I was home.

My Favorite Tradition

LISA STROM
AS TOLD TO KAY MARSHALL STROM

The year I was thirteen, my father was out of work. He lost his job in January. At first it didn't seem so bad. My parents kept saying that it wouldn't be for long, that he would be able to find another job soon. But as the months went by, our lives got harder and harder. My mom worked part time, and we all tried to save every penny we could, but by December, things were really looking hopeless.

Christmas had always been a really special time for our family. We had traditions for everything. We always got the tree the day after Thanksgiving and decorated it together while we sipped hot cocoa, which we stirred with candy canes. Right away the gifts began to appear under the tree.

All of us did our best to make this Christmas seem joyful, too, but it just wasn't the same. We didn't get a tree until halfway through December. It was a small, scrawny thing, one we got for free. We tried to be cheerful as we decorated it, but we got it done as fast as we could. There wasn't any cocoa that year, and no candy canes either. There were no presents to go under the tree, and I wondered if there ever would be.

The last day of school before Christmas vacation, I came home to an amazing sight: There was a whole pile of brightly wrapped presents under the little tree. I hurried to look them over, hoping no one noticed I was trying to see which ones were for me.

Another of our family's traditions was to put a tag on the gift with a made-up name that gave a hint as to what was inside. For instance, if I was getting a flannel shirt, the tag might say:

To: Lisa
From: Paul Bunyan

Because we used that clue to try to guess what might be inside, the person giving the gift tried to be as mysterious as possible.

There was one large gift for me from Frosty the Snowman. That had to be a sweater. Sweaters always seemed to be from Frosty. But there were also many smaller gifts, and they were all from Benjamin Franklin. My brother, too, had a larger one and a whole bunch of small ones from Benjamin Franklin. There were also several like that for my dad and even for my mom. (That was really strange since they were all in my mom's handwriting!)

Trying to guess what was in all those presents put some of the fun back in Christmas. What could Benjamin Franklin be giving every one of us? And why so many from him? And how had my mom managed to afford so many gifts when Dad still didn't have a job?

Well, Christmas morning finally arrived. My first gift was a sweater, just as I had guessed. My mom had gotten it at a thrift store, but I really liked it. My brother and my dad also got clothes from the thrift store. Then it was time to open all the gifts from Benjamin Franklin.

"Before we open them, will you give us a hint of what Benjamin Franklin has to do with it?" I asked my mother.

"Okay," she said. "Here's the hint: Benjamin Franklin was the founder of the public library system."

We tore into the gifts. They were books!

"All of them were withdrawn from the public library," my mom told us. "I got them for twenty-five cents each."

The rest of that day, as the turkey cooked in the oven (some people at the church had given it to us in a Christmas basket), we had a wonderful time reading our "new" books. Some of my all-time favorites came to me that Christmas, books like *The Grapes of Wrath, Black Like Me, Ode to Billy Joe,* and

The Hiding Place.

The next month my dad got a new job, one that was much better than the one he had before. And our Christmases went back to our old traditional ones with a big tree the day after Thanksgiving and a pile of presents under the tree. But now, every year, we also get a stack of gifts from Benjamin Franklin. It's my favorite Christmas tradition of all.

Sometimes love is at its best when it digs in its heels and holds on tight.

WILLIAM COLEMAN

Beauty Restored

KIMBERLY SHUMATE

ADAPTED FROM *STANDING ON THE PROMISES*

How do I explain anorexia? It's like a carnival mirror that distorts your image. No matter what you do or how thin you become, your shape is still grossly exaggerated in your mind. The only way out is to receive new sight.

It started for me at the age of sixteen. It was a traumatic time: My mother had recently been diagnosed with terminal cancer. My world was sliding downward, and I didn't know how to make it stop. When a person loses her balance, the natural inclination is to grab on to something. But in the midst of this surreal and frightening storm, I felt helpless. I could find nothing to stop my slide. I decided, almost subconsciously, to take control of the only thing I could, my body. I began to eat less. Watching the pounds drop away made me feel powerful.

When I was hungry, I suppressed the desire to eat. When other people invited me to eat, I told them that I had already eaten. After a while, the pain in my stomach subsided, and the feeling of emptiness that replaced it became my normal state of being. At five feet six inches tall, I weighed only ninety-three pounds. When my weight fluctuated due to water gain each month, I panicked. More starvation.

Several years went by as I continued this bizarre ritual of starvation and denial. The cramping in my muscles and the tremors in my hands had people concerned that I was a drug abuser, but the symptoms were merely by-products of a nervous system in agony. My ribs were now visible through my chest and my hipbones protruded through my clothes. The real test lay in making certain that my inner thighs didn't touch. I was queen of my domain, and I resolved it that way. When people commented on my weight, my reply was always the same: "I just have a fast metabolism." Lying had become a way of life.

One day I choked on a tortilla chip in a restaurant. I was too embarrassed to tell my friends that I hadn't eaten in three days and that my throat muscles had forgotten how to swallow. If people found out that I was deathly afraid of putting food in my mouth, they might think something was wrong with me. But as far as I was concerned, there wasn't. I just liked being thin. Thin was beautiful. I felt like a strong person, able to exercise amazing self-discipline.

It's funny what the body will do to get your attention. As my blood pressure dropped steadily, I would sometimes faint just getting out of bed. Heart arrhythmia, chest pains, insomnia, hypoglycemia, staggered breathing, internal tremors, muscle cramps, blurred vision, mental lethargy, night sweats, excessive bruising—these were all pleas from my tired body. But it didn't matter. My eyes still saw a fat girl in the mirror, and staying thin was all I could think about. It was what I had become—malnourished, dehydrated, and anemic. I made several emergency room visits, but my perspective didn't change.

If it weren't for several amazing Christian women in my life, I wouldn't be here to tell you this story. They interceded for me when I couldn't pray myself. There were days when I wondered, *How long would it take my heart to stop beating if I just didn't eat again?* The thought of dying was sometimes easier than the thought of continuing on. As my strength continued to ebb, these women were faithful in holding me up. When a walk through the grocery store left me panicked, they were praying. When the mere idea of opening the refrigerator door reduced me to tears, they were praying. When I sat on the couch crying instead of fixing my next meal, they supplied the encouragement to make it through. Because of their persistence, I was eventually delivered.

I humbly report that I have been in remission for four years now. I weigh one hundred twenty pounds, and I'm stronger now than I have ever been. God is the ultimate physician; He healed me from more than just an eating disorder. He gave me a new life and the tools to help other girls with the same devastating disease. I thank those patient, steadfast prayer warriors who never quit standing on His promises.

Faith sees the invisible,
believes the unbelievable,
and receives the impossible.

CORRIE TEN BOOM

UnSpeakable Terror

LAURA McDONALD
AS TOLD TO NANCY JO SULLIVAN
FROM *MOMENTS OF GRACE*

That Wednesday evening, I combed my daughter's hair in front of a gold-framed mirror in her bedroom. As I placed a pink clip on her ponytail, I gazed at her reflection in the glass.

Just an inch over four feet tall, Heather stood proudly in her pink-striped T-shirt and matching pants. Though Heather was eighteen years old, as a Down syndrome teenager she still maintained a childlike appearance.

"We're going to listen to music tonight," I told her as we made our way to the car. She smiled.

Earlier that morning, students from all over the Fort Worth area had gathered around school flagpoles to pray for their teachers and fellow students. To celebrate this prayer event, our church, Wedgwood Baptist, had scheduled a youth rally. Part of the program would include a Christian rock concert. Since I worked at the church as a publications secretary, I had observed the planning of the concert. I knew that over 350 young people would be attending.

What I didn't know is that the night ahead would hold unspeakable terror.

As I helped Heather buckle her seat belt, my thirteen-year-old son, Doug, jumped into the backseat. He'd been on the phone most of the afternoon.

"All of my friends are coming to the concert," he said excitedly.

As the three of us drove to church, we stopped to pick up a sandwich for Sarah, my seventeen-year-old. Sarah was part of the drama team at Wedgwood. She was already at the church practicing a skit. Her performance would take place after the concert.

Arriving at the church a few minutes early, Doug took off to join a group of his middle school friends. After dropping off Sarah's sandwich, Heather and I mingled with friends in the foyer of the church.

"Hi, Mrs. McDonald," a young girl said. Wearing bib overalls, she passed out programs and waved. It was always good to see Mary Beth. She was a smiling blond teenager who was always involved with youth activities.

"I like your pink clip," she told my daughter as she gave her a hug. Heather smiled at her and returned the hug.

As the band began to warm up, Heather and I made our way into the church and took a place in the back row. That night my husband, Bruce, was teaching a mission class. I told him to meet us in the back of the church if he got out early.

The church became crowded with young people, along with several adults. The band adjusted microphones on a platform in front of the pie-shaped sanctuary.

After a few words of introduction, the drums began to beat, electric guitars began to vibrate, and the band members broke into songs of contemporary worship.

The young people clapped and cheered. Some of the adults jokingly put their hands over their ears and rolled their eyes. It was clear their gestures were all in fun.

An unmistakable joy rippled through the church. From wall to wall, young voices of praise were loud and strong and full of irrepressible energy. Seeing so many young people gathered to worship God was quite a sight to behold.

Right next to me, a young woman named Kim was singing so loudly that I began to giggle. Though she was just twenty-three and a seminary student, the two of us had sung together on Sunday mornings in the church choir. I had never seen anyone praising God in such an uninhibited fashion.

As our eyes met, she giggled too. "I can't help it," she laughed as she joined in the next verse.

As I put my arm around Heather, she began rocking to the beat of the band. I thanked God for the gift of life, Heather's life, and all the lives around me.

It was then I heard a series of popping sounds, loud, cracking, banging sounds coming from the foyer.

With the band playing so loudly, most of those gathered in the church were unaware of the unsettling noise. In the corner of my eye, I saw Mary Beth running toward Heather and me from a nearby doorway.

Still holding a stack of programs, she screamed: "There's a gunman in the foyer!"

She rushed to my seat. Her eyes were full of panic.

"Hit the floor!" I yelled.

As Mary Beth and I dropped to the ground, Heather shook her head defiantly. "Noooo...." she called out. Unaware of the danger we were in, she insisted on remaining seated.

When Mary Beth saw me struggling to get Heather down, she put her left arm around my daughter's neck.

"C'mon, Heather," Mary Beth whispered as she tried to pull my daughter to the floor. With Heather still defiant, the two of us huddled over her as the gunman entered the sanctuary and began firing. In between rounds of bullets, he shouted obscenities.

I knew I needed to remain calm, for Heather and for Mary Beth, but deep inside I felt fearful. Where were my other children? Was my husband safe? Would we die at the hands of this evil man?

Amid my private panic, Mary Beth began to pray aloud. She was scared. She didn't realize that the volume of her voice would attract the gunman.

"Shhhh...." I told her as a bullet hit the row ahead of us.

The gunman paced behind our row, shooting and yelling: "You Baptists think you know everything...." I focused my thoughts on protecting Heather and Mary Beth.

A passage from Scripture came to mind, one that I had memorized when Heather was facing a life-threatening operation as a baby: "God is faithful; He will not let you be tempted beyond what you can bear.... He will also provide a way out so that you can stand up under it."

The shooting continued. I smelled the smoldering of spent cartridges. Bullets ricocheted over me and Heather and Mary Beth. I kept repeating the verse.

Then, the church grew eerily still. A man yelled from the foyer: "The gunman is down. Everyone out."

Mary Beth and I looked up and saw the gunman slumped on a pew against the wall right behind us.

"Mary Beth, you're hurt," I said. Her shoulder was covered with blood. As Mary Beth ran toward the outstretched arms of help, I sensed she would be okay. She was conscious and talking coherently.

Taking Heather's hand in mine, I turned to reach out for Kim. I gasped; she was lying lifeless on the church pew. "Oh, please, God…she's too young…too alive," I told myself. But the reality was, she was gone.

"Everyone out…now!" the loud voice commanded.

In response to his commands, Heather and I ran out to join a dazed and confused congregation. My husband came running toward us. "Are you okay?" he asked. Heather and I were covered with blood from Mary Beth's wound. We must have looked awful.

"We're fine, honey," I assured him. Our other children, Sarah and Doug, came running into our arms. We all crowded around Heather, making sure she hadn't been hurt. It was a moment of great relief. God had protected our family from this evil.

Still, in the midst of my relief, I thought about Kim. She had spent the last minutes of her life praising the Lord. For some reason, I felt assured that God's protection had been with her in death, just as it had been with our family in life.

God had rescued her from harm in a different way by quietly ushering her into the kingdom of heaven. Now Kim was in the loving arms of God who promises to "bear us up" when trials come and to provide a way out when there seems to be none.

As the flashing lights of the paramedics surrounded the church, I re-adjusted Heather's pink clip.

I wanted to tell her that she was a person of immeasurable value and worth, that someone had taken a bullet for her. I wanted to explain that Mary

Beth had shown great love, that she had been willing to give her life so that Heather might live. I wanted Heather to know that God's protection had been with her that night just as it had been so many years earlier.

But as I knelt down so that I could look into her eyes, I knew she wasn't capable of understanding these things.

And so I shared a simpler thought.

"God is faithful, isn't He, Heather?" I said softly.

She nodded as if she understood. "Yes," she said.

Tornado!

TIM HEANER

AS TOLD TO LINDA JOYCE HEANER

I grew up going to camp every summer and loved it. Now I was a counselor there, and I was eager to spend the summer outdoors with the kids.

One evening we received tornado and severe weather warnings. Instead of meeting upstairs in the lodge, we gathered the campers in its walk-out basement. Large windows lined the outer walls, and three small storage rooms were along the inside wall.

To keep the kids' minds off the approaching storm, we sang and did skits in our usual lighthearted manner. Suddenly the power shut off, and the air became extremely calm. No siren wailed, but somehow we knew the storm was about to hit.

David, the camp director, gave instructions. "Go into the storage rooms now." The fifty-three third and fourth graders panicked, and so counselors hurried them into the three rooms. Seconds later a roaring sound engulfed the camp, and I felt a painful popping sensation in my ears. Sounds of breaking glass pierced the air. I had never been so scared in my nineteen years of life. And I was responsible for the children, who were scared, too. We crouched on the floor together and prayed hard until the deafening sound stopped. I don't know how long we prayed or what I prayed. I just know that I cried out to God in my need. I put my arms around the campers and prayed. I tried to offer comfort and help them feel protected. We huddled in the room until David opened our door.

"There's glass everywhere," he warned. "Be careful. Have everyone hold hands and walk in a line across the field to the rec hall."

When I stepped outside, I couldn't believe my eyes. Where my cabin and two others had stood, only the concrete foundation slabs remained. Pieces of the buildings were strewn among the trees in a wooded area behind the slabs. I was astonished by the seriousness of our situation, and my mind took off in a zillion directions: *We've got to get these kids to a safe place! I wish I could run to the other camp staff, give them a hug and say 'I love you.' I'll do whatever it takes to get the camp cleaned up. I wonder what God will do here.*

"What happened?" campers asked each other.

"Where's my cabin?" another cried.

I noticed a gas leak on the way to the rec hall. David did, too. "We can't stay here," David told the counselors. "The leaking gas makes it dangerous to start any cars nearby. Let's walk the campers out to the road."

After counting everyone, we walked across a large field to the road. We sat down on the pavement and sang together. My heart's pounding lessened as we prayed with the campers and tried to keep them calm.

The children peppered us with questions.

"Is my family okay?" one camper asked.

"What about my house?" another child questioned.

"And my pets?" another asked tearfully.

"Your families and your houses are far away from here," we reassured the campers. "They're just fine."

We led the children into a soggy field on the opposite side of the road. Mosquitoes swarmed around us, and it was almost dark. We kept talking with the campers, holding them, helping them feel safe. One of the counselors called a local bus driver, and we were relieved to learn that he was coming to get us.

We were singing our camp song when the bus finally pulled into the church parking lot at 1:30 A.M. More than one hundred people crowded around, cheering loudly. Campers hurried into the arms of waiting parents who fervently thanked us for caring for their children. Five life-changing hours had passed since the tornado hit.

Later that morning the staff drove back to camp to retrieve any personal belongings that we could find. Seeing the destruction in its full scope shocked me. Five of the ten cabins were totally destroyed; the others were severely damaged. Part of the lodge roof had collapsed, and another part had blown off. A wall of the lodge dining hall, where we normally met, had blown out. Other sights also stunned me: a mattress impaled on a tree, a canoe wrapped around a tree trunk, our speedboat ruined and paddleboats gone, trees uprooted or destroyed, waterfront docks an unrecognizable tangle of iron. It was obvious that the camp would be closed for the rest of the summer.

When I saw the devastation firsthand, I began to grasp the magnitude of God's awesome miracle. The tornado, with winds over two hundred miles per hour, destroyed the camp. But all sixty-nine of us escaped without injury. God protected us, and now, more than ever, I know that God is my true shelter.

The Road of Life

Don't change yourself for anybody.
You are unique.
Keep your head up high
And continue down the road of life.
There will be obstacles.
There may be a sudden twist in the road.
There will be things that want to stop you,
But God will help you
To get through.
Even though you may be alone,
Don't give up
And you'll reach that goal of life.

JESSICA APPLETON

AGE 14

Craig's Story

≈◎≈

MARTY WILKINS

The September day started beautifully with sunshine, the smell of a campfire, and the sounds of birds echoing through the trees. Dan and his son, Craig, were up early, frying bacon and flipping pancakes. It was Craig's first hunting trip—time with Dad in the great outdoors. Today would mark one of his first steps in becoming a man. He had been looking forward to this day for months, and here it was. For Dan, this was a chance to teach his boy, to laugh and share, and to look at how marvelously God provides for His children.

Dan and Craig set out from camp early, excited about the possibilities for the day. *I'm going to get the biggest buck—the antlers will span sixteen feet, at least! Hmm...I'll have to decide where to display my trophy*, thought Craig.

Father and son were enjoying quality time together, walking and talking side by side in one of those classic Hallmark moments. Suddenly they heard a blast and the sound of rushing wind right above their heads. "Was that you, Craig?" Dan shouted.

"No, Dad, it wasn't me," he replied

In the next moment, as Dan was yelling, "Get down! Get down!" a second blast echoed through the woods, and Craig fell, never to get up again. A tragic moment frozen forever in the mind of a father, Dan held his son, and he wept and prayed.

In the distance was Jarron, a family friend who was also along on the trip. Inexperience and excitement had combined to form a deadly combination. He had mistaken rifle butts for deer antlers and had fired into the bushes. Excitement and thrill gave way to horror when Jarron realized the magnitude of his mistake. He fell to his knees, and he, too, cried and cried and saw no reason to go on. For him, it felt as if his life had just ended with Craig's. It was as if anything good in his life had been cast out and abandoned forever.

A few hours later, Jarron came face-to-face with Craig's father. He also came face-to-face with God-sized love. Dan, whose world had just collapsed in front of him, knew that as terrible as it was, it had been an accident. With tears streaming down his face, Dan opened his arms to Jarron and offered forgiveness before he even asked for it.

At the memorial service for Craig, Dan and his family prayed for Jarron. They prayed for his heart, and they prayed for his mind. They also prayed that the courts would be merciful. Craig's family spent time with Jarron and wept with him. They pleaded with the judge not to jail him.

The words to that old gospel song come to mind: *What a friend we have in Jesus, all our sins and grief to bear.* Long before the accident, Dan and his family placed themselves in God's service and in His love. They love Craig, and their hearts still ache with loneliness. But one day they will see him again in heaven. Jesus weeps with Craig's family, and He weeps with Jarron. He bears both the sin and the grief. Only He could give the power and perspective to love those that we can so easily find a reason to hate. *What a friend we have in Jesus.*

Surprised by God

REBECCA ST. JAMES
FROM *THE DANCE OF HEAVEN*

When my family first moved to America in 1991, we went through a major living-by-faith experience. We moved from Australia to Nashville, Tennessee, because of my dad's job. About two months after coming to America, my dad's job fell through. We were left on the other side of the world with no family, no close friends, no car, no furniture, no income, six kids, and my mum pregnant with the seventh. To say my parents were at a loss and rather humbled would be an incredible understatement. We didn't know what God was doing or even why we were in America. My grandparents even called us from Australia and begged us to come home.

What did we do? We sat on the floor as a family and prayed. We asked God for money, for food—for a car. We prayed specifically for God to provide the things we needed, and we saw miracles happen! Sometimes those specific things would come the same day we prayed for them. People dropped groceries on our doorstep, sent us checks in the mail, delivered truckloads of furniture to our house—somebody even gave us a Christmas tree and presents that first year! One family gave us a car. Someone paid thousands of dollars for my sister Libby to be born in a hospital; to this day we still don't know who that was!

Because of those experiences and others, I know that even when it feels as if life is at its worst and I've come to a dead end in the strength department, somehow God will surprise me with modern-day miracles. It may be as simple as someone saying an encouraging word at the right time or God revealing a Bible verse just for me, right when I need it. Or it may be that He places on my doorstep a houseful of furniture!

Truly, if we are His children and are trusting Him to take care of us—He will! Often when we're going through a hard time, it's not going to feel good in the fire, but God's promise stands that He will be with us.

Once when I was going through a hard time, I asked my pastor about how to deal with the pain. He asked me, "Can God be trusted?"

"Yes," I answered.

I got the point: He's trustworthy, so trust Him. When I am weak, He is strong.

After the Ice Cream Cones

AMY J. WADDLE
AGE 18

My driver's education teacher would have cringed to see me swerving in and out of the freeway lanes and then speeding up the narrow, windy mountain roads. Eventually I jammed the steering wheel hard to the left, sending the tires down the familiar gravel driveway of the camp where I was volunteering for the summer. I swiped hot tears off my face and tried to control my breathing as I opened the car door. "I just need some time alone," I coached myself. "Time to relax, time to read my Bible."

Not five minutes after I had settled on the grass, I was up again, still too upset to sit in one place. I collapsed back into my car and slammed it into reverse. I must have been too agitated to remember the basic rule of looking in my rearview mirror—I suddenly heard a thud and realized that I had backed into a cement wall. I dropped my head on the steering wheel and broke into a fresh round of tears as the reason for my distress erupted. "This can't be happening to my family!" I cried.

My memories were of the times the six of us crammed around a pink plastic table at Baskin Robbins that was meant for only four. What fun that was! Dad made us laugh at his jokes until we almost choked on our sugar cones.

Family meant joining hands around the dinner table to give thanks for the food and talking about our day as we passed the chicken. One time after dinner we spontaneously formed a circle in the middle of the kitchen for a giant group hug. With our arms wrapped around each other we sang the song that had somehow become "ours." "We are fam-i-leeeeee…. Ha ha ha ha ha ha ha haaaaaah." Dad launched into a ridiculous dance, and we laughed and told each other "I love you." *That* was my family.

Now the definition of family was changing right before my eyes. Only an hour before I had read a carefully composed letter from my parents. I could still feel the knot in my stomach that formed when I read the phrases "separate for a while," "moving," and "we love you."

I wasn't blind to the fact that my parents had problems. Recently, "family time" had become "yelling time" because of the increasing tension, and I had begun to dread situations when Mom and Dad were in the same room for longer than ten minutes. Dad had moved a sleeping bag downstairs, and we had long been referring to the master bedroom as only "Mom's."

Mom answered some of my frustrated questions, yet I still couldn't understand what was happening. *My* happy family? *My* parents were separating?

The next several months my sister, brothers, and I tried to adjust to a new and chaotic family life. We were shuffled from one living place to the next, and the feelings of insecurity and uncertainty were almost unbearable.

Stress overwhelmed me, and I lacked the motivation, desire, or stamina to do anything more than sleep. My school attendance slipped, my grades dropped, and my appetite decreased. Depression and loneliness became my constant companions.

In the midst of my pain, I offered God my crushed heart and confusion. In my brokenness, I sobbed in His presence and found peace. And I discovered a beautiful treasure: intimacy with the living God.

The Lord never promised "happy endings" as we would write them. My parents' supposedly temporary separation has already lasted over a year, and trust between them has been lost instead of restored. Although our living arrangements have stabilized, and I again possess the energy to be myself, the story is still far from a happy ending. I can't write that we all laugh or go to Baskin Robbins like we used to, and I honestly don't know what will happen in the future.

Yet, as I reflect on the past year, I am amazed and excited at the increased depth of my relationship with the Lord. He is my shield, my refuge, the lover of my soul. He is my everything. And He is refining my faith to be genuine and as pure gold. Faith that will last long after the ice cream cones have melted away.

I've learned that if there were no problems,
there would be no opportunities.

AUTHOR UNKNOWN

"Since I became a Christian, when someone sneezes and I say 'God bless you,' I really mean it."

"I used to carry a pocket Bible, but then I went through a spiritual growth spurt."

"Prayer is like 'Instant Messaging' with God."

"Dear Lord, bless me indeed. Expand my territory. And keep my dad from freaking out about my grades."

"It's a new reality show about the millions of people who still need to hear about Jesus."

"The bad news is it's a speeding ticket. The good news is
I invited the police officer to come to church with us."

"No...it's called tithing to God, not tipping God."

"Next week the youth group will be doing the service. Complimentary earplugs will be provided."

Love's All in the Family

Feeling at Home

What really makes

a family

is feeling at home

in each other's hearts.

JUDY GORDON

A Father Like That

SANDRA BYRD

Fourth of July fireworks popped like corn in the sky above me as I drove to Brad's house. I was late, as usual, because I'd been working. Every dime that I earned catering was going toward college in another year. Tonight's work was over, and I wanted to be with my friends.

We hung out, eating chips and salsa, talking, and swimming under the stars. Someone turned the music up—it was my favorite song, but I just couldn't get into it. I was too tired.

After saying an early good-night, I rubbed my eyes, grabbed my keys, and headed toward my dad's new car. Dad had let me drive it tonight for the first time. I started the engine, put it into reverse—and crashed into a concrete pillar bordering Brad's driveway.

The shock jolted the car, and as I slammed on the brakes, I flew forward into the steering wheel and threw the car into park. "This isn't happening. I did *not* just smash my dad's new car," I told myself. But the tears started to fall, and I knew the truth: I had crashed.

I ran back into the house to tell Brad that I would pay for the pillar, but that I had to get home now. They didn't want me to drive the few blocks to my house, but I insisted.

Outside again, I looked at the smashed quarter panel; it looked like crumpled aluminum foil. I had to face my dad on my own.

My dad and I had a tangled relationship, always butting heads because I wanted to spread my wings, while he wanted to control where I flew. Recently, though, he had turned his life over to God. He was doing strange things. Holding my mother's hand. Clearing the table. And keeping his words and voice thoughtful when we disagreed.

This will be the real test, I thought. My stomach hurt, and I willed my tears to stop.

I parked the wounded car and sat there in front of our darkened house. I forced myself to get out of the car instead of running away. Opening the front door and walking down the hallway was the hardest thing I'd ever done.

I knocked on my parents' bedroom door. "I'm home," I said. "And I need to talk with Dad."

I waited in the living room. He stepped out a moment later, tightening the belt around his robe.

"Dad," I said. "I was tired tonight from working, and when I left Brad's, I crashed your car."

He leaned forward, and his face softened. "You should have called us! You're okay, aren't you?" He held his arms open, and I ran into them like I hadn't done since I was a little girl. The tears flowed freely again.

"I'm okay now," I said. "And I'll pay for the damages."

"No, I'll pay them for you," he said. "I know you're working hard to save for college."

I didn't know God then, but I wondered for the first time if maybe the love of the heavenly Father was very much like that, wanting me to be safe, wanting me to call Him when I was in trouble. He paid the price and His arms were always open, no matter the time of night, no matter what I had to confess.

My Mom Understands

DANAE JACOBSON
AGE 17
FROM *THINGS I'VE LEARNED LATELY*

When I was in junior high, I was utterly rejected by two of my very best friends. Maybe that doesn't sound all that traumatic. I know it happens all the time, but it was one of the hardest things that had happened to me in my first twelve years of life.

The three of us had been the best of friends, but then one day they decided just to be friends without me. I tried to be brave and pretend it wasn't a big deal. But as I sat on my couch watching them riding their bikes past my house, I started to cry. At first I tried to hold it in because I didn't think my mom would understand, and I wasn't sure I wanted to talk about it with her.

But my mom noticed something was wrong. She came over, sat down on the couch, and held me until I was ready to hear her. Then, with tears in her own eyes at the painful memory, she told me a story about when something similar had happened to her. The circumstances were not exactly the same, but I could tell that she knew what I was feeling. Knowing that someone else had gotten through it meant a lot to me, regardless of the fact that she is my mother.

Since that day in junior high, I cannot count the times when I've felt a certain way or was going through something difficult or overwhelming, and my mom was the friend who was there for me. When I came home from school angry over an argument with a friend, my mom let me express my frustration. When a boy asked me out for the first time, my mom gave me advice on what to do and how to respond. When I was trying to figure out what I really believed about God and why, my mom listened as I searched, questioned, and grew.

While I used to believe that adults couldn't relate because of the "impossible" differences between our generation and theirs, my mom has shown me that this is not always true. And the fact that it was my mom who showed me this makes it even more special. I have not only learned that she really understands, but I discovered in the process that she's become one of my dearest friends.

If you're like most people, you probably have grandparents or know elderly people who say, "When I was your age…" or "I remember when…," and a lot of the time you find it hard to relate to them. They seem so far away, like they can't understand because everything was so different for them. But the older you get, the more experiences and *potential* wisdom you gain. (I've also learned that not everyone who is older is wiser.)

So before you disregard adults, try really listening to what they have to say. Your mom or dad may not always understand, but more often than not, they (or another adult you know) have experienced the same difficult feelings and tough situations. Talk to them and tell them how it really is with you. You might be surprised to discover that it's been that same way with them, too. And your parents just might become two of your closest friends.

Happy Father's Day

ALISON PETERS

I was a good kid. Seriously.

Attending church four times a week was routine at my house. For special services my mom would write poems, and I would stand up in front of the congregation and recite them. I didn't have a nervous bone in my body; stage fright was nonexistent. My mom wrote well, and I was a good memorizer. We made a great team.

In Sunday school, contests were highlights. I would win them. Always. There would be points for learning memory verses, and, boy, did I memorize them all! Points for bringing others to church, points for bringing a Bible, points for answering the most questions, points for simply showing up! The teachers became so accustomed to my winning that they even bought prizes that they knew would most appeal to me.

Eventually, I hit the teenage years, and something went terribly wrong. It was as if I had been shot out of a cannon and hit thirteen running...in the wrong direction.

The first thing that I managed to do was to choose the wrong friends. I cared about pleasing the wrong people. I soon discovered that if I acted like a smart aleck in class, kids would laugh. Getting a laugh and being cool became top priorities. I learned that it was extremely uncool to attend just about anything in the company of my family, and you can guess where church was rated. Suddenly, my solid Christian upbringing and my dedicated

Christian family—even God Himself—did not seem cool.

I fought against anything right, anything moral, anything good. At first, my conscience churned and burned when I told a lie, and all those memory verses stayed with me. *Thou shalt not lie.* Other times I stole from the store or took change off my dad's desk when he wasn't around: *Thou shalt not steal.* I kicked hard against going to church: *Do not forsake the assembling of yourselves together.*

My dad was the most patient, honest man I have ever known. Yet during my early teen years, I showed him no respect at all. I fought against everything he stood for, everything he expected of me. *Honor your parents in the Lord, for this is right.* I wonder how many times I broke his heart, and at the same time I do not want to know.

It was not in his nature to fight. He was not new at this dad business—I had five older siblings and two younger ones—but I challenged him like no other. Only in looking back do I realize how much I put him through…and how much he must have loved me to get us through that time without giving up. Always, always, I knew he loved me.

The June that I was fourteen, my dad and I had a few days of uncommon calm. It could have even been called peace. Perhaps I was sick. It must have been something unusual like that because I got a Father's Day card for him—on my own and without giving it much thought. The night before Father's Day, I left the card at his place at the kitchen table. I knew that Dad would see it the next morning when he and Mom had their coffee.

I had forgotten about it by the next afternoon until my mom pulled me aside. "Your dad cried when he read the card you gave him."

I stared at her. "What? He cried?! Why did he cry?"

"Because you signed it 'With love.' And he thought you had stopped loving him a while back…."

My stomach lurched, and I felt like throwing up. If my face showed anything, I'll never know. My only recollection of that incident was that I was sick of myself.

I was glad that I had told my dad I loved him. He hadn't known! The very thought was heart wrenching. Amazingly, even that was not the worst of it. It was the way that I had told him that tore me up—I had shoplifted the card!

And now I learned that my dad had cried because I had signed it "With love." I let my dad know that I loved him by giving him a stolen Father's Day card.

Not all of the Bible verses I had learned were "thou shalt nots." I had also learned some pretty awesome promises: *"If we confess our sins, He is faithful…to forgive."*

I knew that one, too…by heart.

I'll always be thankful that my dad gave me wings and then made me use them.

MAX LUCADO

Sweet Sixteen

SHELLY TEEMS JOHNSON
AS TOLD TO GLORIA CASSITY STARGEL

H urry and get dressed, Shelly!" Mom's overly cheerful voice penetrated the closed door to my room. "The sun's shining. Let's go riding!"

Mom knew good and well that I was on the phone with my boyfriend. The last thing in all the world I wanted to do on that Sunday afternoon was go horseback riding with my mother. Yet I dared not argue back, not after our blowup the night before. *I'm sixteen years old, for crying out loud!* I seethed. *Why can't she just stay out of my life?*

Sometimes I *hated* my mother. I desperately wanted her to give me a little space. She sponsored my cheerleader squad. She came to every one of my volleyball and softball games. She even taught at my school. Wherever I went, she was there! As if that were not bad enough, she was always ordering me around. Even my friends commented about it.

When I was little, I *liked* it when Mom was protective, when she got involved in my activities. But now I wanted more independence, a chance to make my own mistakes.

The truth was that, in spite of Mom's constant surveillance, I managed to break most of the rules at our private Christian school. And the more I rebelled, the more Mom clamped down. The more she clamped down, the more I rebelled.

Take the night before, when we had the blowup. Okay, so I *was* a few minutes late coming in. Well, maybe it was a little more like an *hour* late. Anyway, just as I expected, Mom followed me into my room. "Where were you all this time, Shelly? I worry about you when you're late. *Anything* could have happened! Why didn't you call me?" On and on and on.

As usual, Mom threw in a little Scripture for good measure, as if she didn't drill me on memory verses at our breakfast table *every morning of the world!* "Remember, Shelley," she'd said that night, "the Bible says, 'Children, obey your parents.' If you honor your father and mother, yours will be a long life, full of blessing."

"Mom!" I had yelled. "Will you just leave me alone?" When she finally left, I slammed the door behind her.

Today she was pretending nothing had happened, trying to make us look like the ideal loving family of her dreams. In the meantime, after hanging up the telephone, I was sitting there thinking, *What is all this horseback riding business? Mom isn't even a horse person! She just wants to know what I'm doing every minute.*

Halfheartedly, I pulled on my riding boots then trudged over to my dresser. Reaching for a comb, my hand brushed against the necklace Mom had given me for my last birthday. *I'd better wear this or she'll ask where it is.* I fastened the silver chain around my neck and straightened the pendant—the silver outline of a heart with its message, in script, suspended inside: "Sweet Sixteen." *Yeah, sure, Mom.*

By the time I got to the barn, Dad had already saddled our paint, Charcey, and Mom was swinging into the saddle. "Mom, *what* are you doing?" I shrieked. "You've never ridden Charcey before! She's a *big* horse." *I cannot believe this woman!* I thought. *She'll do anything to be part of my life. And I just want her out of it!*

While Dad was bridling his Arabian, Mom discovered that her stirrups were too long. Before Dad could turn around to adjust them, Charcey charged away at full gallop. *What has gotten into Charcey?*

Scared and inexperienced, Mom probably reacted by doing all the wrong things. Whatever the reason, Charcey was out of control. Never had I seen that horse run so fast, her mane and tail flying in the wind!

I watched, horrified, as Charcey's hooves beat at the earth faster and faster—like something possessed, a thousand pounds of straining muscle thundering across the pasture.

With lightning speed, Charcey reached a corner of the pasture fence—a place of decision. Should she jump? *No. Too high with a ditch on the other side.* Other choice? *Make a ninety-degree turn.* Charcey turned. Mom flew high into the air, crashed through a barbed-wire fence, and landed with a thud on the sun-parched ground.

Then—*nothing.* Except for Charcey's hoof beats as she tore back to the barn.

Dear God! No! No! This can't be happening! I sprinted across the pasture. "Mom! Mom!" *Please, God, don't let her be dead! I didn't mean it, God. I don't really want her out of my life! Please!*

The barbed wire was holding her in an almost kneeling position. Her right wrist and hand dangled the wrong way, her neck and head were turned as if broken, and blood oozed from gashes on her back. *Is she breathing? Please, God, she thinks I don't love her.* "Mom?"

After what seemed an eternity, I heard a moan, then a weak, "I'm okay, Shelly."

"Mom! Oh, Mom! I didn't mean to be so hateful. I *do* love you, Mom." Ever so carefully, I began untangling her hair from the barbed wire, barely able to see through my tears. "Oh, Mama, I'm so sorry. I'm so sorry."

"I know, Shelly," Mom somehow managed to say while I tugged on her now shredded pink sweater. By then Dad had joined us, and together we freed her from the wire.

"We've got to get you to the hospital," Dad said. "I'll call an ambulance."

"No," Mom said, and because she was a nurse, we listened. "You can carry me to the van."

It wasn't easy, but we did it. Dad barreled down the highway, all the while trying to raise a police escort on the two-way radio. Meanwhile, I did what Mom had taught me—I quoted Scripture, the first one that popped into my head. "Rejoice in the Lord always," I said, close to her ear. "And again I say rejoice." For once I must have done the right thing because Mom, through all her pain, started quoting Scripture, one verse after another, all the way to the hospital.

Mom spent most of the next three months in a wheelchair, and during that time the two of us did a lot of talking. "Mom," I told her, "I know I act a lot like Charcey did that day of the accident. I just want to charge through life without being held back, not missing anything."

"Yes, Shelly, and I always want to be in control, to make sure things go right. To protect you from getting hurt."

We decided that because we were very different, we'd probably *always* clash over one thing or another.

We agreed on something else, too—that we loved each other, no matter what.

Still, I felt a need to do something more to make things right. One day I asked permission to speak at our school's chapel service. I stood on the stage and faced the other students and faculty, including my mom who sat in her wheelchair at the back of the room. I took a deep breath and spoke into the microphone. "I want to apologize for all the mistakes I've made this year, mistakes that have hurt others. Worst of all, they have hurt my mom."

I told them how hateful I had been toward my mother. How I had yelled at her to stay out of my life. Then I told them about Mom's accident. About how, at the thought of losing her, I realized that she is my very best friend. That she wants only what is best for me. "Please, you guys," I begged my fellow students, "tell your mother you love her. Don't wait until it's too late, like I almost did."

I looked back at Mom who was beaming and dabbing at her eyes with a tissue. "Mom," I said, my voice quivering, "I ask you to forgive me. I ask *God* to forgive me."

As if on cue, one of Mom's Bible verses popped into my head. "If we confess our sins, He is faithful and just to forgive us our sins...." *Thank you, God, for believing in me, even when I disappoint You over and over. Just like Mom!*

Instinctively, I reached up and caressed the silver pendant at my neck. My fingers traced the intricate lettering. "Sweet Sixteen." *Sixteen? Yes. Sweet? Hardly! But I will try, Mom.* I smiled through my tears. *I will try.*

Leaving the platform, suddenly I became aware of a new-for-me feeling. One that said, *It's okay, Shelly, to let your mom into your life.*

Even when you're sweet sixteen.

Momma

I cried last night.
Tell me why
I've been so selfish, Momma.
Missing you...
We used to be best friends,
But we are slowly drifting apart.
Pull me back to shore.
I know we have differences,
But more things in common.
I like your serious talks;
They show me you care.
And when you get in my business,
It shows me you're still there.
There are times I wish I were little again;
I don't want to face the world.
What would I do without you, Momma.
I know we have arguments
And that they get in the way.
But I still love you, Momma,
Every day.

PAIGE AICH

AGE 14

Danger: My Mother

ANNE GOODRICH

Back in the mid-sixties my mother was still that stay-at-home mom who baked cookies, sewed, was a Girl Scout leader and a volunteer for our school's Parent-Teacher Association. Life was normal and suburban and good. Good that is, until the Marion Jordan PTA decided to put on a Christmas play. Oh, it's not that putting on a play wasn't a good idea to raise money for the PTA. Everyone thought performing "The Night Before Christmas" would be a great fund-raiser. So did my mom—until they announced who would be playing what characters in their production.

We should have known something was wrong when my mother got home from her PTA meeting by the way the temperature dropped twenty degrees when you got within a two-foot radius of her. We finally took notice of the frosty expression on Mom's face and the firm set of her lips.

"Well, you're in the play, right?" we asked, baffled.

"Yes," was her monosyllabic reply.

"Well...what's the matter then?" one of my braver siblings inquired.

"It's who I am in the play that's the matter."

We knew she couldn't be the father, who would be reading "The Night Before Christmas" to his family.

"Are you the mother?" we asked hopefully.

"No."

"The daughter?"

"No."

We were at a loss here. There was only a father, mother, son, and daughter in this production.

"Well, who are you then?"

My mother stood there, and we felt the temperature plummet another ten degrees.

"I'm the dog," was her curt reply.

"Oh." We weren't sure what to say after that. I don't think we could have said anything that would have made my mother being given the part of the family pet in the PTA play feel any better. Even Zsa Zsa, our Airedale terrier, looked sympathetic.

We three kids suddenly remembered homework that had to be done, and that Zsa's water dish needed filling, and…and whatever we could think of to quickly tiptoe out of arctic range. I mean, we could see the dilemma here. It wasn't as though we could go out bragging to all our friends, "Yep, my mom's going to be in the Christmas play this year. She's the dog." Better to just keep our noses buried in our textbooks.

However, despite feeling insulted by her part, my mother was a trouper. I think it also helped that my father, a thespian in his youth, convinced her that any part was worth playing well. No, my mom didn't give up, and she didn't give in. She went to every rehearsal. (Just what did she practice, we wondered? Different barks?) She even told us that her dog's character had a name, Danger, which we thought was pretty apt, considering. Mom even spent her own money for some kneepads after she started getting sore from running around on all fours on a wooden stage all night. And after a while, it really started to seem that my mother was enjoying this. Yes, there was definitely a gleam in her eye. We guessed that she had decided that being a canine character wasn't so humiliating after all.

It wasn't until opening night that we found out the real reason for that gleam in our mother's eye. We all went to the auditorium that evening to watch Mom perform, and it was a full house. After we settled in our seats, we opened our programs, and there was Mom's name all right—"Jeanne Goodrich: Danger the Dog." We slouched down just a bit lower in our chairs as the houselights dimmed and the audience quieted. Then the big, velvet curtains slowly opened with a whisper, and the play began.

It was a lovely, old-fashioned-looking room, decorated for the holidays, and the Victorian-looking father announced to his family that he would read them the Christmas story. He took his seat in the big rocking chair on stage; his wife gracefully swished her long skirt and slid into the small wingback chair beside him, while the eager-looking children gathered at his feet. In the midst of this gathering around, the father called in the family dog to join them—and then came Mom. Of course, you wouldn't realize it was my mother, as she was in a brown dog costume with a big dog head and floppy long ears, and walking on all fours. But what I did recognize in the first few seconds, when Danger the dog walked out on stage, was that my mother had taken my dad's advice to heart. She was going to play her role to the hilt, with gusto. She didn't just pad onto that stage like some aging canine, but she bounced and wagged her way onto the stage to the sound of the audience's laughter.

Danger (Mom) wiggled her derriere a bit as she stretched and then settled down on the rug behind the father's chair, crossed her paws, and yawned an exaggerated puppy yawn. The laughter faded to a few subdued chuckles while the father took out a large book and began to read the familiar Christmas tale. The two children sat still, gazing in rapt attention. But not Danger. Oh, no. Danger the dog was obviously too enthralled by the story to sit still.

"'Twas the night before Christmas, and all through the house, not a creature was stirring, not even a mouse...."

Danger's head suddenly lifted from her crossed paws. You could almost hear her thoughts as she turned from side to side, ears whipping around. *Mouse?! What mouse? Here? Where? I want a mouse! Where's the mouse?!*

We covered our mouths, trying to stifle our laughter.

"...when up on the roof there arose such a clatter..."

Once again, Danger the dog was suddenly at attention, head jerking toward the ceiling. *What's that noise?! Intruders?! Oh boy, oh boy!* we could almost hear her say.

By this time, it was pretty obvious that most of the audience was not riveted on the recitation by the father in the play, but by the dog whose only line was a tentative "woof." And because Danger was positioned behind the other actors, they couldn't turn their heads and look at her, but it was obvious even to them that something was going on. As the reading continued, you could see how badly they wanted to make a quick backward glance as their eyeballs furtively slid over in Danger's direction.

The reading continued, and so did my mom's dog interpretation, and so did the laughter. I don't know if my mother had spent time studying our Airedale, but she had each dog nuance down pat. At just the right moment she stretched, yawned, burrowed her head in her paws, snapped her head up excitedly, and wagged her hindquarters in perfect canine imitation.

Yes, my mother was a great dog. She took what she thought was a lemon of a role and performed it with a comedic sense that would have made Lucille Ball proud. It certainly made us proud. Almost forty years later, I still remember the time my mother was in a play, spoke not one line, and stole the show. And the Marian Jordan PTA found out that casting my mother in one of their productions was a Danger to contend with.

The Ladder Test

HEIDI HESS SAXTON

My childhood home on Orchard Street was set in a small town in the rolling hills of northern New Jersey. It was a three-story, mint-green stucco affair with forest-green shutters and a shingled roof that was in constant need of repair. Money was tight, and so my father did the repairs himself at night and on weekends. However, when my sisters and I grew into our teens, the roof served another purpose: My father used it to gauge the character of the young men who came to call.

The first time a prospective suitor came to the house, Dad would go outside just before the "guinea pig" arrived, propping his extension ladder against the side of the house. Laying a hammer at the foot of the ladder, my father would then climb up and pretend to do work. When the boy pulled up, Dad good-naturedly called out:

"Hey there! Dropped my hammer. Could you toss it up to me?"

Had the boy refused to get out of his car, I'm certain the date would have been over. (Fortunately, we all had better sense than to invite someone like that home in the first place.) However, if he picked up the hammer, climbed the ladder partway, and tossed it to my father (as requested), the young man got a single star. That was enough for a single date, but not enough for him to be considered a serious contender for our affections.

If the young man climbed the ladder, handed the tool to Dad, and engaged him in a bit of lighthearted banter, that was better: two stars. Enough for a second date. A real conversation earned a guy three stars—and the respect of my father.

One of my boyfriends, a handy young man, was so eager to please that he climbed up and proceeded to spend the afternoon helping Dad tear shingles off the roof, leaving me to stew dateless in the kitchen. Later, Dad tried to smooth my ruffled feathers by exclaiming over the young man's sterling character. I could "keep this one" if I wanted to, he said. My sister's friend John helped my father put the finishing touches on the roof—and he later became my brother-in-law.

The roof completed, my parents sold the house and moved to another state. My younger sisters didn't have the benefit of "The Ladder Test," and I can't help but wonder if all our lives would have been easier had Dad found another roof to fix. Flowers are sweet, and candy is dandy—but nothing says "keeper" to a girl like a guy who's willing to face her father armed with nothing but a hammer.

Planting Love

NANETTE THORSEN-SNIPES

M
other, how could you?" I asked as I opened the screen door of the old clapboard house.

I watched my mother stack another dish, then reach for the cups. She unwrapped newspaper from around a stoneware cup. "This is what your stepfather wanted, Nan. He wanted some land so he could have a garden."

My stepfather! He's nothing but a hick, I thought with contempt. At fourteen, I was horrified by my mother's marriage to a man from the sticks. To top it off, we'd had to move from the sprawling, busy suburbs of Atlanta to a simple house in the country without so much as a dishwasher—except me. That first week I barely spoke to my mother, and I pretended that my stepfather didn't even exist.

The week before Easter there was no school. I was still not on civilized terms with my stepfather, and I observed his every move with anger. On Monday I sat on the back porch steps and watched him shovel dirt in a sunny patch of our yard.

Later that week he broke up the Georgia red clay and tossed rocks and broken limbs into a ditch. The next day he added fertilizer to the topsoil, then raked until it was smooth as could be.

When Friday arrived, I watched him squint against the sun's glare. He held a small plastic bag and began pouring something into his hand. My curiosity loomed at high noon, and I walked over to him, squishing the cool topsoil between my toes.

Without a word, my stepfather placed a dozen seeds into my waiting hand. Before I could even ask, he said, "These are squash seeds. In another few weeks, I'll plant cucumbers, tomatoes, and maybe even some pole beans."

I watched as his callused fingers dug into the cool soil. Almost lovingly, he dropped in a couple of seeds, then pushed dirt on top. To my surprise, I felt my anger begin to disappear as I completed my first row of small mounds.

Spring turned into summer, and with it came harvesttime. I was delighted to find butter-yellow squash hiding beneath dark green leaves. I loved pulling the squash from the plant and putting them into a basket.

When my stepfather suggested that I pick the green tomatoes, I was aghast. "They're not red yet!"

"Go ahead and pull some," he said, "and I'll show you how to fry them."

Thinking that he'd lost his mind, I pulled several of the tomatoes and added them to my already full basket.

Inside our small kitchen, my stepfather taught me how to slice the tomatoes, dip them in cornmeal, and fry them in hot oil. I'll never forget that first sweet bite.

My stepfather also showed me Jesus' love. Little by little he helped tear down the wall that I had built between us. It reminded me of when he had broken up the soil to prepare it for the squash seeds.

As a teenager, it wasn't easy trying to love someone so different from me, especially the man who had taken my father's place. But when I shared in the planting that year, I felt the resurrection of a seed that eventually blossomed into love and respect. And to think…it all began with just one seed.

Bathrobe Lunch

ANNE GOODRICH

It was the winter of my senior year of high school, and I was lying in a hospital bed. I should have been attending classes and basketball games and planning graduation festivities with my friends—not lying flat on my back with a diagnosis of mononucleosis, anemia, and jaundice.

I was happy for one thing, though. My father, who normally traveled for work several days a week, refused to go on any business trips while I was hospitalized. Every day he came and sat with me and talked while I had my meal of chicken broth and Jell-O. I don't think I'd ever had so much time alone with my dad before, and I looked forward to it every lunch hour.

Finally, after almost two weeks in bed, I was told that if I could walk halfway down the hospital corridor and back, I would be allowed to go home the next day. It didn't seem like much of a test to me. My father accompanied me as I made my way in slippered feet down the linoleum hallway. But partway back I felt my strength slipping away. "Dad, I can't make it," I frantically whispered.

"Lean on me," he whispered back. "I want to get you home." So Dad and I, co-conspirators, slowly ambled down the hall, me leaning on my father for support.

The next morning I awoke with great anticipation. I was going home! There were two things I was especially anxious for—street clothes and real food. But when Dad walked into my hospital room around lunchtime, I saw that he wasn't carrying any clothes for me. My mother, practical as mothers can be, had said I should just wear my nightgown and quilted robe home as I had strict orders to go to bed as soon as I arrived. Oh, the disappointment. How I longed for my blue jeans!

We were halfway down the road heading home when my father pulled into the parking lot of a restaurant. "Dad! What are you doing?"

"Taking you to lunch," he nonchalantly replied.

Thinking this was craziness and feeling terribly conspicuous, I slowly shuffled into the restaurant in my robe with a hospital bracelet dangling from my wrist. I got more than a few stares from the suit-clad businessmen dining inside.

It was a wonderful lunch, though. I forgot that I was in a public restaurant in my nightgown as my father and I talked in a way we never had before. Perhaps it was all the time we'd had together while I was sick. Perhaps it was the seriousness of my illness, or maybe somehow my father sensed that I was on the cusp of adulthood. Whatever the reason, Dad talked to me that day as though I were an adult, his equal, and shared things about himself that he'd never discussed before. My father was a distinguished man who had always held inside the tragedies and heartbreaks of his past. That afternoon was a special moment in our relationship. I had the privilege of seeing my father not just as a parent, but as a man.

That memory is especially poignant to me. It was but ten days later that my father suddenly slipped away from this life while sitting in his living room chair. It took me quite a while to recover my health, and it took me even longer to heal from losing the man who was my hero. But I came to realize how much God blessed me with my illness. Without it, I would have never had my "bathrobe lunch" with Dad. My sickness gave me the greatest gift I could ever want—time with my father.

Trunk of Treasures

NANCY JO SULLIVAN

My sisters and I rushed downstairs to the rec room to watch *Wheel of Fortune*. We grabbed floor pillows and staked out places to sit, the six of us encircling the TV like a fan. My oldest sister, Jeanne, sixteen at the time, assumed her usual place of prominence in front of the screen. I sat right next to her.

The game show began, and as soon as the beautiful hostess greeted the TV audience, Jeanne flipped her long blond hair and opened her makeup trunk. Inside were curlers and cosmetics and creams. At fourteen, I was enchanted by her trunk of treasures. I watched her pull a comb from the box and begin to roll her long locks around huge curlers that looked like giant orange juice cans.

Jeanne set her hair in front of the TV every night, and my sisters were getting tired of it. "You're blocking our view," they told her. "Get out of the way!"

Jeanne misted her bangs with hair spray. "I can do whatever I want," she replied.

My sisters may have been disgusted with Jeanne, but I strained to see her reflection in the mirror that lined the lid of the trunk. "She's so beautiful," I said to myself, "not at all like me." I had short dark hair, with bangs that stuck out above my eyebrows. I was skinny and my teeth were crooked. I wanted to be like Jeanne. Beautiful.

One Friday evening, Jeanne set up an easel-like mirror in front of the TV. When she started pulling cosmetics from her trunk—compacts and pencils and blush—my sisters fumed.

They rolled their eyes. "Can't you do that somewhere else?" they cried out in unison.

Jeanne shrugged them off. "I have a date," she said.

While Jeanne carefully drew a line of blue over her eyelids, I leaned over to get a better view. I bumped her. The mirror toppled over. Jeanne smeared eyeliner on her face.

"What a klutz!" she exclaimed. Angry, she wiped the blue smudges off her face.

"You think you're so beautiful!" I yelled. Then I huffed off to my room.

After that night, I didn't watch *Wheel of Fortune* with my sisters anymore. I didn't want to sit next to Jeanne ever again. Instead, I retreated to my room, where I taught myself how to apply lipstick and file my nails. "What does Jeanne know about beauty?" I muttered as I tried to flatten my bangs with hairspray and gel.

Much to my delight, by the time I turned sixteen I had finally filled out. My hair was longer, and thanks to a good orthodontist, my teeth were straight. "I'm not a klutz," I told myself, flipping my hair in front of the mirror.

Then something unthinkable happened to my oldest sister. Just before her high school graduation, Jeanne was severely injured in a car accident. After weeks in the hospital, she came home, hunched over on crutches and hobbling on a thick white cast. That evening my sisters guided her down the stairs to the rec room, and I helped her into an armchair.

Jeanne had stitches in her lips and bruises on her face. Her long hair hung limp. For a moment, my sisters and I stood around her chair in silence. It was hard to believe that this was Jeanne. Suddenly I knew what to do. "I'll get the curlers," I called out, already on my way to retrieve the makeup trunk from Jeanne's room.

My sisters began setting her hair, and I took a tube of eyeliner from the case. I waved it in front of Jeanne. "I know how to use it," I said. Jeanne's battered face broke into a smile. "I'm glad you still love me," she said. Her eyes were bright and shiny. Her smile was warm. Even though her face was scarred, Jeanne looked more beautiful than I'd ever seen her.

Ever so slowly, I etched a perfect line of blue over her eyelids. Thoughts filled my head and heart. *I've been searching for beauty in all the wrong places. The secret to beauty isn't found in a makeup trunk. True beauty is what I'm seeing this very moment...a loveliness that comes from deep inside the heart.*

After I applied her makeup and my sisters rolled the last curler, we all pushed Jeanne's chair close to the TV. Grabbing floor pillows, we each took our places, once again encircling our oldest sister. Even though her cast blocked the screen, my sisters didn't seem to mind. Neither did I. I was glad to be sitting next to Jeanne again.

What a treasured legacy: devoted prayers, lasting love, hearty laughter.

That's the way it ought to be.

CHARLES R. SWINDOLL

Just Like in the Movies

AMANDA BOWERS
AGE 13

I was six years old when my parents divorced. My dad moved to the city while my mom, my two younger sisters, and I stayed at our house in Hilton, New York. Every other weekend we packed up some clothes and went to our dad's apartment.

At school I attended a special class for kids whose parents had divorced. I learned a lot there, especially that you have to just trust God to make everything all right. I used to dream that my parents would forgive each other and remarry, just like in the movies. After a while, however, I realized that it would probably never happen, so I quit dreaming.

For two years my sisters and I went back and forth, from house to house. Then my dad moved to an apartment that was closer to my mom's house. There were no kids around, so we were all alone. I began to dread going to my dad's place. I knew that he loved me, but it wasn't as much fun there.

A year and a half later my dad moved to another apartment only five minutes from my mom's house. I loved that apartment and looked forward to going there with my dad. Everything was going great except for one thing—my parents attended different churches. Now that we were close enough to go to my mom's church, we started begging my dad to take us there. Sometimes he did, but he preferred to go to his church.

One day my sisters and I were at my dad's apartment, and we rented the movie *The Parent Trap*. It was a story about twin sisters whose parents were divorced, and the twins tried to persuade their parents to get back together. In the end the parents reconciled and everyone was happy. The movie ended and my dad started crying. When I asked him why, he said, "Because it had a happy ending."

Soon after that my dad started going to my mom's church and often invited her over for dinner. The months flew by and the next thing we knew, my parents were engaged. The wedding was in October, and my sisters and I were the flower girls. On the day of the wedding we got our hair done and our pictures taken. Then it was time for the ceremony. By the time it was over, both of my parents were crying for joy.

It wasn't the most fancy or expensive wedding I have ever been to, but it will be the one that I will treasure the most for the rest of my life. It has been just over a year since that happy day. Parents who were divorced for five years do not usually remarry, but in this case they did.

Just like in the movies.

I found out I could leave home,
but I could not leave love.

LANE CLAYTON

Dear Daddy

GARY SMALLEY AND JOHN TRENT
FROM *THE LANGUAGE OF LOVE*

An emotional word picture has the capacity to capture people's attention by simultaneously engaging their thoughts and feelings. Along with its ability to move us to deeper levels of intimacy, it has the staying power to make a lasting impression.

When faced with the breakup of her parents' marriage, a hurting teenager named Kimberly used the following word picture in this letter to her father:

Dear Daddy,

It's late at night, and I'm sitting in the middle of my bed writing to you. I've wanted to talk with you so many times during the past few weeks. But there never seems to be any time when we're alone.

Dad, I realize you're dating someone else. And I know you and Mom may never get back together. That's terribly hard to accept—especially knowing that you may never come back home or be an "everyday" dad to me and Brian again. But I want you at least to understand what's going on in our lives.

Don't think that Mom asked me to write this. She didn't. She doesn't know I'm writing, and neither does Brian. I just want to share with you what I've been thinking.

Dad, I feel like our family has been riding in a nice car for a long time. You know, the kind you always like to have as a company car. It's the kind that has every extra inside and not a scratch on the outside.

But over the years, the car has developed some problems. It's smoking a lot, the wheels wobble, and the seat covers are ripped. The car's been really hard to drive or ride in because of all the shaking and squeaking. But it's still a great automobile—or at least it could be. With a little work, I know it could run for years.

Since we got the car, Brian and I have been in the backseat while you and Mom have been up front. We feel really secure with you driving and Mom beside you. But last month, Mom was at the wheel.

It was nighttime, and we had just turned the corner near our house. Suddenly, we all looked up and saw another car, out of control, heading straight for us. Mom tried to swerve out of the way, but the other car smashed into us. The impact sent us flying off the road and crashing into a lamppost.

The thing is, Dad, just before we were hit, we could see that you were driving the other car. And we saw something else: Sitting next to you was another woman.

It was such a terrible accident that we were all rushed to the emergency ward. But when we asked where you were, no one knew. We're still not really sure where you are or if you were hurt or if you need help.

Mom was really hurt. She was thrown into the steering wheel and broke several ribs. One of them punctured her lungs and almost pierced her heart.

When the car wrecked, the back door smashed into Brian. He was covered with cuts from the broken glass, and he shattered his arm, which is now in a cast. But that's not the worst. He's still in so much pain and shock that he doesn't want to talk or play with anyone.

As for me, I was thrown from the car. I was stuck out in the cold for a long time with my right leg broken. As I lay there, I couldn't move and didn't know what was wrong with Mom and Brian. I was hurting so much myself that I couldn't help them.

There have been times since that night when I wondered if any of us would make it. Even though we're getting a little better, we're all still in the hospital. The doctors say I'll need a lot of therapy on my leg, and I know they can help me get better. But I wish it were you who was helping me, instead of them.

The pain is so bad, but what's even worse is that we all miss you so much. Every day we wait to see if you're going to visit us in the hospital, and every day you don't come. I know it's over. But my heart would explode with joy if somehow I could look up and see you walk into my room.

At night when the hospital is really quiet, they push Brian and me into Mom's room, and we all talk about you. We talk about how much we loved driving with you and how we wish you were with us now.

Are you all right? Are you hurting from the wreck? Do you need us like we need you? If you need me, I'm here and I love you.

Your daughter,

Kimberly

With You All the
Way

Love is...

...knowing that people are different
and loving them just the same.

...buying someone flowers for no reason.

...changing your plans for someone.

...listening and giving advice~
and knowing the difference between the two.

...crying for someone when you know they are hurting.

...being there.

DANAE JACOBSON, AGE 17

The Kid with Green Hair

KAY MARSHALL STROM

Well, isn't this just great!" I grumbled as I saw the teenage boy sauntering down the aisle toward me. The seat next to me was just about the only one still open on the flight from Los Angeles to Des Moines, Iowa. I had really hoped no one would sit there because I was tired and had work to do before I arrived at the weekend conference where I was to speak. I just wanted to stretch out and relax, all by myself, no distractions. And now this!

I surveyed the kid out of the corner of my eye as he made his way toward me. About seventeen, I guessed. Dressed in tattered jeans and a dirty T-shirt. Arms and fingers decorated with tattoos. And his hair! It reached down to the center of his back, and it was dyed bright green.

Sure enough, he slumped down next to me. I squeezed as close to the window as I could and buried myself in the book manuscript I was editing.

As the trip progressed, I could overhear passenger after passenger commenting on "that strange guy with the green hair." A couple of children even stopped by to stare. The green-haired kid paid no mind; he didn't even seem to notice. I couldn't see how that was possible, though. I could certainly hear and see them.

When dinner was served, the green-haired kid gobbled up everything on his tray. Since I wasn't going to eat my chocolate cake anyway, I asked him if he would like it.

"Yeah, thanks!" he said as he eagerly took it from my tray. "I'm starved!"

I smiled and nodded.

"Are you going to finish your roll?" he asked, eyeing my plate.

I said I wasn't and handed it to him.

"And the butter?"

I handed that to him, too.

"I saw you reading a manuscript," he said, his mouth full of buttered roll. "It looked kind of interesting. I'd like to write someday."

"Really?" I asked. We talked some about writing.

"Hey," he said, "I'm reading this really funny book. You want to hear some of it?"

"Sure," I said.

He read and we laughed. He read more and we laughed harder. I don't know whether anyone was watching us or not. I didn't really care. We were having a great time, that green-haired kid and I.

When we finished the book, we started to talk about other things. He showed me his tattoos and told me what each one meant and why he had gotten it. I asked him how his mom felt about his green hair. "She's cool," he said. "She helped me dye it. I didn't like the color it came out—it looked like pea soup!—so we did it again." He told me he liked it because it separated the people who accept him for his looks from those who are more interested in who he is. I blushed with guilt.

He was on his way to spend time with his father. "He'll hate my hair," the kid said. "He hates everything I do."

We talked about ideas and values and principles of life. I told him about the place God held in my life and why He was so important to me. The kid said "Hmmmm," but I don't know whether he understood or not.

When the plane landed, the green-haired kid said, "Thanks for talking to me, lady. No one ever does."

"It was my pleasure," I said, and I really meant it.

I hope I encouraged that young man in some way. He certainly encouraged me. I hope I challenged him. He challenged me more than I'd been challenged in a very long time. I hope I built him up a little. He built me up tremendously. I hope, somehow, I helped him come closer to the kingdom of God. He helped me appreciate a heavenly Father who looks beyond tattooed arms and green hair.

Happiness is a perfume you cannot pour on others without getting a few drops on yourself.

RALPH WALDO EMERSON

Letter to My Daughter

ANNE GOODRICH

The phone rang Saturday night. It was Kelly calling from college. "Mom, where were you?" she said. "I tried to call you from a store because I want you to help me make up my mind. I found this beautiful dress for my formal, and I feel like a princess in it, but it's really expensive…. What do you think? Should I buy it?"

I told her yes. But in those few short minutes, I didn't have time to explain why I thought she should have the "princess" dress she'd found.

But there are so many, many reasons I would give my daughter:

Kelly, for growing up without many clothes or vacations because there was never enough money. That would be one reason.

For working so hard to get the best grades you could so you could go to college.

For all those times you passed the soccer ball when you knew that you could have run with the ball and scored, but you were a team player.

For deciding that you had to set an example as captain, and always finding the positive in every game, and refusing to ever lose your temper with another player.

For that fierce determination when you were slammed in the nose and blood poured down your face and you kept yelling, "I'm fine, Coach! I'm not bleeding anymore. Put me in, Coach!"

For that moment when I struggled with a thousand hairpins trying to anchor your tiara, and you turned to me and said, "I hope it won't make my friends feel bad that I was the one who made Homecoming Queen."

For giving up varsity soccer at college because you had to work and you couldn't (wouldn't!) let your grades suffer.

For giving up your spring break to go build houses in Tijuana and coming home scraped and bruised and sick and exclaiming, "Mom, that was the most wonderful thing I've ever done in my life!"

For deciding that even though you're supporting yourself, you could still find the money to sponsor a little girl in El Salvador who has less.

For deciding that prayer is much more important to you than parties.

For telling me when I wish I could give you more, "Mom, I think of you as my angel," and reminding me just how priceless love is.

Yes, Kelly, I do think you should have that dress. And you're right that no one will notice that your shoes don't match (since you have no extra money to go buy new ones). They will only see the shining joy in those big brown eyes of yours and in that radiant smile that could light a midnight sky. But, Kelly, you're wrong about looking like a princess in that dress. You, my darling daughter, are a queen.

The Winner

=◎=

JOHN WILLIAM SMITH

FROM *HUGS TO ENCOURAGE AND INSPIRE*

I was watching some little kids play soccer. These kids were only five or six years old, but they were playing a real game—a serious game: two teams, complete with coaches, uniforms, and parents. I didn't know any of them, so I was able to enjoy the game without the distraction of being anxious about winning or losing—I wished the parents and coaches could have done the same.

The teams were pretty evenly matched. I will just call them Team One and Team Two. Nobody scored in the first period. The kids were hilarious. They were clumsy and terribly inefficient. They fell over their own feet, they stumbled over the ball, they kicked at the ball and missed it—but they didn't seem to care. They were having fun.

In the second period, the Team One coach pulled out what must have been his first team players and put in the scrubs, except for his best player who now guarded the goal. The game took a dramatic turn. I guess winning is important—even when you're five years old—because the Team Two coach left his best players in and the Team One scrubs were no match for them. Team Two swarmed around the little guy who was now the Team One goalie. He was an outstanding athlete, but he was no match for three or four boys who were also very good. Team Two began to score.

The lone goalie gave it everything he had, recklessly throwing his body in front of incoming balls, trying valiantly to stop them. Team Two scored two goals in quick succession. It infuriated the young boy. He became a raging maniac—shouting, running, diving. With all the stamina he could muster, he covered the boy who now had the ball, but that boy kicked the ball to another boy twenty feet away, and by the time he repositioned himself, it was too late—they scored a third goal.

I soon learned who the goalie's parents were. They were nice, decent-looking people. I could tell that his dad had just come from the office—he still had his suit and tie on. They yelled encouragement to their son. I became totally absorbed, watching the boy on the field and his parents on the sideline.

After the third goal, the little kid changed. He could see it was no use; he couldn't stop them. He didn't quit, but he became quietly desperate—futility was written all over him. His father changed too. He had been urging his son to try harder, yelling advice and encouragement. But then he changed. He became anxious. He tried to say that it was okay—to hang in there. He grieved for the pain his son was feeling.

After the fourth goal, I knew what was going to happen. I've seen it before. The little boy needed help so badly, and there was no help to be had. He retrieved the ball from the net and handed it to the referee—and then he cried. He just stood there while huge tears rolled down both cheeks. He went to his knees and put his fists to his eyes, and he cried the tears of the helpless and brokenhearted.

When the boy went to his knees, I saw his father start onto the field. His wife clutched his arm and said, "Jim, don't. You'll embarrass him." But he tore loose from her and ran onto the field. He wasn't supposed to—the game was still in progress. Suit, tie, dress shoes, and all, he charged onto the field, and he picked up his son so everybody would know that this was his boy, and he hugged him and cried with him. I've never been so proud of a man in my life.

He carried him off the field, and when he got close to the sidelines I heard him say, "Scotty, I'm so proud of you. You were great out there. I want everybody to know that you are my son."

"Daddy," the boy sobbed, "I couldn't stop them. I tried, Daddy. I tried and tried, and they scored on me."

"Scotty, it doesn't matter how many times they score on you. You're my son, and I'm proud of you. I want you to go back out there and finish the game. I know you want to quit, but you can't. And, son, you're going to get scored on again, but it doesn't matter. Go on, now."

It made a difference. I could tell it did. When you're all alone, and you're getting scored on—and you can't stop them—it means a lot to know that it doesn't matter to those who love you. The little guy ran back on to the field, and they scored two more times, but it was okay.

I get scored on every day. I try so hard. I recklessly throw my body in every direction. I fume and rage. I struggle with temptation and sin with every ounce of my being, and Satan laughs. And he scores again, and the tears come, and I go to my knees—sinful, convicted, helpless. And my Father—my Father rushes right out on the field, right in front of the whole crowd—the whole jeering, laughing world—and He picks me up, and He hugs me, and He says, "John, I'm so proud of you. You were great out there. I want everybody to know that you are my son, and because I control the outcome of this game, I declare you...the winner."

You Bring the Groom
and I'll Bring the Cake

SUE BUCHANAN

FROM *A PARTY BEGINS IN THE HEART*

One Friday morning, Sandy, one of our employees, tiptoed into my office and shut the door. Self-consciously, she hung her head and covered her mouth with her hand, mannerisms we'd come to expect.

"I need to tell you something," she whispered. "Jake and I are going to get married tomorrow." She glanced up to check out my response.

"A wedding!" I enthused, just waiting for my invitation.

"We really want to please God, but we can't wait to be together. We don't have any money, though. You know Jake's been in prison for possession, but that's good, because he found the Lord there, and I found the Lord too. I know this isn't the right way to do it, but we're going to a justice of the peace, just the two of us, and I thought you should know." Her words poured out followed by a big I'm-glad-I-got-that-over-with sigh.

"Monday I'll be a married lady," she added happily.

When Sandy first interviewed with us, she broke every rule in the book. She was the "how not to" in the human resources handbook. She told us every negative thing about herself she could think of: She didn't look good, her teeth were bad, the only clothes she owned were worn-out jeans and a few T-shirts. With that introduction, most applicants would quickly be shown the door.

"I'll be real good in the back room. I know how to work, but don't bring me out when clients are around," she said. "I don't look good, and I don't talk good," she repeated. "And even if I could afford to buy clothes, I wouldn't know where to begin. I always just wore what was left over." Then, as though realizing that an explanation might be in order, she described her upbringing. Life in a small impoverished Tennessee town, umpteen brothers and sisters, a father long gone, and a mama who supported the large family by working in a boot factory.

When her story was finished, she heaved another glad-I-got-it-over-with sigh, looked me straight in the eye, and with the look of an angel added, "We didn't know we were poor, but we were. We just had a lot of love to make up for it."

What we needed at that point in our business was a Sandy. We hired her! In the film and video business, anyone and everyone who walks through the door (usually straight from a college course in communications) is a self-proclaimed producer looking for a high-visibility position that pays a lot of money. We needed a *worker bee* and Sandy turned out to be a great employee. She was a fast learner, was quick as a flash, had an endearing manner, and we loved her. We knew all about her boyfriend—that he'd been in prison and had come out reformed—but we weren't aware of the seriousness of their relationship.

"Congratulations, Sandy!" I said, "It sounds like you're doing the right thing. Is there any way we can help?" As I said the words, my mind began to race like a horse at the Kentucky Derby.

"Oh, heavens no!" she said. I could sense her embarrassment and her need to disappear to the back room.

"Do you wish you could have a real honest-to-goodness wedding?" I asked. By this time a plan was working in the back of my mind, and the poor girl had no choice but to humor me.

"Well, everyone dreams of a wedding with a dress and a cake, but in our family…" her voice trailed off, "no one has ever had one. Everybody just goes to the JP."

"Sandy, you're going to have a wedding," I said. "I'm not sure where or how, but every girl needs a wedding."

Not much work got done at Dynamic Media that day, unless you call planning a wedding work! Before the day was over, the plan was in place. The nuptials would take place in our family room; our daughter Dana would play the harp. Our daughter Mindy was given a fistful of money and sent off to purchase paper plates, cups, and napkins. Wayne was on the phone arranging for flowers and candelabra, and my assistant, Mel, ran home to get her wedding dress, which turned out to be the perfect size. One of the guys reserved the honeymoon suite at the Marriott and took up a collection to pay for it. Jim, our chief photographer, loaded his bag with cameras and film.

One of our freelance script writers, who just happened to drop by that day, caught the spirit. The next thing we knew, she was on the phone cajoling some temperamental wedding cake designer into doing a rush job.

"I know you only work by appointment! I know how truly fabulous your cakes are. I know they are a work of art. I know you take orders months in advance, but how could I have called you sooner? The wedding was only planned five minutes ago!" We were bent double listening to this one-sided conversation.

The next day, our house looked prettier than it ever had before. The family room looked like a small chapel, and the dining room table was exquisite, with flowers, finger sandwiches, crackers and dips, and the prettiest cake you ever laid eyes on. And even though color wasn't discussed, everything matched as though we'd planned it for weeks on end.

Later, Sandy's family arrived in several very old and rusted-out cars, and it was obvious they had strained to "dress for the occasion." About twenty of her relatives were there, albeit very self-conscious and embarrassed, but also obviously there to enjoy the moment.

Our entire staff of about fifteen was there—it was festively crowded. There were tears of joy on many of our faces as her pastor, from a small country church, performed the ceremony.

It was a joyous occasion—a day we'll all remember for the rest of our lives. The greatest joy of all was to see the happiness in the tear-filled eyes of Sandy's mother and to hear her say, "I never in all my life dreamed that any of my girls would ever have such a day as this."

During that simple ceremony, I couldn't help but think of the day we'll be part of a great wedding feast—a party in heaven—God has spent all eternity planning for His own bride! And you know what, dear reader, we don't do anything to deserve such a celebration. He just wants to do it because He loves us!

A smile is the light in the window of your face to let others know your heart is at home.

AUTHOR UNKNOWN

A Debt of Hope

JULIE B. GIBSON
FROM *SMALL MIRACLES FOR WOMEN*

When I was in eighth grade in Ohio, a girl who rode the same school bus that I did had a terrible accident. As she was racing to the bus so as not to miss it, she slipped on ice and fell under the rear wheels of the bus. She survived the accident but was paralyzed from the waist down.

I went to see her, and in my thirteen-year-old mind I thought that she wouldn't have much of a life now. Over the years, I moved, married, and had children, and didn't think much about Helen after that.

Three years ago, in Florida, my oldest son was hit by a car while riding his bike. He was thrown ninety feet and landed on his head, suffering a horrible brain injury. While semicomatose, he was transferred to a rehabilitation center.

I was in my son's room when the phone rang. It was a lady who said that she was the rehab's social worker. It was a particularly trying day. I burst into tears for no reason and heard the click of the call being disconnected.

A short time later, a beautiful woman in a wheelchair rolled into my son's room with a box of tissues. After sixteen years, I still recognized Helen.

She smiled, handed me the tissues, and motioned for me to come closer. I did, and she hugged me. I told her who I was, and after we both got over the shock of finding each other after sixteen years, she told me about her life since we had last seen each other. She was happily married, had children, and had gotten her degree so that she could smooth the path for those less fortunate than herself. She told me that if there was anything she could give me, it would be hope.

Looking at this wonderful, giving person, I felt small. But I also felt the hope she gave me, the first I had since learning that my son had been hurt. From this person whom I thought would have no quality of life, I learned never to give up—ever. And I learned that where there is life, there is hope.

My son miraculously recovered and we moved back north, but I owe Helen a debt that I can never adequately repay.

Mrs. A.

HEIDI HESS SAXTON
FROM *TOUCHED BY KINDNESS*

I never saw Peggy's mom make cookies, like other moms I knew. When we came home from school, Mrs. A. would always be on the couch, smoking a cigarette. She had a bad back that made it hard for her to get around. When Peggy joined our high school Bible study group, we sometimes prayed for her mom.

From time to time I would chat with Mrs. A. while waiting for Peggy. Unsure that she was a Christian (she attended a different church than I did), I would try to help God along a bit by explaining how to know for sure she was going to heaven. Mrs. A. was always very nice, but firm. "Now, Heidi, go downstairs with Peg. I've got my church, and you have yours." I always did what she said. I knew better than to talk back to an adult.

The winter after I graduated from high school, I was in a bad car accident. Hospitalized and bedridden for over a month, I grew more and more depressed. Friends came by and brought cheery cards and flowers, but all I wanted was a shower. My hair was dirty and stringy, and I felt gross all over.

Then one morning the door to my room opened and in walked Mrs. A. I was surprised that Peggy's mother even knew I was in the hospital—I had been out of touch with her daughter since Peggy had left for college the previous fall. "Mrs. A.! What are you doing here?"

Smiling, Mrs. A. went into the bathroom and got a basin. Taking a garbage bag from her purse, she pushed back the covers from my bed and arranged the bag and the basin under my left shin. Then she squirted my leg with a can of shaving cream, rubbed it around, and carefully shaved me from my ankle to my knee, chatting all the while. It was glorious.

Pouring a little water into the basin, she swished the razor around to get rid of the hair, then bent over her task again. First one leg, then the other, chatting amiably the whole time. When she was done, she lowered the head of my bed and rigged another contraption so she could wash and blow-dry my hair. Then, as a final touch, she painted my nails a cheery pink—fingers and toes. For the first time in a month, I felt like a human being. Admiring my newly pinked fingernails, I asked her, "What made you think of this, Mrs. A.?"

"Oh, I know what it feels like not to be able to reach your toes. I figured you might need a little help. That's what it's all about, right? 'Love one another.'"

A pang of guilt hit me. How could I have doubted that she loved God? Mrs. A. had shown me more kindness in a half hour than I had shown her in two years. But she just brushed aside my apologies. "Here. Have a little ice cream." And from her magic bag she pulled out a pint of my favorite lemon sherbet—and soon the world was right again.

Smile

Smile!
It costs nothing, but creates much.
It enriches those who receive it
without impoverishing those who give it.
It happens in a flash,
and the memory of it sometimes lasts forever.
None are so rich they can get along without it,
and none so poor but are richer for its benefits.
It creates happiness in the home,
fosters goodwill in a business,
and is the countersign of friends.
It is rest to the weary, daylight to the discouraged,
sunshine to the sad, and nature's best antidote for trouble.
Yet it cannot be bought, begged, borrowed, or stolen,
for it is something that is no earthly good to anyone until it is given away!
And if you should meet someone too tired or sick or depressed to give you a smile,
make sure you leave them one of yours.
For no one needs a smile so much as those who have none left to give.
A smile is always welcome
for it opens doors and hearts as if it were a key.
Smile!

AUTHOR UNKNOWN

The Day Cheering Stopped

JOHN C. STEWART
AS TOLD TO GLORIA CASSITY STARGEL

It happened on a cold day in January, midway through my senior year in high school. I tossed my books into the locker and reached for my black-and-gold Cougar jacket. From down the corridor, a friend called out, "Good luck, Johnny. I hope you get the school you want."

Playing football meant more than a game to me. It was my *life*. So the world looked pretty wonderful as I headed up the hill toward the gym to learn which college wanted me on their team.

And how I counted on the resulting scholarship—had for years! It held my only hope for higher education. My dad, an alcoholic, had left home long ago, and Mom worked two jobs just to keep seven children fed. Already I held down part-time jobs to help out.

But I wasn't worried. I had the grades I needed. And ever since grammar school, I had lived and breathed football. It was my identity.

Growing up in a little Southern town where football is king, my skills on the field made me a big man in the community as well as on campus. I pictured myself right up there on a pedestal.

And everybody pumped that ego. The local newspaper mentioned me in write-ups; at football games exuberant cheerleaders yelled out my name; people said things like, "You can do it, Johnny. You can go all the way to professional football!" I mean, that was heady stuff and I ate it up. It kind of made up for my not having a dad to encourage me along the way.

Hurrying to the gym that day, I recalled all those football games—and all those *injuries!* I never had let any of them slow me down for long—not the broken back nor the messed up shoulders and knees. I just gritted my teeth and played right through the agony. I *had* to.

And now came the reward. A good future would be worth the price I had paid. So with a confident grin on my face, I sprinted into Coach Stone's office.

Coach sat behind his desk, the papers from my file spread before him. Our three other coaches sat around the room. No doubt about it, this lineup signaled a momentous occasion.

"Have a seat, Johnny," Coach motioned to the chair beside his desk.

"Johnny," he started, "you've worked really hard. You've done a good job for us. A couple of colleges want to make you an offer."

Something about his tone made me nervous. I shifted my sitting position.

"But, Johnny," he said, holding my medical records in his hands, "Doctor Kendley can't recommend you for college football. Johnny, one more bad hit and you could be paralyzed for life. We can't risk it."

A long silence followed. Then Coach Stone's eyes met mine. "I'm sorry, Johnny. There will be no scholarship."

No scholarship?! The blow hit me like a three-hundred-pound linebacker slamming against my chest. Somehow I got out of that office. I could not understand that they were thinking of my welfare. Instead, in my mind a voice reverberated like a punching bag, "You're not good enough. You're not good enough. You're not good enough."

For *me,* the cheering stopped. Without the cheering, I was nothing. And without college, I would *stay* a nothing.

After that, I just gave up. And in so doing, I lost my moorings.

At first I settled for beer and marijuana. Soon I got into the hard stuff: acid, PCP, heroin, cocaine—I tried them all. Graduation rolled around, and I wonder now how I ever made it through the ceremonies.

Several older friends tried to talk to me about God. Yet even though I had grown up in church and had even served as an altar boy, I couldn't grasp the fact that God cared about my present problems.

A couple of buddies and I decided to hit the road. We had no money and no goal. Along the way, we got into stealing gas to keep us going. When we got hungry enough, we picked up some odd jobs. No matter how little food we had, we always managed somehow to get more drugs.

My anger continued to fester. It wasn't long until I got into a bad fight and landed in jail thousands of miles from home. It caused me to take a good look at myself and see how low I had sunk. *God,* I prayed for the first time in years, *please help me. I'm lost and I can't find my way back.*

I didn't hear an immediate answer. Nor did I clean up my act. We did head toward home, but the old car had enjoyed enough. It quit.

I went into a garage, hoping to get some cheap parts. *Maybe I can patch her up enough to get us home.* I was tired, hungry, dirty—and very much under the influence. Yet a man there extended a hand of friendship. Even took us to supper. After we were fed, Mr. Brown called me aside, "Son," he said, "you don't have to live like this. You can be somebody if only you'll try. God will help you. Remember, He loves you. And so do I."

I was buffaloed. He seemed really to care about me. And he called me "son." It had been a long, long time since anyone had called me "son."

That night in my sleeping bag, I gazed up at the star-filled Texas night. The sky looked so close, I thought maybe I could reach up and touch it. And once again, I tried to pray. *Lord, I am so tired. If You'll have me, I'm ready to come back to You.*

In my heart, I heard Him answer, "I'm here. Come on back, son. I'm here." He called me "son," just like Mr. Brown did! I liked that.

On the road again, I began thinking, *If Mr. Brown, a complete stranger, thought I could make something of myself, maybe I can.*

I didn't straighten out all at once. But at least I started trying. God kept sending people to help me. Like Susan. In September, this cute young thing—a casual friend from high school—came up to me at a football game of all places. She kissed me on the cheek. "Welcome home, Johnny."

The day she said, "Johnny, if you keep doing drugs, I can't date you anymore," is the day I quit them for good.

Susan and I married and today have three beautiful children. We're active in our local church and operate a successful business. I can tell you it means the world to me having earned the respect of my community.

All these years later, I still can feel the sting of that day—the day cheering stopped. The hurt doesn't linger, though, as I've learned I can live without the cheers. After all, I have a caring heavenly Father who calls me "son."

Which reminds me, I *do* have a cheering section—a heavenly one. Check out this Bible verse I came across: "There is rejoicing in the presence of the angels of God over one sinner who repents" (Luke 15:10).

How about that?

Angels! Cheering for *me!*

I like that.

The Eco-Challenge

REBECCA ST. JAMES
FROM *THE DANCE OF HEAVEN*

I t was a race I will never forget. It was the kind of event you didn't have to participate in to be moved and inspired by. In fact, you didn't even have to be there to "get it." The truth is that I watched the race from half a world away in the safety and comfort of our motor home on the road, months after the event actually took place.

Set in my homeland of Australia, this particular adventure caught my interest from the beginning. Known as the Eco-Challenge, this tax-your-body-to-the-limit quest is incredibly tough, to say the least. How does this sound—three hundred miles of nonstop kayaking, hiking, mountain biking, cliff climbing, walking, and rafting? It's exhausting to even think of! The race takes seven to ten days, with teams stopping only for the rest needed to survive. Organizers say that the key ingredients in this race are honest communication, compassion, and remaining mission-oriented. Part of the goal of Eco-Challengers is simply to finish the race, as some do not.

With contestants coming from all around the world, obviously I was rooting for my home team to win. But it was not the Australians or their courage that impacted me so greatly. It was a Chinese team, three guys and a girl, that inspired me so much.

The race had begun, and the Chinese team was progressing through the rough Australian land. Then the nightmare began. It became clear that the lone female member was in pain—one foot began to weaken noticeably. Still she kept on. Finally, after many miles, she could go no farther. She could not put weight on her foot, let alone hike the distance still remaining. It was a disaster, and the Chinese team was looking at the very real possibility of not finishing the race.

One of the most important rules in the Eco-Challenge is that all team members must cross the finish line together. So do you know what they did? Instead of quitting, seeing this misfortune as the end, they found another way to keep on with the race. The strong loaned their strength to the weak. The men on the team took turns running ahead and resting so that when the team caught up, a "rested" member could take the woman from the back of his teammate and carry her. To see their commitment to finish together and not give up brought tears to my eyes. They even had to pack her up mountains, help her over rocks, and carry her through the forest. It was so inspiring!

To me, their story is such a vivid picture of what the true Christian family should look like. Jesus says there is no greater love than when a man lays down his life for his friends (John 15:13). I truly believe that God often uses you and me to help give His strength to other members of the body. We are to carry each other's burdens—but ultimately it is God who carries us.

Billy's Triumph

ERN GROVER

They mocked him as he rode by on his bicycle.

Their stinging words burned in Billy's heart as he fought back his tears. Soon he'd be home and far away from his tormenters.

Billy was born of alcoholic parents in a small coastal village in Maine. Doctors concluded that he and his siblings would reap the harvest of his parents' indulgence. He was a slow learner and was plagued with stuttering and a drool.

Lack of hygiene at home kept most people at a respectable distance. Billy had a kind heart, but he had very low self-esteem, especially when confronted by his peers. I was Billy's only friend during childhood.

We lived only a short distance from each other, so it was natural that we found ourselves running through the woods or swimming under the bridge during the summer months. Billy joined the Boy Scouts with me when we turned eleven.

I arrived in my uniform, but Billy arrived in tattered, dirty clothes. His parents couldn't afford to give him new clothes, and a Boy Scout uniform didn't fit into their drinking budget.

My dad, the scoutmaster, saw his plight, so he rummaged through some packed clothing and came up with my older brother's uniform. It didn't fit very well, but after a few alterations, it became respectable.

I felt his anguish during our first Boy Scout meeting. A couple of boys behind us snickered and made some cutting remarks.

When we were dismissed from formation, Billy and I were assigned to the Wolf Patrol. We eagerly opened the flexible covers of our new Boy Scout handbooks to see what adventures lay before us. I read the introduction, and Billy looked at the pictures.

As the weeks passed, Billy became more discouraged. Boy Scouts was difficult for him because of his disability. The jeering by our peers continued, but it was his inability to read and comprehend that hindered him the most.

One day, Billy and I watched my dad pulling on the mooring ropes of a boat. We gave him a hand, and Billy grabbed the loose end and tied it around a tree. My dad looked up.

"Where did you learn to tie a knot like that, Billy? I'm all thumbs with knots."

Billy took that as a compliment. With a smile on his face, he stuttered his response. "I…I…I've got lotssss of time on my hands."

My dad's eyes lit up, and I could visualize his brain gears turning. Over the next few weeks, Dad worked with both of us from the Boy Scout handbook so that we could pass our requirements.

What Billy couldn't read, he was finally able to memorize after repeated drilling by my dad. In turn, Billy showed my dad how to tie knots and splice rope ends.

Billy's moment came during our awards banquet that fall. My dad congratulated Billy for his achievement. Then he shocked the entire assembly of Boy Scouts and parents.

With his hand upon Billy's shoulder, he announced, "Billy is my number one Scout for knot-tying. From this night on, no one passes the requirements for knot-tying and rope work unless Billy qualifies you."

A tear began to trickle from the corner of Billy's eye as he stood there, proud and smiling, and a few onlookers sniffled during his moment of triumph.

Author's note: I saw Billy again last year. He's doing well, still stutters, and is happily married with children.

My Brother's Keeper

SHANNON KYLE MORROW

I crept into my younger brother's bedroom in the early morning darkness, careful not to wake our parents. Before I even reached his bed, Kalen awoke and immediately got up. We quickly dressed in the jeans and flannel shirts that we had laid out the night before and silently made our way to the front of the house, where our full backpacks were waiting. Excitement filled us as we eased out the front door into the chilly morning. We threw our packs into the bed of Dad's pickup and headed out of town.

This adventure had been planned for weeks. Over the next three days, Kalen and I would be backpacking in a nearby national forest. I was seventeen and had been backpacking for the past ten years, but this was Kalen's first time. He was ten and trusted me to lead him safely through the mountains.

We stopped at a coffee shop for pancakes and eggs, and then left the last little town behind us. Kalen's anticipation began to build as we started winding up the steep mountain road.

"How many times will we have to cross the river today?" Kalen asked.

"Five or six, but the crossings aren't that bad. There are good rocks to jump across on most of them, so we should only have to wade once or twice."

"But didn't you say that the water came up to your waist? That'll be almost to my neck!"

"I don't think the river will be as high this year because we haven't gotten as much rain. But if it is, I can carry our packs across and then carry you across, just like Dad used to do with me."

Kalen's concern reminded me of my own fears when I went on my first backpacking trip. I realized how much he was depending on me.

"Don't worry, Kalen. I'll take good care of you. We're going to have a great time."

I reviewed my mental checklist one more time to make sure I hadn't forgotten anything: matches, wilderness maps, Swiss army knife, first-aid kit. I knew I had packed plenty of food, but I had purposefully left the tent at home. The weather forecast promised clear skies.

The road turned to dirt as it took us deeper into the forest. Dark mountains covered with evergreens hid the morning sun. I parked the truck at the trailhead, and we strapped on our packs. For the first couple of miles, we sped along the trail with fresh legs. Once the novelty wore off, our pace slowed slightly, and we settled into a rhythmic stride.

After a while Kalen suddenly stopped. "My pack is so heavy!"

His comment surprised me because I was carrying most of the gear. I inspected his pack. "Tighten up your hip belt and loosen your shoulder straps," I said, helping him with his buckles. "You want to carry most of the weight around your waist."

"Whew! That's so much better. Thanks!"

Towering pine trees surrounded small meadows, still wet with dew. After a few hours the sun had reached its full strength, and beneath our packs our T-shirts were soaked with sweat. We had shed our flannels much earlier.

"I'm starving," said Kalen. "When can we stop for lunch?"

"We'll reach the river again at the bottom of this canyon. It'll be cooler there, and we can refill our water bottles."

Our pace grew faster down the switchbacks, and we soon heard the crashing of white water. At the river we left the trail and picked our way upstream to sit on some large boulders shaded by an overhanging tree. We took off our boots and rested our feet on the smooth, cool granite and savored our trail lunch of peanuts, beef jerky, dried fruit, wheat crackers, and chocolate.

When we hoisted on our backpacks again, Kalen groaned. I laughed. "You think it hurts now—just wait till tomorrow morning!" A few hours later we reached the campsite I had chosen for our first night. An old fire ring was still there, and I sent Kalen to gather wood while I set up camp. He soon had a good pile of branches, and I showed him how to start a fire. Dusk settled in as we set a pot of water on to boil.

After our supper of ramen noodles, I said, "Let's go for a night hike."

Kalen hesitated. "But we can't see anything. Where would we go?"

"Just up the trail a little. Our eyes will adjust to the dark once we get away from the fire."

"Okay, but let's not go too far."

The path was barely visible as we followed it uphill. Our campfire shrank to an orange speck below us. We sat down on the trail and leaned back against the slope, our faces turned upward. The brilliance of the stars washed me with wonder. I had forgotten how intensely they shone in the wilderness, miles away from other lights.

"Aren't the stars incredible," I said. "I'm so amazed by God's creation."

Kalen agreed. "Looking at all these stars makes me feel really small."

"It's awesome how God made this entire universe, but still cares about each one of us," I said. "I'm glad that someone so powerful loves us so much."

We continued to gaze at the night sky and talk, and I was suddenly aware of how much influence I had over Kalen. If he relied on me this much while backpacking, how much did he look to me in everyday life? I realized that my responsibility toward Kalen would continue long after we were out of the mountains.

Later that night, after a cup of hot cocoa by the campfire, we stretched out in our goose-down bags, exhausted from our long day of hiking. The cold vapor of our breath dissipated as it rose toward the stars overhead.

"Thanks for taking me backpacking," Kalen whispered in the darkness.

"Thanks for coming. Sleep well, brother."

I soon heard Kalen's even breathing, and I took one last look at the ceiling of shimmering stars. I breathed a prayer in the blanket of darkness. *Thank You, God, for Kalen and for the honor of being his big brother. Thank You for this opportunity for us to spend time together.* I rolled over on my side and saw that the glowing embers of the campfire matched the warm satisfaction in my heart.

I've learned that if you want to cheer up yourself, you should try cheering up someone else.

AUTHOR UNKNOWN, AGE 13

Chocolate Cake Mystery

HEIDI HESS SAXTON
FROM *TOUCHED BY KINDNESS*

It had been a rough winter. My ten-year-old sister, Chris, had lost her leg in her long battle with cancer. As the bills continued to pile up, the belt my parents had drawn tighter and tighter around our family finances had left us all more than a little winded.

The summer of my sophomore year in high school, things got a little brighter. I had always wanted to be an exchange student. As a concession to my wanderlust, my parents agreed to host a student that year. Jaana was from Finland—a junior, blue-eyed, blonde, and beautiful enough to make even the senior boys swoon. I enjoyed the novelty of having a Finnish friend and especially liked that at last I had an identity I could live with. I was no longer the four-eyed Christian geek who didn't wear makeup or cool clothes. I was Jaana's little sister.

That winter, Jaana's parents wrote to tell us that they were hoping to visit America at Easter, and my parents immediately wrote back to invite them to stay with us.

Then tragedy struck. One month before Jaana's parents were to arrive, Chris wound up back in the hospital for another operation that sucked the family bank account drier than last week's soup bone.

The week before our guests arrived, I overheard my parents talking one night when they thought everyone was asleep. "What are we going to do?

How will we feed our guests? Should we find another place for Jaana to stay?" Not wanting to hear the answers to those questions, I covered my ears with my pillow and went to sleep with an uneasy gnawing in the pit of my stomach.

The next morning as we sat down to our traditional Sunday morning donuts, Dad announced that we were going to ask God to help us. "You will not ask anyone at church for help," Dad reminded us. "They've done enough." Then he bowed his head and implored almighty God to do something.

Three hours later, when we returned from church, we discovered that someone had propped open our front porch door. Dad ordered us to stay in the car until he made sure everything was all right. The next thing we heard was the sound of my father's deep, booming laugh.

On the porch, just to the right of the door, sat ten large boxes of food—enough to feed us for months. And on top of the largest box was the biggest miracle of all: a huge, delectable three-layered chocolate cake—my favorite. There was no note, and everyone who heard the story looked as surprised as we had been.

"God must have sent His angels to take care of us," my mother said later that evening. My dad just nodded, took a sip of tea, and buried his nose back in the newspaper. That special delivery from God's compassionate angel (whoever it was) did more than feed our bodies. It fed our souls with the reassurance that God loved us and had not forgotten us—and that as long as we trusted Him, we would always have a little left over for the stranger at the door.

Another chance

Rainbow of Hope
The brilliant
rainbow
promises newness ahead,
vibrant hues
coloring our world
with hope.

JUDY GORDON

choices

MATT JOHNSON
AS TOLD TO JANET SCHREUR COCKRUM

I had been drunk for more than a week when I found myself sitting in my truck with two of my so-called friends.

One of my buddies began to speculate about how easy it would be for us to rob the local store. Because I was still inebriated, the foolishness of his words didn't register; instead, the urgency to get money for more booze drove me to grab my gun and rob that store. The next day I woke up sober enough to realize that I had committed a crime. I knew that the police would be looking for me.

Six months later, while hiding out in another state, I was caught, arrested, and jailed. A judge sentenced me to fourteen years for armed robbery. In my home state, North Carolina, the Fair Sentencing Act meant that my jail time was immediately cut in half, but I would have to serve all seven years without opportunity for an early parole.

As a young man of twenty-two, I couldn't believe that I was going to spend the best years of my life rotting in a prison cell. How had I sunk to such a low point in my life? I had been reared in a loving Christian family. I had attended church and had been a well-mannered, polite kid. I even owned a Bible.

But in spite of my upbringing, I had made some very bad choices. I can still remember being at a friend's house when I sneaked my first drink of alcohol. I was twelve years old. When I turned sixteen and was able to have a driver's license, I had many opportunities to get alcohol. As my addiction to liquor grew and as its power over my life intensified, my love for basketball and my dreams of playing college and professional sports diminished.

After struggling through high school, I enlisted in the military where I became even more dependent on liquor and became an alcoholic. Three years later, when my tour of duty was up, I came home. Through drinking and partying, I wasted the money that I had saved in the military. That was when I made that decision to rob the liquor store. The decision took only a few seconds to make, but it cost me seven years of my life. I was angry at myself for being so stupid. I felt as if my life was wasted, and I saw no hope for my future.

One of my few pleasures in prison was playing basketball. One day an opportunity came to the inmates at our prison facility. A Christian basketball team was coming to our facility and had challenged our best players to a game. I didn't care who those guys were, but I thought that if I made the prison team, I could have a good game of basketball.

I tried out and made the team. I felt sure that we could beat a group of Christians. But when I saw the Spirit Express basketball team, I knew that their six-foot-ten-inch and six-foot-eleven-inch men were going to be hard to beat. They didn't look like a bunch of wimpy Christians!

By halftime the Christian guys were easily beating our team, and they had earned my respect. Because of their athletic abilities, I listened to what these men said after the game as they talked about God's love and forgiveness.

At that time I didn't want God in my life. But the testimonies I had heard left me questioning my life and what was lacking in it. Now I felt even more miserable than I had before the team came, but I didn't understand why.

Two months later I returned from my work detail to find a large Christmas card waiting for me. All the guys on the Christian basketball team had signed it, telling me how much they loved me and, more important, how much God loved me.

Suddenly I knew why I had been so unhappy. God had been dealing with me. Right then I got onto my knees beside my bunk and prayed to receive Jesus Christ as my Savior and Lord. Instead of seeing despair and hopelessness in my future, I now sensed that God had good things in store for me. I was going to make it through prison. I knew that when I was released from jail, God would give me purpose and direction for my life.

Immediately I began to read my Bible and to grow as a Christian. The president of the Spirit Express basketball team began to correspond with me, and that helped me to grow stronger in my faith.

I began to feel a burden for kids. I thought that if they could hear my story about drinking, they might think, *That sounds like me. I don't want to end up in prison. I need to make good choices and not bad ones that I'll regret for years.*

Even while I served the last three years of my prison term, God brought opportunities for me to tell my story to young people. I was invited to speak to kids in schools, in youth detention centers, at sports banquets, and in churches. A guard would escort me there, and I would tell my testimony. I told the kids that growing up in a good home doesn't protect them from making bad choices, and I emphasized to them that making bad decisions can lead to serious consequences. And I told the kids that prison didn't rehabilitate me: Jesus Christ alone changed me and made me new.

Four years ago I was released from prison, and God immediately provided the opportunity for me to join the Christian basketball team that had come to my prison. Now I tell prisoners how God changed my life and gave me hope and a future. In the summers I lead basketball camps for kids, and in recent months, God has provided opportunities for me to tell my story at inner-city youth rallies, chapel services at Christian schools, and church group meetings. I've even told my story on radio.

My message is the same one that I heard back in the prison yard in North Carolina. My message is simple: God loves you, and no matter how many bad choices you have made, He can change your life…just as He did mine.

Sudden Death

WENDY DUNHAM

Who would have thought that some of my best friends—the ones I stole pumpkins with, painted water towers with, and partied with—were the friends I met at my church youth group.

I know that sounds hypocritical, but just because you go to youth group doesn't mean you're a Christian.

In our youth group, there were kids at all levels of Christianity: those who were fully committed and carried their Bibles even at school, those who were forced to attend by their parents, and those like me, with one foot in the door of Christianity and one foot out. We were the ones who formed our clique. We were the ones who got together after youth group and had all the fun, so we thought.

One time my friend Eric and I decided to skip out early from youth group and see what kind of fun we could discover. It was perfect timing, as I had recently gotten my license and I had my parents' car. We drove around for a while, then ended up stopping at a community auction—it was just one of those spontaneous things to do on a hot summer evening. Anything seemed better than sitting in that muggy youth group room. We bought tickets and had fun bidding on things we didn't want—it was just fun raising the bid when we knew other bidders were willing to pay big bucks for an item.

On the way home afterward, I said to Eric, "My parents will kill me when they find out I bought a piano!" (That time, no one had bid past twenty dollars.) "I don't even have a way to get it home. And even if I do get it home, there's no room for it in the house. Maybe I can keep it in the garage?"

"You're crazy, girl," said Eric. "At least I ended up with something practical. My parents can't complain about an old suitcase. I'll be able to use it for college next year."

"Maybe," I said, "if you can get the dust off it. That thing is old."

We continued laughing as I drove along the open country road. Soon we approached the large hill near Eric's house. When we were almost at the top, a car came out of nowhere, roaring over the crest of the hill—in our lane—heading right toward us.

There was little time to react, and from that moment on, everything took place in slow motion, like we were in a movie. I felt my hands deliberately turning the wheel to the left, swerving away from the oncoming car. The cars' right front ends danced slowly around each other, with no space in between. Then my hands turned the wheel to the right, swerving back into my lane. Everything happened as if we lingered in time. I felt that something, or someone, had helped me turn the wheel—I couldn't have reacted that quickly on my own. It was intense. We were a breath away from a head-on collision, a breath away from death.

I pulled over to the side of the road, my body trembling, my hands still gripping the wheel. I tried to speak, but my words made little sense. Eric could see I was no longer able to drive, so he put his hands on my shoulders and guided me around to the passenger's seat. He drove the rest of the way, and I closed my eyes and took several deep breaths to relax.

When we arrived at his house, Eric got the suitcase out of the trunk and carried it into the kitchen. Feeling something shift inside, he set it on the table to open it. As he unzipped it, we expected to find a smaller travel bag, but instead found an old board game. The name emblazoned on the box leaped out at us—*Sudden Death*. As I read the words, chills slid down my spine. Eric and I stared at the game and then at each other. Nothing before had ever seemed so strange, yet so real. We said nothing. Eric picked up the game and shoved it deep into the garbage. Neither he nor I wanted anything to do with that game.

Still without saying a word, we joined hands, faced each other, and sat down at the table. We knew what we had to do. We started praying, thanking God for His protection and for a second chance. In rededicating our lives to God, we asked Him to help us put two feet in the door, not just the one we had before. We learned firsthand how sudden death could be…. We wanted to make sure we were ready—wouldn't you?

Change is what happens when the pain of holding on becomes greater than the fear of letting go.

AUTHOR UNKNOWN

Carl's Garden

AUTHOR UNKNOWN

arl was a quiet man. He didn't talk much. He would always greet you with a big smile and a firm handshake. Even after living in our neighborhood for over fifty years, no one could really say they knew him very well.

Before his retirement, he took the bus to work each morning. The sight of him walking down the street alone often worried us. He had a slight limp from a bullet wound received in World War II. Watching him, we worried that although he had survived World War II, he may not make it through our changing uptown neighborhood with its ever increasing random violence, gangs, and drug activity.

When he saw the flyer at our local church asking for volunteers for caring for the gardens behind the minister's residence, he responded in his characteristically unassuming manner. Without fanfare, he just signed up. He was well into his eighty-seventh year when the very thing we had always feared finally happened.

He was just finishing his watering for the day when three gang members approached him. Ignoring their attempt to intimidate him, he simply asked, "Would you like a drink from the hose?"

The tallest and toughest looking of the three said, "Yeah, sure," with a malevolent little smile. As Carl offered the hose to him, the other two grabbed Carl's arm, throwing him down. As the hose snaked crazily over the ground, dousing everything in its way, Carl's assailants stole his retirement watch and his wallet, and then fled. Carl tried to get himself up, but he had been thrown down on his bad leg.

He lay there trying to gather himself as the minister came running to help him. Although the minister had witnessed the attack from his window, he couldn't get there fast enough to stop it. "Carl, are you okay? Are you hurt?" the minister kept asking as he helped Carl to his feet. Carl just passed a hand over his brow and sighed, shaking his head.

"Just some punk kids. I hope they'll wise up someday." His wet clothes clung to his slight frame as he bent to pick up the hose. He adjusted the nozzle again and started to water.

Confused and a little concerned, the minister asked, "Carl, what are you doing?"

"I've got to finish watering. It's been very dry lately," came the calm reply. Satisfying himself that Carl really was all right, the minister could only marvel. Carl was a man from a different time and place.

A few weeks later the three returned. Just as before, their threat was unchallenged. Carl again offered them a drink from his hose. This time they didn't rob him. They wrenched the hose from his hand and drenched him head to foot in the icy water.

When they had finished their humiliation of him, they sauntered off down the street, throwing catcalls and curses, falling over one another laughing at the hilarity of what they had just done. Carl just watched them. Then he turned toward the warmth giving sun, picked up his hose, and went on with his watering.

The summer was quickly fading into fall. Carl was doing some tilling when he was startled by the sudden approach of someone behind him. He stumbled and fell into some evergreen branches. As he struggled to regain his footing, he turned to see the tall leader of his summer tormenters reaching down for him. He braced himself for the expected attack. "Don't worry old man; I'm not gonna hurt you this time." The young man spoke softly, still offering the tattooed and scarred hand to Carl.

As he helped Carl get up, the man pulled a crumpled bag from his pocket and handed it to Carl. "What's this?" Carl asked.

"It's your stuff," the man explained. "It's your stuff back. Even the money in your wallet."

"I don't understand," Carl said. "Why would you help me now?"

The man shifted his feet, seeming embarrassed and ill at ease. "I learned something from you," he said. "I ran with that gang and hurt people like you. We picked on you because you were old, and we knew we could do it. But every time we came and did something to you, instead of yelling and fighting back, you tried to give us a drink. You didn't hate us for hating you. You kept showing love against our hate." He stopped for a moment.

"I couldn't sleep after we stole your stuff, so here it is back." He paused for another awkward moment, not knowing what more there was to say. "That bag's my way of saying thanks for straightening me out, I guess." And with that, he walked off down the street.

Carl looked down at the sack in his hands and gingerly opened it. He took out his retirement watch and put it back on his wrist. Opening his wallet, he checked for his wedding photo. He gazed for a moment at the young bride that still smiled back at him from all those years ago.

He died one cold day after Christmas that winter. Many people attended his funeral in spite of the weather. In particular, the minister noticed a tall young man that he didn't know sitting quietly in a distant corner of the church. The minister spoke of Carl's garden as a lesson in life. In a voice made thick with unshed tears, he said, "Do your best and make your garden as beautiful as you can. We will never forget Carl and his garden."

The following spring another flyer went up. It read: "Person needed to care for Carl's garden." The request went unnoticed by the busy parishioners until one day when a knock was heard at the minister's office door. Opening the door, the minister saw a pair of scarred and tattooed hands holding the flyer. "I believe this is my job, if you'll have me," the young man said.

The minister recognized him as the same young man who had returned the stolen watch and wallet to Carl. He knew that Carl's kindness had turned this man's life around. As the minister handed him the keys to the garden shed, he said, "Yes, go take care of Carl's garden and honor him."

The man went to work and, over the next several years, he tended the flowers and vegetables just as Carl had done. In that time, he went to college, got married, and became a prominent member of the community. But he never forgot his promise to Carl's memory and kept the garden as beautiful as he thought Carl would have kept it.

One day he approached the new minister and told him that he couldn't care for the garden any longer. He explained with a shy and happy smile, "My wife just had a baby boy last night, and she's bringing him home on Saturday."

"Well, congratulations!" said the minister, as he was handed the garden shed keys. "That's wonderful! What's the baby's name?"

It was Carl.

Nothing can stop God from loving you.

RITA ROBINSON

A Prisoner of Hope

DARRON SHIPE
AS TOLD TO RICK CONNER

I was handcuffed and sitting in the back of the sheriff's car, with the words of the juvenile judge haunting me. "Darron, I find that you should be awarded to the state juvenile system for an indefinite period." The image of Mom, sitting in the front row crying, tormented me. Dad, who had a history of drinking and violence, remained unemotional and seemed relieved of a burden and responsibility that he had never wanted.

On Sundays, Mom came to the juvenile facility to visit. Her eyes were always on the brink of tears, filled with pain and disappointment, especially when she had to say good-bye. She would choke, quickly turn away, and never look back. I'd push my head up against the barred window until she was out of sight, knowing that she was crying all the way to the car.

After four years in the juvenile facility, I was set free. But the freedom lasted a little less than a year before I was arrested again. This time I was charged with four armed robberies. For the next eight years, I remained incarcerated in a maximum security prison. On Saturdays when Mom would come to visit, I walked out to the visitors room, filled with pain. I knew how disappointed she was, seeing me as a failure and not being able to make it in life. A few times I told the guards to tell her that I wasn't available, because I just couldn't face her.

After I was released, I hit the streets, and I was in trouble again with the law. This time I was charged with fourteen counts of grand larceny, and I faced ninety years in prison. Surprisingly, the judge admitted me into a drug program for rehabilitation. I stayed four months before walking out the door. On September 14, 1983, the judge issued an APB on me as a fugitive from justice.

For the next year I stayed on the run, always having to look over my shoulder. No place was safe. One Monday morning I stopped by my mom's house and went to the shed in the backyard, where I hid my weapons and ammunition. I decided that I would go out like a gangster; at least the guys in the prison would be able to read about me in tomorrow's headlines. I was planning to go out and rob everybody that got in my way, and when the cops cornered me, I'd shoot it out.

I was putting on my shoulder holster for my shotgun and loading my pockets with ammunition when I noticed Mom coming out onto the back porch. She sat down holding her old, worn-out Bible and appeared to be praying. I watched her sitting there, with no idea as to the new troubles that I was about to bring her way.

I felt sorry for her, knowing that I could never be the son that she would be proud of in life. And now, I was going to downtown Baltimore to shoot it out with the cops. Suddenly I changed my mind. I just couldn't leave her with that legacy.

A few months later, I was caught in a high-speed chase with a stolen car. I was arrested and charged with an array of crimes. While in jail, all the felony warrants from Maryland were charged to me.

About an hour's ride from the prison lived a man by the name of Mr. Gravitt. One afternoon while he was praying, God spoke to him through Matthew 25:35–36. "'For I was hungry and you gave me something to eat, I was thirsty and you gave me something to drink, I was a stranger and you invited me in, I needed clothes and you clothed me…I was in prison and you came to visit me.'" After reading those verses, the Lord directed him to go to the Caroline County Jail and visit Darron Scott Shipe with a message from God.

In all my years in prison, I had been able to control the depression and hopelessness that came from being incarcerated. But for some reason, this imprisonment was finally getting to me. I had lived a wasted life, without purpose, without reason, and now I was paying the price. I looked out the barred window, over the razor wire, and wondered if there was any hope for me beyond these prison walls.

At that hopeless and depressed moment, Mr. Gravitt cautiously peeked around the corner of the cell block. The guard had warned him of the violent rage I had been in earlier. He approached my cell. "Darron, can I talk with you a minute?"

I told him to come over. He began to share how God had a purpose for everyone's life. He declared in a loud voice, "God said this afternoon that you're not going back to prison. But you'll be a witness to His power and grace, and you'll come back as a testimony of what He can do in someone's life."

"Look, there's no hope for me. I've already been sentenced, and I'm going back to prison," I said sadly.

I watched the old man ease closer, using the bars to lower himself to a prayer position. He reached through the bars, grabbed my hands, and began to pray like he believed every word he spoke. Something happened that day that changed my life forever. I felt like the old man had made contact.

Going from one courtroom to another, I was finally released into a Christian program. After completing it, I returned for a re-evaluation. To the amazement of all, God had totally changed me.

For the past sixteen years, I have been a successful businessman and the president of my own company in Richmond, Virginia. On weekends, I speak at churches and prisons on how God can change a person for His glory. My mom had the pleasure of seeing God change my life as I began serving Him. In her final days, she was proud to see me make something of myself and become successful. In fact, one day she read a letter that I had written to her from prison: "One of these days, Mom, you'll be proud of me. Just wait and see."

With tears in her eyes, she said, "I am, son. I'm really proud of you." A few months later, in March 1996, she died of cancer. I had the honor of standing by her graveside one sunny afternoon to preach her funeral, sending her home to meet her Savior, the Lord Jesus Christ.

Driving back to Richmond, all I could do was cry and hum that old gospel song, "Amazing grace! how sweet the sound that saved a wretch like me! I once was lost, but now I'm found; was blind, but now I see."

Thank you, Mom, for never giving up on me. Forever I remain, a prisoner of hope.

The great thing in this world is not so much where we are, but in what direction we are moving.

OLIVER WENDELL HOLMES

MY STORY

I am not the person I always dreamed I'd be.
I am not the person I pretended to be.
But I am not the person I will yet be
Because my Jesus loves me,
and He is renovating my life.
Here is the truth:
This house is under reconstruction
by the master carpenter.
So come on in and don't mind the mess.
I have nothing to hide,
nothing to fear,
nothing to lose.
My Jesus loves me,
and He is not finished with me yet.

OLIVIA

FROM *STORIES THAT COUNT*

Vacation from God

TERESA J. CLEARY

The final bell of the school day rang, and I breathed a sigh of relief. "No more pencils, no more books...." I recited under my breath as I dialed the combination to my locker. Today was the last day of my senior year, and it hadn't arrived a moment too soon.

No more getting up at 5:30 A.M. to get ready for school, I thought gleefully. *No more riding the bus when everyone else drives. No more long hours spent on homework when I'd rather be out with friends.*

Ever since my eighteenth birthday two weeks before, I'd felt a growing sense of rebellion. Suddenly my parents seemed too strict, school too boring, youth group too conservative, and life too dull. As I saw my friend Jenny, who lived next door, going to parties and on dates, I began to feel that I was missing something.

All that's going to change, I thought as I slammed my locker and headed for the bus for the last time.

"My life is so dull," I told Jenny later as we sat on her front porch munching on potato chips. "I feel like the world is passing me by."

"Maybe it's all the time you spend doing church stuff instead of going out and having fun," Jenny replied. "Retreats, youth group, service projects—give yourself a break!"

Normally I would have dismissed Jenny's comments. After all, I'd heard them often enough in the past. Jenny's family hadn't attended church in the ten years we'd lived next door to them, and Jenny said that the only time she'd ever gone was with me.

With the way I'd been feeling lately, her words seemed to make sense. Even though I enjoyed spending time with my friends from youth group and liked the meetings and retreats, I was beginning to think that there had to be more to life than church.

"What are you doing this weekend?" Jenny asked, interrupting my thoughts.

"I was going to help out at the church picnic," I said with a sheepish smile.

"Forget it," Jenny said. "You're going with me."

And so began a summer of weekends spent at parties, movies, and just hanging out. I filled my life with these new experiences hoping to find what I thought was missing.

After my late Saturday nights out with Jenny and my new friends, I'd be too tired on Sunday for church and youth group. Yet I always reasoned my way out of feeling guilty. *Everyone takes time off during the summer. I'm sure God understands how busy I am. Anyway, He'll still be there when things slow down.*

Somehow I got the idea that from June through August, God was on vacation too. Although I pretended He didn't exist for three months, He was as busy as ever. Every time I saw a friend from church, I'd hear about the great youth group meetings and the fun service projects they were doing.

When they asked me how things were going, I'd mumble an embarrassed "fine" and make a quick getaway. My spiritual life was at an all-time low. I hadn't read my Bible or gone to church in weeks and talking to any of my new friends about spiritual things only brought disinterested stares and as change of subject.

All through the summer, I had a nagging sense that what I was doing wasn't right, but I told myself that I was having too good of a time to care. I missed church and my old friends, and one Sunday I realized how much.

On that weekend, Jenny had gone out of town with her folks, leaving me to make my own decisions about how to spend my time. Instead of calling one of my new friends, I found myself heading for the church building where I'd heard they were holding a car wash to raise money for a guy at school who'd been injured in an accident.

All my old youth group friends were there, laughing and carrying on as they cleaned car after car. I joined the fun, and soon the old feeling of camaraderie was back. *It's just like old times,* I thought, until my friends started discussing how they'd grown spiritually over the summer through youth group meetings and retreats.

Don't ask me how I've grown, I thought, trying to look busy with a particularly stubborn smudge on a windshield. *My spiritual life dried up over the summer.*

No one asked, and I breathed a sigh of relief. *A reprieve,* I thought.

The reprieve didn't last long. After the car wash, the group formed a circle to pray for the surgery for the accident victim and to thank God for the money they'd raised that day. As everyone joined hands, I hung back, unsure if I'd be welcome.

"Pray with us, Teresa," one of my friends said with an encouraging smile. "We've missed you."

I looked at the group around me and at their outstretched hands as they invited me to pray. Even though I'd ignored God all summer, He was still there anxiously awaiting my return.

What is it I want for the rest of the summer? I asked myself. *Parties or prayer?*

I'd had a good time with Jenny during the past weeks, but I still felt something was missing from my life. All the parties and new friends hadn't helped me find what I felt was lacking. I'd tried to use new experiences to fill a void that was never really empty. God had never left me. I'd been the one who'd turned my back on Him.

In that moment I made my decision. What I thought was missing from my life was what I already had. I walked forward and joined the circle of outstretched hands.

The Haunting Smile

MICHAEL W. SMITH
FROM *IT'S TIME TO BE BOLD*

I read once that a famous Roman senator went to the Colosseum as a spectator during Nero's persecution of the Christians. He had joined in similar gruesome festivities before, but this was his first contact with the new religious sect, and he was curious about how these people would face death.

Not far from where he was seated, a ferocious lion stalked a young Christian girl, and the wealthy Roman was spellbound as he prepared to watch the slaughter. Just a few yards away from him, the girl bravely faced the beast in grim silence.

The senator later wrote in his journal that just as the girl was about to die before his eyes, she did something that changed his life forever. She smiled at him. The Roman was haunted by that smile for days afterward, until he could no longer run from "the God who teaches men how to die." It is said that he faced the lions himself after he publicly trusted in Jesus.

The Robber's Return

TERESA ROBOTHAM

O n a fall Sunday in 1995, nurse Kim Bracken completed two early morning home visits before heading downtown to First Baptist Church of Fort Lauderdale.

As she pulled into the city parking garage, it was about 9:30 A.M. Bible study was already under way; the worship service wouldn't begin for another hour.

Kim noticed how empty the garage was as she stepped out of her car. Reaching in the backseat for her viola, she hummed a hymn she'd heard on the radio.

Before Kim could shut the car door, she suddenly heard a voice. "Don't move!" threatened an unwelcome stranger. Kim tried to get a glimpse of the man, but she changed her mind when she felt the jab of a gun against her temple.

Was this a joke or the beginning of a life-and-death ordeal? "Give me all your money," the man demanded, "and your jewelry, too."

"Sure," Kim answered. "Take anything you want." Then she added, "And if you're hungry, there's some fresh grapefruit in the backseat."

What a foolish thing to say! Kim thought, her fear increasing as the man ripped away all her belongings.

Then she heard a click. *Was that the safety on the gun? I can't believe this is happening to me.* Kim did not know whether she would live or die. A Bible

266

promise came to mind. "To live is Christ and to die is gain." *If this man pulls the trigger,* Kim thought, *I'll be immediately in heaven.* The idea stirred courage she didn't know she had.

Kim, in her midthirties, had always had a heart for evangelism. *If I have to die, at least he will hear the name of Jesus,* she decided. *After all, I'm not going to die for nothing.* Quickly turning around, Kim's movement startled her assailant. He stood frozen with wide eyes. She noticed unusual tattoos on his face and arms. Her next words were filled with compassion. "It's okay. I forgive you because Jesus loves you."

The man jumped back with a flustered and confused look on his face. He may have been armed, but he was no longer dangerous. God had intervened.

The man quickly ran away, disappearing behind a tall building down the street. Frozen, Kim felt like she was trapped in a nightmare. *Run. Just run!* she thought, but her legs would not move.

Before she had a chance to regain her composure, Kim saw the man in the distance. "Oh no," she whispered, "he's coming back." The closer he got, the more apprehensive she became. Now just a few feet away, with head down and eyes averted, the man handed everything back to Kim—including his gun! She clumsily accepted it, putting the gun in her car.

The Holy Spirit gave her the strength to introduce herself. "My name is Kim. What's yours?" Once more he became fearful and looked as if he were going to flee.

Kim grabbed him by the arm.

"My name is Jimmy." He glanced up with tears in his eyes.

"Hi, Jimmy," Kim said. "I believe God brought us together for a reason. I'm on my way to church, and I would consider it a privilege if you would be my guest."

Jimmy glanced at his blue jeans and T-shirt, then said, "I can't go to church looking like this."

"I don't care what you're wearing, and I'm sure the Lord doesn't mind," Kim assured him. "But if it means that much to you, I can drive you home to change."

"No!" Jimmy retorted. *Who was this woman and where did she get the courage?* he must have thought. "I'll run home and meet you back here in ten minutes," he promised.

Kim questioned his sincerity but agreed. "Okay, I'll be waiting right here." As he left, Kim took a deep breath and felt like collapsing.

People started arriving for the 10:30 service. As a teenage girl passed by, Kim thought it might be a good idea to notify security. She called out, "Hi, Shawn. Could you do me a favor and mention to the guard that there is a suspicious looking character in the area?" She was purposely vague so as not to alarm the young girl or risk any unnecessary confrontations between Jimmy and security. The teenager hurried off with the message.

A few minutes later, a car pulled into a nearby parking spot and out stepped David Lowe, Sr., one of the church ushers. "Good morning! How are you today?"

"I'm fine," Kim answered guardedly. David started walking up the street, but when he neared the church and noticed Kim still in the parking garage, he decided to go back and investigate. "You're not fine, are you?" he asked.

"No, I'm not," Kim confessed. She told him the whole story and asked him to stand by in case something went wrong. David slipped out of sight behind a concrete pillar.

When Jimmy reappeared, Kim almost didn't recognize him. Wearing a crisp white shirt, tie, a pair of dark knit pants, and polished black shoes, he approached her.

"You're back," she nervously announced. "Jimmy, I hope you don't mind, but I shared what happened with a friend." David stepped out from behind the pillar. Once again, fear flashed on Jimmy's face, but he didn't bolt. He nodded uneasily as he and Kim walked with David a few blocks to church.

Once inside, David tried his best to make the new visitor feel welcome. Jimmy relaxed when he realized nobody was going to arrest him.

After a quick tour of the building, David suggested that they sit in the balcony where he ushered.

As thousands of worshipers filled the large sanctuary, the minister of music stepped up to the podium. The pipe organ vibrated the pew where Kim and Jimmy were sitting. To Kim's surprise, Jimmy knew all the words to the hymn. As the music played, Jimmy began to sob. "Why are you crying?" Kim whispered.

"It's the only hymn I know—and I know every word of every verse," Jimmy muttered. It was a song Jimmy learned as a child in vacation Bible school.

It was time for the sermon. As the pastor turned to the large multimedia screen behind him, words appeared on the screen. The pastor read, "Robbery. Today we are going to talk about robbing God."

Tears streamed down Jimmy's face. Clearly, this message was no accident. God had Jimmy's undivided attention.

After the service, Kim found out that Jimmy had been raised in a Christian home but did not have a personal relationship with Jesus Christ. Kim led Jimmy in a prayer to ask Jesus to forgive his sins and take charge of his life.

Kim and Jimmy joined another church friend, Bob Henderson, for lunch. Quickly briefed on what had happened that morning, Bob asked, "Jimmy, what were you thinking when Kim reacted the way she did?"

"I have never been so afraid in all my life," he said. Jimmy's voice quavered. "When Kim mentioned Jesus, I remembered a Bible verse that said God's Word was a double-edged sword, and at that very minute the sword went right through my heart. I felt so ashamed."

At the restaurant, the three were surprised to see the pastor. Kim and Bob tactfully introduced Jimmy as a "first-time visitor to church" and found an empty table.

During lunch, both Bob and Kim could sense that Jimmy was still burdened with shame.

"Jimmy, you don't have to be ashamed anymore," Kim encouraged him. "God has forgiven and forgotten all your sins." Then she added, "And so have we."

In the following weeks, Bob, who was involved in the church's outreach ministry, helped Jimmy with food and other necessities. Besides meeting Jimmy's physical needs, Bob also extended his friendship by giving him rides to church. When Kim would see Jimmy at church, she'd always make a point to greet him.

On November 12, 1995, Jimmy made a public commitment to Jesus Christ. He joined the church and was later baptized. "Jimmy was really sincere and genuine—repentant for what he did," said Bob Henderson.

Soon after, Jimmy returned to Chicago to reconcile with his mother and three small children. Though the Christians Jimmy met in Florida have lost contact with him over the last couple of years, people have not forgotten the dramatic testimony of his changed life.

It's never too late to be what you might have been.

GEORGE ELIOT

A Treasure Within

S. J. BARKSDALE

Louie was a fearless sixteen-year-old boy who approached life with dangerous enthusiasm. Long labeled a macho kid whose booming voice could stop an attack dog in midlunge, he seemed destined for a career as a barroom bouncer or an alligator wrestler, whichever challenged him the most. Much to my mother's dismay, he was my best friend.

Each time he roared up our lane in his old hot rod, its exhaust spewing black smoke, radio at full blast, the cats ran for cover, and my mother braced herself for the incoming turbulence.

Louie and I somehow managed to graduate from high school. At the end of summer, we took separate roads—I to college in California, he to new adventures. Except for a spurt of postcards, we soon lost touch. Afterward, I remained in California and became a drafting apprentice. Sometimes when I sat in my office on my nine-to-five schedule, I remembered my free-spirited best friend and felt a stab of envy for the exciting life he must be enjoying— always on the edge, taking dangerous risks.

One day my dad called to tell me that Mom was in the hospital and maybe I should come home. Things didn't look good. She had suffered a severe allergic shock while on her daily walk and barely made it back to the house before collapsing into a coma. My dad called 911, and in minutes a paramedic fire truck was rushing her to the hospital.

Despite all odds, Mom survived, thanks to the firefighters' prompt emergency procedures and the chain of prayers that swept through our community. Soon after her release from the hospital, a fire truck rumbled up our lane, lights flashing and siren wailing. Puzzled, I opened the door to three brawny firefighters, looking trim in their dark blue uniforms. The one with the biceps the size of cantaloupes slapped me soundly on the back and said, "Hey there, Buddy."

I stared, bug-eyed and openmouthed. "Louie?" He'd filled out, his frame finally fitting his size thirteen shoes, but I'd know that look of cheerful impudence anywhere.

"Right," he said. "The same Louie who used to send your mom into hissy fits. We're the team that answered the 911 call, and we decided to drop by to see how your mom's doing."

My mother appeared in the kitchen doorway. Her eyes widened. "This has to be Louie," she said. "Who else would come barreling up our lane making such an alarming racket?"

Mom led us into the kitchen and, just like in our high school days, gave us cookies and lemonade. It was then that I told her that it was Louie who had come to her rescue. Tears rolled down her cheeks. "Louie, I always figured you'd be the death of me. I never dreamed that one day you'd be my guardian angel."

During our brief visit, we learned that he had tried many jobs before becoming a firefighter. He took good care of his aging parents and, with an eye on the future, developed a flourishing tree farm on the side.

"Wow, Louie," I said. "All this time I pictured you tearing around the country on a Harley, wearing black leather, with a biker chick behind you."

He laughed. "Well, you didn't miss it by far. On my days off I load up my five-wheeler and head for the mountains. And I've got plenty of chicks— a wife and three daughters. I tell you, man, it's the way to go."

On my flight back to California, I thought of Louie and all the people who had misjudged him. They had failed to recognize the brashness and daring of his youth as the very leadership qualities needed to become a man of bravery, a responsible husband and father, and a shrewd business entrepreneur.

How much we miss, I thought, *when we see only the packaging and not the treasure within.*

Guns 'N' Prayer

TOM
AS TOLD TO MURIEL LARSON

What are you doing to my brother?" screamed the teenage girl, running into the street.

"I'm going to kill him, and now I'll have to kill you, too!" I cried.

I had recently been released from prison after serving time for manslaughter. But I couldn't seem to stay out of trouble. While living at a halfway house, I had gotten into a fight with a man. The next morning I bought a gun, loaded it, and headed to the man's house. When he answered the door, I lunged in and grabbed him by the collar. Pulling him into the deserted street, I shoved him to the ground, jabbed a foot into his throat, and took aim. That's when the teenage girl ran into the street. She fell to her knees and bowed her head.

Her posture startled me, but I held on to my victim and cocked the gun. As I debated which one of them to shoot first, I heard the girl pray.

"Dear Lord," she said softly, "this man must be the most miserable person in the whole world. I pray that You will save him and give him the happiness he must be searching for."

I stared at her. She wasn't praying for herself. She wasn't praying for her brother. She was praying for me!

My hand began shaking and I loosened my finger on the trigger. Releasing the man, I walked over to the girl and handed her the gun. "Take this thing and throw it away," I mumbled.

Back at the halfway house, I threw myself on my bed. The girl's prayer kept replaying in my mind. I tried to get ahold of myself. I hadn't broken once during my long years in prison. Now I was out, and I didn't want to turn soft. Yet this was the second time in a few days that something had gotten to me.

Recently, Gene, a counselor at the halfway house, had come to my room to talk to me about starting my life over again. I had let Gene talk for a while, then interrupted.

"Hey, Gene," I said. "I know you're interested in me. I think you really want to help me. But you—or anybody else—don't mean a thing to me. If I thought you were a threat to me, I'd kill you." I reached under my pillow and brought out a hatchet.

Gene's face turned pale.

"But then I know you're not here to hurt me," I admitted.

"Then give me the hatchet," Gene said. He breathed deeply when I handed the weapon over. "Do you know what your problem is, Tom?" he asked.

"What's my problem?" I mocked.

"You don't know the peace and love and joy of God."

I knew the words were true.

"You're lost in your sins," Gene went on. "If you died tonight, you'd be lost forever. You need Christ as your Savior."

Gene looked at me for a moment. "You've never known real happiness, have you, Tom?"

"No, I haven't," I agreed.

"Well, why don't you receive Jesus as your Savior right now? You will find peace and joy."

I shook my head. "I'm not ready." I was glad when Gene finally left.

I had felt smug about my coolness then, but now…after that girl's prayer…

Later that afternoon I barged into Gene's office. "I went out to kill someone this morning," I blurted out when I saw him. "I was ready to pull the trigger when his sister came out. I told her I had to kill her, too. Then she fell to her knees and started praying for me! Not for herself or her brother, but for me!" I was too choked up to go on.

"That girl loved you, Tom," Gene said, "because she's experienced the love of Christ. She wasn't afraid to die. She was concerned about your soul. That's why she prayed for you."

I nodded in agreement.

"Tom," Gene said softly, "are you ready now to accept what Jesus did for you on the cross when He died for your sins? He can give you the same peace and faith that girl has."

The battle was over. "Yes," I replied. "I'm ready."

As we knelt in prayer, I experienced peace in my heart—a peace I had never known before. My whole attitude toward life changed when I received Christ. Instead of wanting to hurt people, I wanted to help them. As I got into the Bible, I learned more about Jesus Christ, and He not only gave me peace, but also gave me understanding.

I have since become the manager of the halfway house. The Lord has enabled me to help other men fresh out of prison start new lives as I did. I know the problems they're facing. I also know the only certain help for them. But I wouldn't be serving there today if it hadn't been for a teenage girl's timely prayer.

A Christmas Eve to Remember

=◎=

T. SUZANNE ELLER

The kids poured out of church like wild kittens running from a barn. Our neighborhood outreach had so far proved to be a mixed success. Getting the kids to come was easy, but corralling them once they arrived was tricky.

One Wednesday night I sat in youth church and watched one kid in particular. Brandon was thirteen, and he had dirty blond hair tied in a backward ponytail so that it hung between his eyes. Within a few minutes, he sauntered outside to take a smoke.

I felt discouraged and frustrated. How could we impact the lives of these young kids if we couldn't keep them in the church for more than fifteen minutes?

That night I offered to take Brandon home. I walked him to the door, and a hugely pregnant woman ambled out to the porch. She looked barely old enough to carry the child inside of her, much less to be the mother of a teenager. A little girl peeked out from the doorway, her bangs hanging to her nose. Her tiny, beautiful smile lit up the darkness.

The house was smack in the middle of a crack neighborhood. One window was clamped shut with a piece of plywood, and the porch we were standing on was rotted and sagging.

The mother pushed a blond strand of hair behind her ears. She glanced at me and smiled, but quickly looked away. "We're really glad Brandon is coming to youth group," I said.

She hesitated, then asked, "Would you like to come in?"

I stepped inside a dimly lit room. An old brown couch was shoved against the wall, and a tiny TV with rabbit antennas sat snug under the wheezing heater. Brandon's mom, Tina, motioned for me to sit down. "Would you like a glass of water?" She opened the refrigerator and I could see that its only occupants were a pitcher of water and a half gallon of milk.

She came back with our water and sat down next to me. Hopelessness and desperation filled her eyes. I felt out of place, my church clothes too fancy, but I smiled as she rubbed her protruding stomach. "I carried twins," I said. "I was huge." She laughed and told me that her baby was due in the next few weeks.

"Do you want a boy or girl?" I asked.

"A healthy baby," she said. "I have hepatitis C."

Total silence. I wasn't sure how to respond. Then I covered her hand with my own. "I will pray for your baby," I said, meaning it.

"I've given up on praying a long time ago, but feel free."

Then she opened up to me, and my heart nearly broke when I heard her story. Tina had grown up in an average family and had been a practicing nurse. Her ex-husband, Brandon's father, was a former military officer; they divorced when Brandon was young. Then Tina met and married another man who assured her of his love. He introduced her to drugs, and now he was in jail for dealing meth. Tina had contracted hepatitis C through drug use, and she was struggling in every realm of life.

After that evening, I picked up Brandon every week for church, and eventually the rest of the family. One night I took the kids to see the Christmas lights. As we drove through town, Brandon's little sister tapped me on the shoulder. "Can we go to Burger King?" she asked. Brandon shushed her from the backseat. "When we're in school," she said. "I get to eat breakfast and lunch. But on Christmas break, I only get breakfast."

My heart dropped, and I swung the car toward Burger King. While the kids were eating, I called the church and arranged to raid the pantry and take food to Brandon's house.

A few days before Christmas, I told a friend about Brandon's family. I was a struggling writer at that time and had enough money to buy a few things, but I wished out loud that I could do more. My friend grabbed her keys, and then my arm, and ignored my protests. "Come on," she said. For the next few hours we shopped. By the end of the day, my trunk was completely packed.

On Christmas Eve night I drove to Brandon's house. It was dark and gloomy. Men stood in groups outside smoking, the tips of their cigarettes the only lights around. I knocked on the door, and Tina answered, holding her new baby in her arms.

A tree that would have made the Charlie Brown tree look grand stood at an angle in the corner, one strand of popcorn wrapped around its bare-of-needles branches. No presents were in sight.

Tina helped me unload my trunk, tears running down her face. "I didn't have anything to give my kids," she said. "It was either pay the rent or buy Christmas presents. I had given up on Christmas." She stared at all the presents, the joy in her eyes unmasked.

"These are not from me, Tina," I said. "I'm only the delivery girl."

Tina wrapped her arms around me. "I can never thank you enough," she said.

I smiled at my friend. "Please don't tell the kids I dropped these by," I said.

"What do I tell them?" she asked.

"Tell them, 'Merry Christmas!'"

Over the next months the family sought God more and more. Tina asked questions, searching for answers to the tough challenges she faced every day. Brandon's little sister joined me at the altar when I prayed, tucking her tiny frame under my arm, her mouth quietly moving as she prayed in unison with me. Brandon changed the most, losing the backward ponytail and T-shirts splashed with the heavy metal logos or obscenities. But it was the heart changes that encouraged me the most. He showed up for every church event. He talked about his new faith and even brought other teens to church with him.

One night I arrived at the house, and it was strangely empty. I talked to a neighbor and discovered that Brandon and his family had left in the middle of the night because of threats directed at Tina.

For months I heard nothing, and then one night I received a collect phone call. It was Brandon. "Where have you guys been?" I asked as soon as I accepted the charges.

"We moved closer to my stepdad," he said. "He's up for parole soon, and Mom wanted us to be close to him." He paused. "And guess what? Some people came to the jail and preached. My stepdad was saved. He's telling everybody in the jail that he's changed. Mom went to visit him, and it's true. He's really different."

I quickly wiped away a tear. "That's great, Brandon."

He went on to tell me about his new church with its great pastor and youth group. It made me so happy to hear how well the family was doing.

Brandon is now sixteen and helps the youth pastor in his church. His mom's hepatitis is in remission, and she is working again as a nurse. After his release from jail, Brandon's stepfather reconciled with his family and is now an active member of their church.

I talked to Brandon a few weeks ago, and the topic of Christmas came up.

"Do you remember that Christmas when I got my new shoes?" he asked.

"Sure I do," I said, remembering the glow on his face when he showed them to me.

"I believed that Christmas and birthdays were for other kids, not kids like us," he said. He told me how it felt to wear brand-name shoes to school the following week—shoes that didn't pinch his feet or allow the icy water to soak his sockless feet.

I will never forget the night when I saw new light in the eyes of a mother who had given up on Christmas. Whenever I reflect on the true meaning of Christmas, I think of that moment. Seeing hope reborn in a young mom's eyes was the best present I had ever received—and every Christmas Eve I remember it once again with joy.

Worth Thinkin' About

The Future

Dreams wait to unfold.
What will I do? Where will I go?
All the "what ifs" crowd my mind.
There are so many possibilities,
So much potential.
Lord, please show me the way.
I know not which path is right.

MELISSA ANN BROECKELMAN, AGE 17

The Father's Anguishing Decision

CARLA MUIR

After a few of the usual Sunday evening hymns, the church's pastor gave a very brief introduction of his childhood friend. With that, an elderly man stepped up to the pulpit to speak. "A father, his son, and a friend of his son were sailing off the Pacific Coast," he began, "when a fast approaching storm blocked any attempt to get back to shore. The waves were so high that even though the father was an experienced sailor, he could not keep the boat upright, and the three were swept into the ocean."

The old man hesitated for a moment, making eye contact with two teenagers who were, for the first time since the service began, looking somewhat interested in his story. He continued, "Grabbing a rescue line, the father had to make the most excruciating decision of his life...to which boy he would throw the other end of the line. He only had seconds to make the decision. The father knew that his son was a Christian, and he also knew that his son's friend was not. The agony of his decision could not be matched by the torrent of waves. As the father yelled out, 'I love you, son!' he threw the line to his son's friend. By the time he pulled the friend back to the capsized boat, his son had disappeared beyond the raging swells into the black sea. His body was never recovered."

By this time, the two teenagers were sitting straighter in the pew, waiting for the next words to come out of the old man's mouth. "The father," he

Stories for a Teen's Heart 3

continued, "knew his son would step into eternity with Jesus, and he could not bear the thought of his son's friend stepping into an eternity without Jesus. Therefore, he sacrificed his son. How great is the love of God that He should do the same for us." The old man then turned and sat back down in his chair as silence filled the room.

Within minutes after the service ended, the two teenagers were at the old man's side. "That was a nice story," politely started one of the boys, "but I don't think it was very realistic for a father to give up his son's life in hopes that the other boy would become a Christian."

"Well, you've got a point there," the old man replied, glancing down at his worn Bible. A big smile broadened his narrow face, and he once again looked up at the boys and said, "It sure isn't very realistic, is it? But I'm standing here today to tell you that that story gives me a glimpse of what it must have been like for God to give up His Son for me. You see…I was the son's friend."

284

Winning the Gold

DAVID BARNETT

I've been watching the Olympics off and on over the last couple of weeks, and I enjoyed the gymnastic events. The strength, agility, and talent of all the athletes really impressed me.

The women's team gymnastics and the individual all-around competition were especially interesting. Many of those favored to win kept making mistakes. "The judges will deduct a tenth for that" was probably the most frequent comment made by the announcers during the competition.

In addition to the mistakes being made, there were also equipment problems. The vaulting horse was discovered to be four centimeters shorter than regulation. It seemed like such a small deal to a non-athlete like me, but it caused some of the world's best gymnasts to make bad landings.

In the midst of these games, I got to thinking about the game of life that we are all players in. In my opinion, the ultimate prize—the gold medal—is eternal life with our Lord and Savior, Jesus Christ. If my quest for the gold was televised, this is probably what you'd hear from the announcers:

Announcer 1: Well, he's off to a pretty good start. The way he helped that old man across the street was really something.

Announcer 2: Uh-oh, did you see that? He lied to his parents. They'll deduct a tenth for that.

Announcer 1: Yes, dishonoring his parents is definitely frowned upon in this competition.

Announcer 2: Oh, did you see that? Did you see the way he looked at that girl? That will be at least a tenth off, if the judges caught it.

Announcer 1: He was off to a great start, but lying to the police officer about why he was speeding…that will be a tenth.

Announcer 2: This is unbelievable. He was favored going into this competition, but I just don't see how…

Announcer 1: Holy cow! The clerk gave him a twenty-dollar bill instead of a ten for change, and he saw it but didn't say anything! You're right, I don't think he can even hope to win any medal, much less the gold.

Announcer 2: Quick to anger, that's a tenth.

Announcer 1: Failure to love his neighbor as himself. Another tenth.

Announcer 2: Pride. A tenth.

Announcer 1: Did you hear what he just said? I don't remember the last time I heard language like that from a gold medalist.

Announcer 2: Selfishness. A tenth.

Announcer 1: Underage drinking. Breaking the law. A tenth.

Announcer 2: Materialism. A tenth.

Announcer 1: I'll tell you, I haven't seen a performance this poor in a competition…. Well, I can't remember ever seeing this. He is definitely out of the gold medal picture.

Announcer 2: Yes, it is amazing. The score will definitely be very low.

Announcer 1: Wait, he's going into the final move of his routine. What's this? I don't think anyone expected this…. He's getting on his knees…he's praying…he's repenting. He's asking forgiveness…he's inviting Jesus Christ to be his Lord and Savior and accepting His gift of salvation!

Announcer 2: He's getting up and he's smiling.

Announcer 1: I don't see why. His life has been full of errors and mistakes.

Announcer 2: How the judges will look at this performance is anyone's guess. The scores are coming up now.

Announcer 1: I can't believe it! He got…

Announcer 2: Perfect tens! Incredible!

Announcer 1: Yes, it is incredible, but it was that last move that really impressed the Judge. In the end, nothing else really mattered.

The Party

LISSA HALLS JOHNSON

At lunch, Jade made herself the center of attention as usual. She threw back her head and laughed at what Nate said. Then she looked at me. "What are *you* doing this weekend, Megan?"

I swallowed my anger. "*Not* going to your stupid party," I wanted to scream. Instead, I forced out a calm, "Oh, nothing much." I faked a smile, then turned my attention to my turkey sandwich, pretending I didn't know she was having a party. Pretending I didn't know I wasn't invited. Pretending it didn't hurt.

"Sounds like *loads* of fun," she replied sarcastically. I didn't look at her, but I knew Jade well enough to know she probably grimaced and did an exaggerated rolling of her eyes for her audience.

Some of the girls giggled knowingly. I wanted to scream at them all. But I was also mad at myself. After all, Jade was allowed to invite anyone she wanted. There was no law that said she had to invite me. I popped the last bit of sandwich into my mouth, then sucked Capri Sun through a straw to wash it all down.

Jenn slid onto the bench next to me. "So you're not going to the party?" she whispered.

I shook my head. "I wasn't invited."

Jenn dropped her jaw in surprise. Her eyes widened. "But you and Jade have been friends since sixth grade."

I hoped I could keep winning the fight against my tears. I shrugged, hoping to make it look like it didn't matter.

For the zillionth time, I went over the invitation list in my mind. It seemed everyone I knew was invited. We all hung out at youth group and ate lunch together every day. The strangest part was that my longtime friend Nate, who had just moved to our town, was invited—and he and Jade hardly knew each other.

I went over every encounter I'd had with Jade for the past month, hoping to discover some slight against her that I'd missed in my previous reviews. I came up with nothing. I crumpled my lunch bag and threw it away.

At youth group, I tried to be my usual friendly self. I eventually gave up fighting my feelings and sat off to one side, hoping no one would notice. I stayed lost in my own thoughts until the lights went out in the room. I snapped to attention as Nate sat next to me. "Our film debut," he teased.

"Oh no," I groaned. "Not tonight."

"It won't be so bad. I think it will be fun to hear what everyone has to say."

I wasn't in the mood to preview the video our youth pastor had made. He had interviewed the kids in the youth group individually so he could make a video montage of testimonies to show the adults on Youth Sunday.

The television screen flickered to life. Jenn's face wobbled a moment, then stabilized. "How have I grown this year?" she asked, repeating the question given her. Her response was drowned out with hoots of laughter from the audience.

"Jenn hasn't grown since kindergarten," someone yelled.

"Anyone pick up those five-inch platforms for her yet? Maybe then we could find her in a crowd of third graders."

Even Jenn laughed.

As my friends' faces appeared one by one on the screen, I became absorbed in hearing how God had been working in their lives. I felt privileged to be friends with people concerned about knowing God better.

Then Jade popped up, and my good feeling faded fast. "I've learned how important it is to be like Christ," she said, tucking a stray strand of hair behind her ear. "And so I've started to make choices the way Christ would and do things He would do."

Anger and hurt burned within me. I didn't know whether to scream or cry. I thought my head would explode. I leaned over to Nate and whispered, "And I suppose Christ would have eliminated one of the disciples from His party without telling him why."

Nate leaned toward me. "I won't go to the party either," he said, trying to comfort me.

I shook my head. "That wouldn't solve anything."

"Hey, look," he said suddenly, "it's you!"

I heard the televised version of myself say, "Lessons God teaches are never easy. I hate being in the middle of a lesson, but I'm glad once I've gotten to the other side and can see what I've learned and how it's changed me into a better person and a stronger Christian."

Nate whispered in my ear. "Who was that girl? She's smart and honest— I think she's great!"

I ignored Nate and stared at the TV, still seeing and hearing myself even though a new face had taken my place. I didn't like the words that had come out of my mouth. I didn't like that God was going to use my own words from a video to teach me another lesson I did not want to learn.

"I'll be right back," I said to Nate and slipped out of the room. In the church library, I paced back and forth, talking softly to God. "I don't like this one bit, God. Not one bit. I really want to go to the party Little Miss Christlike is having. I want to know *why* she didn't invite me."

Staring at the floor, I said, "Jesus, the Bible says You know how I feel. But I think someone forgot to let You in on this one." I chewed on my cheek and paced at least eight more rounds, stewing over what I knew was the right thing to do—I just didn't want to admit it.

Growing up, I realized that God's way often doesn't make sense. But right now I wanted God to make my life smooth. Instead, He took the rough parts and smoothed *me*. I knew I had two options. I could fight Him and end up with no invitation to the party. Or I could let Him work in me and still have no invitation to the party.

"As much as I hate to say this," I said to God, "teach me something through this situation. Help me to do what's right, even if Jade doesn't do the right thing. And—" I sighed and shook my head—"help me to forgive Jade and be nice to her."

The library door popped open. "Hey! I caught you!" Nate said, teasing. Then he became serious. "I wanted to make sure you're okay."

"I am and I'm not," I said honestly. "I wonder if the hurt over being excluded from the party will ever go away."

"Can I help?" Nate asked.

I smiled. "I just hate learning these lessons. It's like eating brussels sprouts for every meal."

"Yum!" Nate said.

I whacked him on the arm.

"The worst thing you can do is let it eat you up inside," Nate said. "Look at my Grandma Margaret."

I smiled. Grandma Margaret made every day of her life miserable by recalling past wrongs. "I certainly don't want to get like that."

"I don't either. So I try to figure out how Jesus felt in similar circumstances and ask Him what He did about it."

I frowned at him. "Yeah, like He was ever excluded from a party."

"Two of his closest friends betrayed Him. Judas sold Him; Peter denied Him. That didn't hurt?"

"But it all seems so far away," I said softly. "It doesn't seem to connect with what I'm looking at today."

"I know you've been a Christian long enough to know that it *does* connect," Nate said. "You just have to let God show you how."

I nodded.

"I'm going to leave you alone with God, and I'll bet you'll hear from Him if you let Him speak."

Nate closed the door gently. I put my head on my arms and prayed. *God, I don't want to become like Grandma Margaret. Lots of bad things are going to happen to me. I don't want to collect them all.*

I looked up at a small cross someone had taped to a bookshelf. The cross—where Jesus was deeply wounded by our sins. And what about during His life? Wasn't He wounded by all the people who lied about Him, cursed Him, and denied who He was? That didn't hurt?

I began to think about the difference between Jesus and Grandma Margaret. Jesus took His hurts to the cross and still had compassion toward people. He didn't ask for anyone to feel sorry for Him.

God, as I go through this hard place, heal my hurt and use it to make me stronger and more compassionate toward others. Help this experience to make me more like You.

I left the library feeling a weird peace. The hurt wasn't gone, but the peace made it feel different.

I took a seat next to Nate again in the youth room.

"Enjoy your brussels sprouts?" he asked.

"Never better," I said, smiling.

The Red Convertible

LARRY CHRISTENSON
FROM *THE RENEWED MIND*

A young man named Sinner once received from his Father a beautiful, bright red convertible. He named it Salvation—sparkling, new, clean, modern, powerful.

It delighted the young man so much, especially because it was a gift. He could never have afforded it. So delighted, the boy even changed his name from Sinner to Saved.

He polished his car every week. Took pictures of it. Sent it to friends. Looked it over—front, back, under, top, bottom, inside out. Never, never tired of telling others about the gift. "My Father gave it to me. It was free!"

Some days later, Saved was seen out on the highway, pushing Salvation. An individual named Helper walked up and introduced himself and asked if he could assist.

"Oh, no thanks. Just out enjoying my new car," as he wiped the sweat off his face. "Just had a little trouble because my bumper kept cutting my hands, especially on these hills. But then a nice man helped me. Showed me how to mount little rubber cushions here, underneath the bumper, and now I can push this thing for hours without a blister. Also, I've been trying something new lately. They use it over in England. You put your back against the car, lift, and it works like a charm, especially on muddy roads."

Helper asked, "Have you pushed the car very far?"

"Well, about two hundred miles altogether. It's been hard, but since it was a gift from my Father, that's the least I can do in return to thank Him."

Helper opened the door on the right side and said, "Get in."

After hesitation, he decided it was worth a try and he slid on the passenger side and rested for the first time since he'd been given the car. Helper walked around, opened the door, slid behind the wheel, and started the car.

"What's all that noise?" he said. Moments later they were moving down the highway quietly, at fifty or sixty miles an hour. He was taken aback. It all seemed to fall into place. It was even exciting. He knew he needed this salvation car to be admitted through the gate at the end of the highway. But somehow he felt that getting there was *his* responsibility.

God has a purpose for my life.
No other person can take my place.
It isn't a big place, to be sure,
but for years I have been molded in a
peculiar way to fill a peculiar niche
in the world's work.

CHARLES STELZLE

Finding God in Colorado

=◎=

KELLY MCGUIGGAN
AGE 16
AS TOLD TO NANCY JO SULLIVAN

I was going to Colorado to find God. As our Greyhound bus wound through a mountain pass, my friends and I chatted excitedly. We were a long way from home on our way to a Christian camp. I glanced outside my window. *I'd hate to crash here,* I thought. Beneath the winding highway were steep ravines, towering pine trees, and large rocks with jagged edges.

I brushed off my fears. It felt good to have some time to think about my life. The last few months had been hard. Weeks earlier, my thirteen-year-old brother had been diagnosed with a serious kidney disease. "We're not sure if Steven will ever play sports again," the doctors had said. This news devastated my brother. He played football, basketball, and baseball. My parents took it pretty hard. I did too. Sometimes I'd stand outside his hospital room and just cry.

My heart hurt. *Where are You, God?*

When Steven came home from the hospital, the doctors put him on six weeks of bed rest. Slowly, Steven began to recover, though his prognosis remained uncertain.

"You need a break, Kelly. Go to that camp in Colorado," my mom told me.

Now, eighteen hours away from home, I dozed off to sleep, cuddling a pillow my mom had given me just before boarding the bus in Minnesota. "I hope you find God," she had told me.

Suddenly, the bus began to slide and swerve. I opened my eyes. At first I thought we were going on one of those windy freeway ramps. "Oh God!" someone shouted in a loud voice. The bus lurched to the right where there was a three-hundred-foot drop. I heard screams.

"We're going to crash!" another voice called out. Again, the bus swerved to the left.

I tucked myself into a ball. I heard broken glass as I fell down, down, down.

The next thing I knew, I was crouching in a pile of shattered glass and my leg was bruised and bleeding. A few feet away from me, the bus rested on its side, dented and crumpled like an accordion, every window blown out and broken.

Everywhere I looked I saw someone in pain. My friends were lying on top of the bus and underneath trees. They were bleeding and crying. Some were unconscious. I was so stunned I could barely move.

I looked up toward the highway and saw a van stop. People jumped out and ran down the embankment to help us. "We're doctors. We were on our way to a convention," they called out. I watched as this assorted group of doctors and nurses began caring for the most severely injured.

Ambulances started arriving. Helicopters soared above. "Where are You, God?" I whispered, tears filling my eyes.

Once more, I looked up toward the highway where a woman in a gray car had stopped. As she hiked down the hill, she saw me crying. "I'm a pastor," she said as she started gathering some of my less-injured friends into a circle. "Lord, we know that You are with us," she prayed.

Just before I was loaded into an ambulance, the pastor ran to the bus and found my pillow, the one my mom had given me. Inside the pillowcase, I found the old tattered quilt that I had slept with ever since I was a kid. My mom packed it at the last minute.

Later that night, those of us with minor injuries left the hospital to stay with a youth group in Denver. There, an entire group of kids from Colorado brought us toothbrushes, clean clothes, and basically anything we needed. One girl from Denver walked up to me and handed me a shirt that had Columbine High School printed on it. "I'm praying for you," she told me.

There was a light sparkling from her eyes. Somehow, I knew she understood what we were going through.

Two days later, most of us flew home to Minnesota. (Though some of my friends had to stay in Colorado hospitals for treatment, eventually all of us came home.) When I arrived at the airport, my entire family was there to greet me: my mom and dad, my two little sisters, even Steven—and he looked stronger than ever.

In between smiles and hugs, my mom asked, "Honey, you didn't make it to camp, but did you find God?"

In that moment, I thought about all that I had experienced in the last few months: Steven's diagnosis, the bus crash, and, of course, my ongoing quest to find God. Suddenly, I realized that I had not only seen God at work in the doctors who had cared for us on the mountainside, but also in the doctors who were continuing to care for my brother at home. I had felt God's presence in the unknown pastor who had prayed for us at the accident site and in my mom's tenderness when she had tucked the old quilt into my pillowcase. I had known God's love when a stranger from Columbine High School gave me prayers and clothes. I had learned to trust in God.

"Mom...I didn't find God in Colorado," I said. My mom looked at me curiously as a smile overshadowed my tears. "I didn't find God...but He found me."

The Man in Your Eyes

As the wind blows your sweet perfume in my direction,
I notice your eyes hold a brilliant reflection.
I do not know that face,
the echo of your heart's embrace.
I must be asleep, this image is so deep.
Don't let me wake;
the memory will not take my breath away
as it does now
as I look into your eyes.
What I see is not of this earth.
It offers dead souls rebirth.
How can this be?
How do I receive this love you believe?
I want to know;
I want the seed inside to grow;
I want to meet the One you love.
You say His name is Jesus?

ROSS GUNN IV

AGE 17

A Cross to Wear

N. BAYLESS

I was chowing down my second taco when my little brother, Sam, kicked me under the table.

"Hey, Nate, look at that old lady over there. She's got on the same cross you gave Mom for her big 4-0 birthday. I bet she swiped it from her," he hissed.

"No way!" I snarled, gulping ice water to cool the sizzling salsa cremating my throat.

"Yes, she did! Yes, she did!"

"Knock it off, will ya, Sam!" I kicked him back. Then I looked at the jade cross hanging on a gold chain around the neck of the grandma-type lady at the table next to ours. Parrot-brain had scored again. The crosses were identical.

"Hey, Mom!" I called to her at the end of our table. "Are you wearing your jade cross?"

"No, honey. It's in my jewelry box. The clasp is broken. Maybe Dad can fix it when he gets home from his trip."

While I sopped up the juice from my taco with a hunk of leftover tortilla, I couldn't stop thinking about Mom's jade cross. *Man, I worked hard to buy it for her. Raking and weeding. Getting blisters. A yard slave to our neighbors.*

I kept staring at the old woman with the jade cross. When she caught my eye, she smiled. I looked away.

She and her husband finished eating and left their table. He opened the outside door for her, then he took her hand. Suddenly, I raced after them.

When I caught up, I touched her arm. "Where did you get that cross?"

She looked surprised. "My husband gave it to me for a wedding present." She smiled at the man.

"I bought my mom one just like it for her fortieth birthday."

"What a wonderful gift! Is your mother a Christian?"

"Uh...sort of, I guess, but she doesn't wear her cross very often. Do you wear yours a lot?"

"I never take it off," she said. "It reminds me that Jesus loves me. Tell me, young man, are you a Christian?"

I shrugged.

She touched my cheek. Her hand felt cool and dry. Her brown eyes looked right at me. "Jesus is my best friend," she said. "I asked Him to take over my life on my fifteenth birthday. Are you about fifteen?"

"I'll be fourteen next month, but I never heard of having Jesus for a best friend!"

Her husband laughed. "Well, now you have," he said. "Jesus is my best friend, too."

The man stood there grinning, and I noticed his white and even teeth. *I bet he puts them in one of those plastic-jaws boxes at night.*

He grabbed my hand and squeezed it. He acted as if he wanted to say something else, but he didn't, so I turned and walked away.

Hmm. What a trip! Jesus. Best friend? Sounds like the soaps. My friend, God. Who'd believe it?

Maybe it could be true.

Man! I need something. Sam bugs me so much, and Dad always takes his side. I'm angry all the time.

I stood on the curb watching the traffic. The old couple passed in their car: A VW Bug convertible with the top down. Cool!

They waved. The jade cross flapped against her white sweater.

At the park across the street, three guys were huddled around a picnic table smoking pot. A couple of homeless men pawed through a dumpster, stashing stuff in torn garbage bags.

I'd rather grow up like that old couple than like those guys.

I went over and leaned against a tree. It seemed weird to think about talking to God. I'd never prayed except when my dog, Scoobie, got hit by a car. Then I asked God to let her live, and He did.

I looked around to see if anyone was watching me. With all the crazy stuff going on in the world, I guess having Jesus as a friend would be an okay idea. Maybe He'd be my bodyguard, too.

"Hey, Jesus. I don't want to blow it and end up like those guys over there. Can we be friends? Could You be my best friend?"

Talking to Him made me feel good. I waited for something to happen, but nothing did, so I crossed back over to the restaurant.

The door crashed open, and my little brother bolted out. Mom stormed out right behind him. She had on her what-has-he-done-now face.

Maybe Jesus is running with me. I hope so. I need all the help I can get.

Who can fathom the depth of those words:
"God so loved the world"?
We can never scale the heights of
His love or fathom its depths.

DWIGHT L. MOODY

Lighten Up!

JENNIFER KNAPP
RECORDING ARTIST

In recent years, I've done a bunch of concerts in amusement parks. My band would typically arrive in the morning for a gig that night and spend much of the day getting ready for the show. But I never took the time to ride any of the roller coasters.

Don't get me wrong. I love roller coasters. But since I take my work so seriously, I've always felt like I had to be at the stage all day long, making sure every little detail was perfect for that night's concert. I figured I just didn't have time for something as trivial as a three-minute thrill ride.

Then one day a friend said, "You know, Jen, it wouldn't kill you to take an hour and go ride a few roller coasters. The road crew will get the stage ready. Everything will be fine. Just go on out there and have some fun for a while, okay?"

I didn't realize at the time, but that's exactly what I needed to hear. I guess I just needed somebody to give me "permission" to lighten up.

So I took that advice and went out and rode some coasters. And I had a blast.

I've never been the type to "lighten up" very easily. I'm very driven, and I always like to go, go, go. I've always felt this hyper-responsibility for making everything just right. I was that way in high school and in college. And for the most part, I'm still that way.

But I'm learning. God is teaching me that I don't have to push, push,

push all the time. I don't see any place in the Bible where He says, "Work harder." Yes, He tells us to run the race and to give our best effort. But He also says, "Be still, and know that I am God" (Psalm 46:10).

God also says He'll finish what He's started in me (Philippians 1:6). I sometimes get this idea that I'm the one who has to finish everything I'm trying so hard to do, but God tells me to relax in His peace. He loves me because of His grace, not because of what I do—or don't do.

I have to constantly remind myself of that. And thankfully, I have friends who remind me too. They encourage me to stop and smell the roses and let me know that it's okay not to have to slam dunk everything I do.

So I'm learning to lighten up.

And I'm enjoying the ride—literally. On roller coasters everywhere. I just wish the lines weren't so long!

I do not want merely to possess a faith;
I want a faith that possesses me.

CHARLES KINGSLEY

My Senior Year

HEATHER MEZEL
AS TOLD TO ROBIN JONES GUNN

I've always been shy. One time when I was a high school freshman, a teacher asked me a question. I didn't know the answer, so I didn't say anything. My throat squeezed closed, and my face turned red. The whole class laughed.

Because I'm so shy, I was always afraid to witness for Christ—especially at school. I had quite a few friends, but I was a listener, not a talker. I cruised through my first three years of high school. Then, the summer before my senior year, everything changed.

It started on a Wednesday night when our youth pastor talked about witnessing. He said that we were all missionaries, that our mission field was our high school campus. I didn't feel like a missionary, and I certainly didn't think I had much to say. I figured somebody else could be the missionary—like Brian. He was bold, and people respected him because of his good grades. People knew that he was a Christian.

That night I left feeling guilty. I knew that my friends needed Jesus, but how could I express that to them? I still had two weeks before my senior year would begin—two weeks to be transformed from a mouse into a missionary.

The next day my best friend, Denise, came over. She'd been crying. She had a rough family situation, and that afternoon she had left her house during a fight and had run the five blocks to my house. We talked a long time. I said I'd pray for her and that the Lord knew her so well that He knew what she was going through. For me, that was a big step in witnessing, but it didn't seem that Denise had even paid attention to what I had said.

A few days later I read a poem about telling our friends about Jesus. If we don't, when we all stand before Him on Judgment Day, our friends will say, "If you were really my friend, you would have told me."

That got to me. I closed myself in my bedroom and prayed. I told God that I was willing to be His missionary at my high school during my senior year. If He wanted to say anything through me, that would be fine, I'd try not to get in the way. After I prayed, I started a missionary list of my friends. These were my friends who needed Jesus. I wanted to make sure that each one heard the gospel by the end of my senior year.

The first person on my list was Denise. Then Elaine, Dean, Candy, Alan, Kay, and Aletta. As I looked over their names, I laughed! If any of these friends ever became Christians, it would be a miracle!

I started praying. The first miracle came a few days before school started. Our youth group went to a water slide park for the last big event of the summer. Denise came with me and spent most of the day talking with Larry, an older guy from the youth group. When we were ready to leave, Larry said to me, "Denise is super close to accepting Christ." I couldn't believe it!

That Sunday night, Denise came to church. After the service she talked to some of the adults. About twenty minutes later she and my youth pastor's wife walked out to the parking lot.

"Tonight I asked Jesus into my heart," Denise said. We burst into tears and I hugged her. The next day we would be in our senior year together, and tonight we were in eternity together.

Before I went to bed, I pulled out my list. "Thank You, Lord! Who's next?"

Elaine. I didn't have a lot of classes with Elaine our senior year, but I did invite her to church a couple of times. She came to a New Year's Eve party that our youth group put on. At midnight our youth pastor gave a short message and Elaine seemed to be listening intently. When response cards were passed out, Elaine told me that she wrote on hers, "When you gave the invitation tonight, I prayed and gave my life to Christ." What a happy New Year!

What surprised me most during those first few months of school was how my boldness increased. I wasn't even saying things that were intensely witnessing. If someone would ask if I were going to a school activity on a Friday night, instead of just saying no, I would reply, "No, I'm going on a hayride with my church youth group," or whatever.

Then my friends would ask, "Oh, where do you go to church?" Some even asked, "What do you believe?" I started to talk from my heart about my relationship with God. It was slow, but it came out naturally, and my face didn't even turn red.

But Dean knew how to get the red back into my face. One day he asked why I hung around with Brian, "the Jesus freak."

"Because he's my friend," I said.

"I suppose you're a 'Jesus freak' too," Dean snarled.

My face turned totally red and I barely squeezed out, "Yeah, I am."

Dean laughed. "You should stick with me—your friendly neighborhood pagan. I could show you some real fun."

Actually, I was having fun—more than I'd had in all my previous high school years put together. As Easter vacation approached, I started getting excited about our youth group's outreach to a Mexican village. I had gone to Mexico the year before and had learned so much. Now I kept talking about it at school and, to my surprise, both Alan and Candy said they wanted to go. I told them that they would have to go to a month of training and start coming to church with me.

The first night of training they were there, and they showed up faithfully every week. The third week of training, when we practiced giving our testimonies with an interpreter, Candy raised her hand and said, "I don't think I have a testimony. How do I get one?" That night both Alan and Candy surrendered their lives to Christ. A few weeks later, when they shared their testimonies with the people of the Mexican village, I thought my heart would burst!

When we came back to school after Easter vacation, Alan put me to shame with his boldness in witnessing. I walked into calculus class one morning and heard him loudly telling another guy all about Mexico and how he had become a Christian. When Alan saw me, he said, "Heather, tell Brent how great it is knowing Jesus and having Him as King in your life."

I felt my face turning red, but my voice stayed steady as I said, "It's the greatest thing that could ever happen to you. I wouldn't trade it for anything." Twelve people must have heard me say that! I couldn't believe how easy it was or how good it felt to identify myself publicly with Christ.

At our yearbook signing party, Aletta, an exchange student from Finland, wrote a long message. She was going home in a few days, and I promised to visit her some day. She had come to church with me a number of times, but I didn't know if she had really understood the gospel message. She and Dean were still on my missionary list of friends.

My attempts to witness to Dean had been weak. Every day in photojournalism class he asked tough questions about my faith in Christ and made me think about my faith harder than anyone else had.

Kay asked tough questions too and liked to argue. One day I finally said, "I believe that Jesus Christ is God's only Son. He came to earth and died on a cross, carrying with Him all the sins ever committed. Three days later He came back to life, proving His power over sin and death. His Word, the Bible, says that if I believe in Jesus and ask Him to forgive my sins, I will have a relationship with Him that will last for all eternity."

"What if you're wrong?" Kay challenged.

I felt the color crawling up my neck into my cheeks, but I asked her, "What if you are wrong, Kay?"

That night I realized I had been a witness to Kay. I could mark my list that way. My goal was to tell my friends about Jesus and explain how to become Christian, not to force them to make a decision. They were responsible for that. I just wanted to tell them that they had a choice.

On commencement day I thought back over the year and how I had told the Lord that I was willing to be His missionary. I guess God took me seriously, because four of my friends were now Christians. I hadn't really done that much. I was just available.

At the end of our graduation ceremony, four of the people who hugged me were Denise, Candy, Elaine, and Alan—my Christian friends. Even though our high school days were ending, I felt happy knowing that our friendship in Christ would continue.

Gotcha!

STEVEN J. LAWSON
FROM *ABSOLUTELY SURE*

A soldier who was a Christian made it his practice to conclude every day with Bible reading and prayer. As his fellow soldiers gathered in the barrack and retired for the night, he would kneel by his bunk and offer prayers to the Lord.

The other soldiers saw this and began to mock and harass him. But one night the abuse went beyond verbal assault. As the soldier bowed before his Lord in prayer, one antagonist threw his boot through the dark and hit him in the face. The other soldiers snickered and jeered, hoping for a fight.

But there was no retaliation.

The next morning when the taunting soldier awoke, he was startled to discover something at the foot of his bed. For all to see, there were his boots, returned and polished.

No Accident

CARLIN HERTZ
FROM *GOD ALLOWS U-TURNS*

January 27, 1994, was no ordinary day for Alabama State University. It was a day the whole Hornet football team would never forget. This day would forever be etched in the minds of sixty-six young men. It would change many lives for good.

The day was cloudy and a bit chilly. It had rained all day, but the rain let up just in time for the football team's daily conditioning session on the track. The players hated running in the cold on a slippery track.

"Zo, I do not feel like running today," I said to my roommate as we both laced up our running shoes and headed outside. I threw on a thick black sweatshirt to keep warm. We listlessly trotted over to Hornet Stadium. Within minutes, a gang of tired and complaining football players all walked in unison toward the track. Puddles splashed on our legs, dampening our clothes. We ignored it. Our minds were focused on the eight laps we would have to run.

The conditioning coach greeted us with a sinister smile. "Good afternoon, 'ladies.' Welcome to my house." He laughed as he rubbed his thick beard and blew his whistle to get our attention.

I was stretching my hamstrings, trying to loosen up, when Darnell walked over to me and asked me to help him stretch. I didn't really know him that well, but he was a teammate. Besides, I'd heard nothing but good things about him. He extended his long, muscular arm to help me off the ground. He smiled, and then he sat down on the wet grass.

Darnell was no ordinary football player. He was a slender six feet six inches, 265 pounds of solid muscle. He had the biggest feet I had ever seen. His size would intimidate most men. But Darnell was different. Despite his massive frame, he was gentle and the nicest guy I had ever met. I didn't know much about God then, but I heard that Darnell was a Christian. He never messed around with girls. He always went to church. If you had a problem, you could go to him, and he would help you through it. Darnell was a good influence on us all.

"You ready to knock these laps out, Carlin?" he asked as I stretched his hamstrings for him.

"I guess," I replied.

"Well, just keep up with me, and I'll get you through," he said as he jumped up and smacked my hand. The coach blew his whistle, and we all started running on the track.

We had to run eight laps, and then we had to do some sprints. I didn't know how I was going to get through it, but I stayed close to Darnell, like he told me to do. His presence kept my mind off the laps.

We were coming on the last lap, and I was a few feet behind Darnell. His long strides covered so much ground that I knew my baby strides would never catch him. I was determined to catch him, though, so that I could brag about it later at dinner.

Darnell was running at a good pace, not looking tired, when all of a sudden, he just collapsed. He crashed to the ground. I thought he was just tired and had fallen out, but he didn't get up. We all stopped and ran over to where he lay.

The student trainer ran over and frantically tried to help him, but she didn't really know what to do. By now, we could see Darnell was fighting for his life. His fists were balled up tight, and he struggled to breathe. Finally, he just stopped. The trainer kept trying to talk to him, "Darnell, stay with me." In the distance, we could hear the blaring sounds of an ambulance siren.

By the time the ambulance got there, though, I think it was already too late. He just lay there as the paramedics tried to revive him. They placed him in the ambulance. We were told to go back to our rooms and wait for further instructions. We left the track in tears, hugging each other and praying, something many of us had never done. We were stunned.

A couple of us decided to go to the dining hall together instead of to the solitude of our rooms. As we sat down, a teammate ran over to us. "Everybody needs to go to the meeting room now!" From the look on his face, I knew that Darnell was gone.

"Hey, Kenny," I asked, "is Darnell all right?"

Kenny just looked at me and broke down.

Without thinking, I threw the glass in my hand, sending glass flying everywhere. "No! He can't be gone!" They had to hold me, because I couldn't control myself. People who didn't know what was going on looked at me like I was insane.

They told us Darnell had died of a massive heart attack. Apparently he had high blood pressure, but he wasn't taking his medication. I didn't want to accept his death. He was just twenty-two years old. I had just talked to him. Yeah, I had been to funerals, but to witness somebody alive one minute and dead the next was spooky. I had talked to him only minutes before.

During this time, a stranger from Cleveland arrived on campus. He was a missionary and had come to Montgomery to set up Bible studies on the campus. Jeff befriended a lot of the football players at a time when we really needed him and what he had to say. Learning that we had just lost a teammate, he set up weekly Bible studies in the football dorm. Every Wednesday night, the room where the Bible study was held would be packed with football players searching for answers. Many of my teammates had been very close to Darnell, and we couldn't figure out why he would die like that.

Through God and the Bible, Jeff soothed a lot of our pain and suffering. He told us the truth, and he told us about salvation through Jesus Christ. A lot of football players were saved during those Bible studies. Jeff and I became good friends. He told me that when he left Cleveland, he didn't know what to expect. He said that God told him to take nothing with him, get on a bus, and head to Montgomery. He came right at the time we needed to hear God's Word the most. It was no accident he was here.

The good thing about Darnell's death was that he went to heaven. He was saved. The rest of us weren't, though. Any one of us could have died on the track that day. Where would we have ended up? Suppose Darnell had not died? Would a lot of those players have given their life to Christ? I doubt it.

Like Christ, Darnell died so that many of us might live. His death was the wake-up call it took to bring our entire team to Christ. I think Darnell is pleased.

Faith is daring the soul to go beyond what the eyes can see.

AUTHOR UNKNOWN

Teen Santa

MARJORIE GORDON

H ey, Josh," I said as I plopped my cafeteria tray on the table. "I finally got a job for the Christmas season."

"Doin' what?" Josh asked, just before digging into his meat loaf and mashed potatoes.

"Would you believe a shopping mall Santa? Yours truly, Brandon Brady, will arrive at the Super Mall parking lot in a helicopter next week."

Josh grinned. "A two-hundred-pound lineman won't need much stuffing to fill out the red suit! You're gonna get paid for sitting on a throne and giving away candy canes? Right on!"

"Tough job, but someone's gotta do it." I filled my mouth with salad. I didn't tell Josh, but I hoped my cushy job would impress some of the super-jocks here at Riverside High. I played an okay ball game, but I also spent time on the sidelines. At least I wasn't sitting in the bleachers like Cody Harrison. He's the guy I beat out for my position. He hates my guts.

Josh finished his second carton of milk and looked across the cafeteria. "Here comes Courtney with Matt. I thought she was goin' out with you."

"Nah. I took her to a party last Saturday night, but it was no big deal. Coach, not to mention my parents, would have a cow if they knew the guys had a keg there. Courtney was so impressed with the other guys, I left her with one and went home early."

Josh piled his dishes into a tower on his tray and gave me a mischievous smile. "So now you can get to know Jenny Phillips better. I saw you with her after biology."

I felt myself turn three shades of red. "I'd like to know her better. She acts like she really cares about people—doesn't use them like someone else I know."

We dumped our trays. "So, Brandon, when do you start 'Ho, Ho, Ho-ing'?"

"My chopper ride's Saturday morning, the day after our last game. See ya in Spanish."

The next few days went by quickly. Word spread about my upcoming debut as a teen Santa. I took a lot of teasing but suspected most of the guys would have loved to trade places with me. Biology became more interesting, too—once Jenny became my lab partner. Our conversations showed me how smart she was.

"Brandon, did you know that centuries before people discovered the purpose of blood, God told His people 'the life of the flesh is in the blood'? If George Washington's doctors had read the Bible and believed it, they wouldn't have killed him by bleeding out his 'bad blood' to cure an infection."

I smeared a drop of blood on my glass slide. "You believe the Bible? I'm not even sure there's a God."

"Hey, the evidence is all around you. Didn't our teacher just tell us the heart is far more efficient for its size and output than any pump invented by man?" Jenny's green eyes twinkled when she got excited. "What hydraulic engineer wouldn't like to invent a closed system for a liquid that repairs its own leaks? The Bible says all this was God's design. He even knew you before you were born, Brandon."

She made some good points. Too good. I changed the subject. "Do you have a job over the holidays?"

Jenny wrinkled her freckled nose. "Yep. I'm working at the Super Scoop Ice Cream Bar."

"You're gonna be a super scooper, huh?" I said with a laugh. The teacher glared at us. We lowered our heads in front of our microscopes. "Will you be working this Saturday when I step out of the chopper to meet my eager little subjects?" I asked as quietly as I could.

She mimicked a bow. "Yes, your highness. When the shopping center deity arrives, I'll salute with my ice cream scoop."

Saturday morning I put on my new outfit. I felt like a different person. The fur-trimmed red velvet suit was cool, and the white hair and beard looked almost real. Once up in the helicopter, I saw a huge crowd gathered in the mall parking lot, waving and pointing.

Seconds later we were on the ground and the door opened. I'm sure I was beaming. Television cameramen and newspaper photographers welcomed me. I, Brandon Brady, was the center of attention. I could get used to being visiting royalty.

A long line of kids and parents waited beside my little North Pole house. A tiny girl with blond curls put her thumb in her mouth. I lifted her onto my lap and asked questions. The cameras flashed. I gave her a candy cane and she slid down—the first of hundreds. Or was it thousands?

Those December Saturdays tended to be long. Kids dropped ice cream cones on me, and mothers sat wet-bottomed babies on my lap. Didn't they know I had feelings, too?

The next several days were incredibly busy. School. Homework. Tests. Evenings at the North Pole. The best part was getting to know Jenny. Whenever we worked at the same time, she'd give me a wave from the Super Scoop counter. Sometimes I gave her a ride home, and we had the coolest conversations.

"You wouldn't believe the crazy things these kids unload on me...well, Santa, actually," I complained one snowy night.

"Do I detect disillusionment?" she asked as she fastened her seat belt and brushed snowflakes from her brown curls.

"Yeah. A six-year-old asked for a husband and a baby. A seven-year-old wants his own computer in his bedroom. A nine-year-old in mascara and purple lipstick demanded a fourteen-piece French Provincial bedroom set—whatever that is." I carefully drove out of the parking lot.

Jenny teased, "Wow, Santa, you're really going to be busy Christmas Eve."

I searched for the right words. "There's something wrong with this Santa gig. One little girl had tears in her eyes when she asked me to make her daddy well so he can be home for Christmas. Who do they think Santa is? God?"

"The problem is they don't know who *God* is. He's a lot more dependable than Santa," she said with a grin. "Sorry."

"Don't be," I said as I stopped in front of Jenny's house, wishing we had more time to talk. "See you in biology tomorrow."

The first day back at school in January, Jenny waved for me to join her at lunch.

I slid my tray beside hers and plopped into a chair. "How's the retired super scooper?"

"Richer, but glad it's over. How about Santa? You sure look different in khakis and a T-shirt," she said with a grin.

I sighed. "I feel different, too. Being Santa should have been a blast. Instead, it left me with a gazillion questions."

"I noticed lots of students from Riverside paid to have their picture taken with Santa just because you were under that suit."

"I guess I have more friends than I thought," I said as I stared at my pizza. "Well, that's not exactly what I mean."

Jenny finished her fries. "So what's bugging you?"

"How come people act like Santa is real?" I burst out. "His kind of gifts aren't fair. Rich kids get lots of presents. Poor kids get few—maybe none. The joy and surprises Santa brings last only for a short time."

Jenny looked serious. "We discovered a phony fifty-dollar bill in our cash register one night. I couldn't tell the difference, but the manager could tell."

"What does that have to do with me and Santa?"

"You had a problem with a counterfeit, too. Look, Brandon, God's the problem solver, not Santa," Jenny said and then hesitated. "God has the answer for the child with the missing father and the one with the sick mother. His gifts are for everyone, in every season. Best of all, He wants to be our helper and friend."

"You seem to know Him pretty well." With a loud slurp, I drained my milk carton.

"Disgusting!" she said with a laugh. "Good thing God loves people whether they're bad, good, or disgusting. Jesus died to pay the penalty for every crummy thing we've ever done. All you need to do is tell Him you're sorry and that you want to live for Him."

I leaned back in my chair and said, "I don't have to clean up my life before I get to know God? Just being sorry seems too easy."

"I know. But when we tell God we're sorry and invite Him to take charge of our lives, He does," she said. Her green eyes twinkled. "I bet you'd like our church youth group. We meet every week for fun and food. How about coming with me this Wednesday night?"

I thought it over. Jenny was special. She never gossiped or put people down. She was friendly and cared about others—look how she listened to me. If God could make that kind of difference in someone, I'd like to learn more about Him. I smiled at her. "What time should I pick you up?"

It's a God Thing

He is...
the Wind beneath my wings,
the Treasure that I seek,
the Foundation on which I build,
the Song in my heart,
the Object of my desire,
the Breath of my life~
He is my All in All.

ANNE GRAHAM LOTZ
FROM *JUST GIVE ME JESUS*

God, Is That You?

AUTHOR UNKNOWN

A young man had been to Wednesday night Bible study. The pastor had shared about listening to God and obeying the Lord's voice. The young man couldn't help but wonder, *Does God still speak to people?*

After service he went out with some friends for coffee and pie, and they discussed the message. Several different ones talked about how God had led them in different ways. It was about ten o'clock when the young man started driving home. Sitting in his car, he just began to pray, *God, if You still speak to people, speak to me. I will listen. I will do my best to obey.* As he drove down the main street of his town, he had the strangest thought to stop and buy a gallon of milk. He shook his head and said out loud, "God, is that You?" He didn't get a reply and started on toward home.

But again came the thought, *Buy a gallon of milk.* The young man thought about Samuel and how he didn't recognize the voice of God and how little Samuel ran to Eli. *Okay, God, in case that is You, I will buy the milk.* It didn't seem like too hard a test of obedience. He could always use the milk. He stopped and purchased the gallon of milk and started off toward home. As he passed Seventh Street, he again felt the urge. *Turn down that street.* He thought, *This is crazy,* and drove on past the intersection. Again, he felt that he should turn down Seventh Street. At the next intersection, he returned back and headed down Seventh. Half jokingly, he said out loud, "Okay, God,

I will." He drove several blocks when suddenly he felt like he should stop. He pulled over to the curb and looked around. He was in a semicommercial area of town. It wasn't the best, but it wasn't the worst of neighborhoods, either. The businesses were closed, and most of the houses looked dark like the people were already in bed.

Again he sensed something. *Go and give the milk to the people in the house across the street.* The young man looked at the house. It was dark, and it looked like the people were either gone or they were already asleep. He started to open the door and then sat back in the car seat. "Lord, this is insane. Those people are asleep, and if I wake them up, they are going to be mad and I will look stupid."

Again he felt like he should go and give the milk. Finally he opened the door. "Okay, God, if this is You, I will go to the door and I will give them the milk. If You want me to look like a crazy person, okay. I want to be obedient. I guess that will count for something, but if they don't answer right away, I am out of here."

He walked across the street and rang the bell. He could hear some noise inside. A man's voice yelled out, "Who is it? What do you want?" Then the door opened before the young man could get away. The man was standing there in his jeans and T-shirt. He looked like he just got out of bed. He had a strange look on his face, and he didn't seem too happy to have some stranger standing on his doorstep. "What is it?"

The young man thrust out the gallon of milk. "Here, I brought this to you."

The man took the milk and rushed down a hallway speaking loudly in Spanish. Then from down the hall came a woman carrying the milk toward the kitchen. The man was following her, holding a baby. The baby was crying. The man had tears streaming down his face. The man began speaking and half crying. "We were just praying. We had some big bills this month, and we ran out of money. We didn't have any milk for our baby. I was just praying and asking God to show me how to get some milk."

His wife in the kitchen yelled out, "I asked Him to send an angel with some. Are you an angel?"

The young man reached into his wallet and pulled out all the money he had on him and put it in the man's hand. He turned and walked back toward his car, and the tears were streaming down his face. He knew that God still answers prayers.

If you ask me why God should love us,

I cannot tell.

I suppose it is because He is a true Father.
It is His nature to love;

just as it is the nature of the sun to shine.

DWIGHT L. MOODY

A Father's Love

=◎=

MICHAEL T. POWERS

H is name was Brian, and he was a student at the small high school I attended. Brian was a special education student who was constantly searching for love and attention, but it usually came for the wrong reasons. Students who wanted to have some "fun" would ask, "Brian, are you the Incredible Hulk?" He would then run down the halls roaring and flexing. He was the joke of the school and was "entertainment" for those who watched. Brian, who was looking for acceptance, didn't realize at times that they were laughing at him and not with him. One day I couldn't take it anymore. I told the students I'd had enough of their game and sternly told them to knock it off. "Aw, come on, Mike! We are just having fun. Who do you think you are, anyway?"

The teasing didn't stop for long, but Brian latched on to me that day of my sophomore year. I had stuck up for him, and now he was my buddy. Thoughts of: "What will people think of you if you are friends with Brian?" swirled in my head, but I forced them out as I realized that God wanted me to treat this young man as I would want to be treated.

Later that week I invited him to my house after school to play video games. Pretty soon he started asking me questions like, "Hey, Mike, where do you go to church?" I would politely answer his questions, all the while turning my concentration back to the video games. He kept asking me questions about God and why I was different from some of the kids at school.

Finally my girlfriend pulled me aside and said, "Michael, he needs to talk. How about you go down to your room where you can talk privately?" She had picked up on the cues better than I had.

As soon as we arrived in my room, he asked, "Hey, Mike. How come you're not like some of the other kids at school?"

I knew I needed to share with him the difference that God had made in my life. I got out my Bible and shared John 3:16 and some verses in Romans with him. I explained to him that God loved him just the way he was and that He sent Jesus down to earth to die on a cross for him. All the while, I did not know if he was comprehending anything I was telling him. When we were done, I asked Brian if he wanted to pray with me. He said he would like that.

We prayed together: "God, I know I am a sinner and that even if I was the only person on earth, You still would have sent Your Son down to die on the cross for me and take my place. I accept the gift of salvation that You offer and I ask that You come into my heart and take control. Thank You, Lord. Amen."

I looked at him and said, "Brian, if you meant those words you just prayed, where is Jesus right now?"

He pointed to his heart and said, "He's in here now."

Then he did something I will never forget as long as I live. Brian hugged the Bible to his chest, lay down on the bed, and let the tears flow down his face. When I cry, my sobbing is very loud. Brian was unearthly silent as the faucet behind his eyes let loose. Then he said to me, "Mike, do you know that the love that God has for me must be like the love a husband has for his wife."

I was floored.

Here was someone who had trouble comprehending things in school, but had now understood one of eternity's great truths. I knew now that he understood what I had shared with him.

He lay there for another five minutes or so as the salty drops continued to flow.

I don't remember now if we went back upstairs to finish playing video games or not. But I do remember the incredible feeling I had at that moment.

A high, higher than anything a substance could ever give me. The high of knowing that God still works miracles in everyday life. John 10:10 immediately came to mind: "I have come that they may have life, and have it to the full."

It was about a week later that everything came into perspective for me. It was then that Brian really opened up to me. He explained that his dad had left him and his mom when he was five years old. As Brian stood on the porch that day, his dad told him he was leaving and that he couldn't deal with having a son like him anymore. Then he walked out of Brian's life and was never seen again....

Brian told me that he had been looking for his dad ever since.

Now I knew why the tears kept flowing that day in my bedroom.

His search was over. He found what he had been looking for since he was five years old.

A Father's love....

Silent Reminder

CHARLES R. SWINDOLL
FROM *THE TALE OF THE TARDY OXCART*

I't's tough to live a focused life. From every direction, something or someone clamors for our attention. A distraction draws our eyes, and the next thing we know, we've swerved off the road and headed down another detour.

One Chicago youth pastor came up with a clever way to keep his group on track. Concerned that the balmy beaches of Florida—the site of their upcoming evangelism trip—would lure the teens from their purpose, he fashioned a cross from two pieces of lumber. Just before they climbed on the bus, he showed it to the group.

"I want all of you to remember that the whole purpose of our going is to glorify the name of Christ, to lift up the cross—the message of the cross, the emphasis of the cross, the Christ of the cross," he announced. "So we're going to take this cross wherever we go."

The teenagers looked at one another, a little unsure of his plan. But they agreed to do it and dragged the cross on the bus. It banged back and forth in the aisle all the way to Florida. It went with them into restaurants. It stayed overnight where they stayed overnight. It stood in the sand while they ministered on the beach.

At first, lugging the cross around embarrassed the kids. But later it became a point of identification. That cross was a constant, silent reminder of who they were and why they had come. They eventually regarded carrying it as an honor and privilege.

The night before they went home, the youth leader handed out two nails to each of the kids. He told them that if they wanted to commit themselves to what the cross stood for, they could hammer one nail into it and keep the other one with them. One by one, the teens drove their nail into the cross.

About fifteen years later, one fellow—now a stockbroker—called the youth leader. He told him that he still keeps that nail with him in his desk drawer. Whenever he loses his sense of focus, he looks at the nail and remembers the cross on that beach in Florida. It reminds him of what is at the core of his life—his commitment to Jesus Christ.

Every day I live is an opportunity to reach out to others who need Jesus.

JESSICA BROWN
AGE 17

The Bible Smugglers

LINDSAY WILLIS

AGE 18

T he door creaked as the last person entered the back staircase where twenty of us sat clustered together for warmth and reassurance.

The air was heavy with anticipation as we awaited instructions. Each of us held a crumpled piece of paper in our shaking hands. The tiny typewritten message that had led us to this secluded house for a Bible study contained few details, yet it still included the bone-chilling warning: "Do not let this paper fall into the wrong hands. Your life depends on it." But despite our best efforts to keep the meeting undercover, our secret had been leaked, and the police were out in full force, hunting us down. Speaking in a hurried whisper, our leader revealed the plan to us.

"We can't be sure that we're not being watched even now as we speak, so I'll make this brief. We will drive you to the park where you will split up to throw off any followers. You will see a lady walking her dog in the park, and you must talk to her to get further directions. If you are stopped and questioned by the police, do not tell them where you are going, and above all make sure your Bibles are well hidden!"

The quivering in her voice scared us enough that no one spoke as we crept outside to meet the cars waiting to take us to the park. Katie, Will, Michelle, and I were told to get on the floor in the backseat of our vehicle and cover up with blankets. If we were stopped en route to the park, we were to remain perfectly still and allow the driver to do all the talking. Full of anxiety, we huddled as far out of sight as possible and prayed we would not be found. Thankfully, we arrived at the first stop without incident, but as the car sped away, we were left standing on a dark street feeling alone and vulnerable under the city lights.

As we walked into the park, we saw other members of our group being stopped by tough-looking officers who questioned them. We felt helpless as we watched friends escorted to waiting police cars. All we could do was walk past as if we didn't know them.

Though full of fear, we continued on. We came to an abrupt halt when we spotted a lady with a small dog wandering slowly through the trees. Nervously, we approached her, and Katie mumbled the secret code. The lady acted like she had not even heard us and kept walking. Then she paused, turned slightly and nonchalantly replied with the answer to our code. Excitedly, we dug our Bibles from their hiding places underneath our layers of clothing. When she saw them, she handed each of us a map.

"The dog's name is Sparky," she said, and then she was gone.

Thrilled we had made it this far, we began to decipher the directions. The map would supposedly lead us to a house where we were to look inside the mailbox. There we would find a newspaper with more directions wrapped inside.

We twisted and turned our way through side streets and finally found the designated house. Searching inside the mailbox, we found the news-paper and the address. This was the last clue. We were almost there! Heading for our final destination, we walked with confidence and even dared to talk quietly. It looked like everything was going to be all right.

Then suddenly an officer stepped from behind a tree and blocked our path. Terrified, we looked for an escape, but there was nowhere to run. With suspicion in her eyes, the policewoman approached us.

"Where are you kids headed tonight?" she asked with an icy tone.

"Oh, just going to visit a friend," Michelle said, trying to keep her voice steady.

"Well, it's kind of dangerous to be walking around the park at night.

Maybe I should escort you to your friend's house," she said as she checked our pockets for Bibles.

We began to sweat. We had no choice. If we didn't let her escort us, we'd arouse suspicion. Attempting to mask our desperation, we tried to make pleasant conversation with the officer. As we neared our destination, it looked like we were going to have to turn ourselves in, but then her walkie-talkie buzzed, calling her to another assignment. Our hearts soared as we watched her disappear down the street. As soon as she was out of sight, we raced to the front door of the house where the Bible study was being held.

We had not even knocked when the door flew open. Mouths wide with shock, we looked up into the steely glare of not one, but three officers. We looked at each other questioningly. Did we have the wrong house? When they hauled us into the living room, we knew that couldn't be it. Other members of our group already sat on the couches looking defeated. Somehow, despite all our precautions, they had found us.

The policemen huddled at the front door discussing what they were going to do with us. Still feeling a little stunned, I glanced sadly around the room. The look in Will's eyes caught my attention. I could tell a plan was forming. Katie and Michelle noticed it, too, and we watched to see what he was trying to show us. First he looked at the group of officers cluttering the front hall, then slowly his eyes rolled to the back door. No one was there. With the officers' backs turned, we would have a good head start. As if reading one another's minds, we gave each other silent nods. Then with a burst of adrenaline we bolted for the door. The policemen yelled after us, ordering us to stop, but it was too late. Running full speed, we flew across the yard and over the fence. We ducked behind a garden shed and lay flat against it until the sounds of pursuing officers faded.

We crept out of hiding with caution. That's when we noticed some people we knew sneaking in the back door of the next house. When we got to the door, the man standing guard asked for the password. Still panting from our great escape, Michelle spoke up.

"The dog's name is Sparky."

The doorkeeper smiled and welcomed us inside. We followed him up to the attic where the rest of the group sat in a circle reading their Bibles by candlelight so as not to draw attention to the house. Having a Bible study had never been so exciting!

It had been the most outrageous Saturday night any of us had spent together in a long time, and we all agreed that we would like to do it again some time soon. But as I looked around at the smiling, dirt-smeared faces, I began to wonder. If this whole underground game had not been make-believe, would we still have had the courage to come? If those officers were real, rather than parents who attended our church, would we still have risked running into them or running away from them? Would we have taken the chance of being arrested in the name of God had this not been just another creative Saturday night social event for the youth group?

As we prayed, we thanked God for giving us a chance to experience what it might be like to stand up for our faith in a country where we're not free to do so. We also thanked Him that our country is free, because none of us knew how we would have acted if it hadn't been a game.

When I Say, "I Am a christian"

When I say, "I am a Christian,"
I'm not shouting, "I am saved!"
I'm whispering, "I was lost."
That's why I chose His way.

When I say, "I am a Christian,"
I don't speak of this with pride.
I'm confessing that I stumble,
Needing God to be my guide.

When I say, "I am a Christian,"
I'm not trying to be strong.
I'm professing that I'm weak
And pray for strength to carry on.

When I say, "I am a Christian,"
I still feel the sting of pain.
I have my share of heartaches,
Which is why I speak His name.

When I say, "I am a Christian,"
I do not wish to judge.
I have no authority;
I only know I'm loved.

CAROL S. WIMMER

The Inscription

LINDA M. WALL

She writes his name boldly on the palm of her hand, proof of her devotion. She would give anything if he would only notice her!

But he hurries past her every day in the hallways of school, never really seeing her at all. He hardly even knows she exists.

She watches him with hopeful eyes, praying someday he will turn and see her—really see her. Maybe then he'll smile and say her name. And just maybe—when he sees how much she cares for him—maybe he will take her hand and walk beside her.

Maybe someday he'll know how much he means to her, and how she wears his name on the palm of her hand.

Someone else watches *her* with hopeful eyes, her name boldly inscribed in the palms of His hands. It isn't written in with ink that will one day fade, but is carved there for all eternity with nails of love.

He gave *everything* for her to notice Him.

Instead, she hurries past Him every day, never really seeing Him at all. She hardly knows He exists.

He watches and waits for the day that she will turn and see Him—really see Him. Maybe then she will finally smile and whisper His name. And just maybe, when she sees how much He loves her, maybe then she'll take His hand and walk beside Him.

Maybe someday she will know how much she means to Him—and the price He paid to bear her name on His hands.

Behold, I have inscribed you on the palms of My hands....

ISAIAH 49:16, NASB

Freedom Behind Bars

=◎=

NEELY ARRINGTON
AS TOLD TO CANDY ARRINGTON

My stomach tightened into a knot as the iron door slammed shut behind me. I never dreamed I'd be in a place like this. The guard ordered us to walk, hands behind our backs, to the end of the hall.

"Turn left," he shouted.

Rounding the corner, I heard a noise that sounded like three gunshots. I jumped and grabbed the hand of the girl beside me. She suddenly screamed, and I turned and saw two eyes peering through a tiny window in the lockdown cell next to me. The mouth that belonged to those eyes yelled a barrage of the worst swearing I have ever heard.

The offensive verbal assault continued as the inmate punched and kicked the cell door. I heard him threaten to wring my neck. I had never been so scared.

The guard motioned for us to go on. I thought about how angry and afraid that person must be. I had fears of my own, but I was here to try to make a difference for people like him.

In preparing for the prison ministry choir tour, I was not sure what to expect. We spent countless hours learning songs, choreography, and speaking parts in order to present the gospel of Jesus Christ. When the week finally arrived, we visited ten juvenile detention centers in Florida. We left each one with a different story.

Our first experience seemed like a disaster. Pouring rain canceled our outdoor performance. Instead, we squeezed into a tiny meeting room. There was not enough space to set up all the risers and sound equipment. Initially, we felt uneasy because we were so close to the prisoners. We totally blew the first song, messed up the choreography, and missed speaking parts. The prisoners mocked us and made fun of our dancing. I was unprepared for their hostility. Only a few of the inmates seemed to be really listening.

One girl in the back row caught my eye. She watched me as I sang and danced, and she even tried to sing along with me. When our pastor began to talk, she started weeping, and I knew God was speaking to her. During the invitation she raised her hand, indicating that she wanted to accept Christ. It broke my heart to think that a girl who seemed so sweet had to live her life in prison. I glanced her way as we left, and she mouthed "thank you." That let me know that God still worked in spite of our mistakes.

In another prison, we were allowed to interact with the inmates. After the performance, the superintendent let a few girls from the choir talk to the female inmates. We had only fifteen minutes, but we made the most of it. Even though these girls were behind bars, I realized that they were like me. They had hopes and dreams, fears and frustrations. The only difference was the wrong choices that had brought them to this place.

One girl struggled with a drug problem and asked us to pray for her. She was to be released the next day. That afternoon she made a decision to follow Christ. If we had been at that prison one day later, she wouldn't have heard us. I saw that God was in control and that His timing was perfect.

One of the chaperones was an interpreter for the deaf. At one of the prisons she learned from a guard that a boy there was deaf and had no interpreter. She was given permission to interpret for him. He never took his eyes off her, and during the invitation he accepted Christ. If she hadn't been with us, he might have never "heard" the gospel.

The most intense experience occurred in our ninth prison. Our performance was going well when suddenly one of the younger teens sitting right in the middle got sick and vomited. The prisoners around him began to laugh and make fun of him. A guard came and led him out of the room, and three more came to clean up the mess. I prayed that God would keep the inmates focused as our pastor began speaking.

A sudden hush came over the room and I knew that God had heard my request. Our pastor gave the same basic message at every prison, but that day he spoke with greater emphasis, and his words had more power. I looked across the sea of faces and saw a boy who looked about sixteen. He was crying so hard that a guard brought him a towel to wipe his tears. A teen guy in our group got permission to talk with him. The inmate told him that for a long time he knew who God was but was confused about Jesus and didn't know what to believe. Through us, his questions had been answered. He finally understood who Jesus is and the message of salvation. He was so thankful that we had come and for his new understanding. He joyfully accepted Christ.

We were still concerned about the young teen who threw up. Our pastor and his son went to the infirmary to see him. They told him how much they cared about him and how much Jesus loves him. He responded to their words, and our pastor watched prayerfully as his son led this boy to Christ.

There are so many more stories I could tell. Over and over we saw God at work. We saw angry, lonely, hopeless teenagers understand and respond to the good news of Jesus Christ. We touched the lives of many prisoners, but our lives were changed too. We came home with a new sense of gratitude for our blessings and for the freedom we have in Christ.

Most of those prisoners are still behind bars, but because of our ministry and God's grace, many now have a personal relationship with Jesus Christ. They may live behind bars, but they are experiencing true freedom in Christ.

Spray Painting for Jesus

BEN BRYDEN
AGE 17
AS TOLD TO BARBARA MAJOR BRYDEN

Armed with stencils and bright yellow and white spray paint, we stepped out of the air-conditioned bus. Justin and I hurried toward the first condo on the short street. The other high school teams spread out to cover the rest of the buildings.

"Hey, Ben. If you talk to this family, I'll talk to the people at the next house we go to," said Justin breathlessly.

"Sounds good," I answered.

Dodging a large hanging plant, I rang the doorbell. A man with a little girl in his arms opened the door. "We're painting house numbers on curbs," I said. "Could we do yours? If you have your house number on the curb, it's easier for emergency vehicles to find your home. And it's free."

The man gave me a puzzled look and asked with a Spanish accent, "What do you want?"

I realized the man hadn't understood.

Wow! I finally get to use my Spanish. Hope I know enough words to explain. I switched to Spanish, searched for the right words, and explained again slowly.

The man next door came over when he heard us talking and started listening.

"Sure. Go ahead. What group are you with?" asked the little girl's father in a mix of Spanish and English.

"We're attending the Christian youth conference at the university."

"Oh," said the man settling into a chair on the porch with his daughter on his lap. "My wife is cooking for your group. That's why I'm taking care of our daughter."

We painted the numbers on the curb as the two men watched from the shade. "Good thing you can speak Spanish, Ben," Justin whispered to me as we worked. When we finished painting, I peeled the tape back, Justin pulled the stencils off, and we walked back to the porch where the little group was sitting.

"Thanks. Do you mind if I ask you some questions? We're supposed to fill out this survey form."

"What do you want to know?"

I read each question slowly, translating the English into Spanish. Both men began to discuss the questions: How do you like living so close to the university? Are the young people at the conference too noisy? Do you believe in the God of the Bible? Do you attend church? Do you have any questions you would like to ask?

"I always wanted to hear about Jesus, but there was no one to ask," interrupted the next-door neighbor, moving closer.

I looked at him and saw real hunger in his eyes. *Lord, he wants me to tell him about You! I'm not sure I have enough Spanish to tell him what he needs to know. Somehow, Lord, give me the right words,* I prayed.

First, I told him everything I could think of about Jesus. Then I went through the plan of salvation we were taught at church. I was still worried my high school Spanish didn't include all the words I needed to witness about Jesus, but the words came. I was using words I couldn't remember learning in Spanish class, but the men understood and so did I. Finally, I asked the neighbor man if we could pray with him to accept Christ into his life.

"Yes. You're the first one to explain it to me so I can understand."

"Repeat this prayer after me," I instructed him. I was trembling all over with excitement as I began the prayer of salvation in Spanish.

"I know Jesus loves me! I know it!" The neighbor man said, shaking our hands. "What do I do now?" His eyes were dancing, and he looked like he heard angels singing.

We pulled out our list of area churches. We were so excited it was hard to concentrate. Finally we found a church close to his home. Then we prayed with him again.

As Justin and I started back to the bus, my thoughts were whirling. *I can't believe that happened to me! I didn't know those words.*

Oh, Lord, I prayed excitedly, *that was the most amazing thing that ever happened to me! You gave me words I didn't have, didn't even know, and gave me the translation for them, so I could tell him about You. I trusted You and You gave me what I needed. Now I want to tell more people about You. Thank You, Lord.*

Pray the largest prayers.
You cannot think a prayer so large
that God, in answering it,
will not wish you had made it larger.
Pray not for crutches but for wings.

PHILLIPS BROOKS

The Love Note

KEN JONES

My Midwest bones were frozen on that late January day as I boarded a plane for Bethany College near Santa Cruz, California. I would be preparing for full-time ministry there. As I buckled my seatbelt, I looked forward to seeing palm trees and the ocean.

Within days of arriving on the campus I met Randee, and my interest in palm trees and the ocean diminished immediately. She was different than other girls, I thought. Quiet and shy and deep in the things of God. We went out for coffee several times, sitting and talking about our families: hers, the Smiths; and mine, the Joneses. We talked about school and friends and the future. We talked about the Lord, who was leading us both into full-time service, and I sensed such a wonderful spirit in this girl, such a warm love for God.

My feelings for her intensified. Actually, I was in love—severely in love. Unfortunately, she was not—at least not yet. And so I plied her with candy and flowers and notes telling of my devotion to her. She smiled and nodded and thanked me. And she seemed to notice me, but very, very gradually.

One rainy morning, I worried that Randee would not have an umbrella to walk to her 7:30 class. I got dressed, grabbed my umbrella, and waited outside her dorm until she came out. We walked together under the protection of my umbrella across the campus. We walked down the hill toward the gymnasium. We talked as we walked, about the rain and wet books and our schedules. When we arrived at the door of her classroom, she handed it to me.

A card with my name on it. She said, "I saw this and thought of you." Then she turned and walked into her class.

I ran toward the campus coffee shop with my card. When I got there, my wet fingers fumbled to carefully open the envelope without damaging its precious contents.

On the front of the card, there was a cartoon of a little girl with blond hair, her face and hands covered with chocolate. Beneath the picture, in crayonlike, crooked printing were these words: "I like you better than chocolate-covered graham crackers."

I stared at the damp card for a few seconds before I looked inside. There, in the same, crayonlike printing, were these words:

"And I *really like* chocolate-covered graham crackers!"

The card was signed "Love, Randee."

I leaned back and looked up at the ceiling, smiling. I just sat there in the coffee shop in wet clothes, alone with a cup of cold coffee.

I enjoyed the caption: "I like you better than chocolate-covered graham crackers...and I *really like* chocolate-covered graham crackers!" I thought the sentiment and idea were terrific. But the part of the card that sent me into orbit was the handwritten part; *her* handwritten part that read: "Love, Randee." I thought that note—the first love note I ever got from my Randee—was the most beautiful love note I had ever read. But that was before she shared the other love note with me. It was written to Another: Someone who had captured her heart before I came along. It was obvious by reading the note that she was involved in an ongoing relationship, and that her feelings for this significant Other were deeper than her feelings for me.

She had written it on the first blank page of her Bible, from her heart, in her own hand. A vow to the Bridegroom:

> "I, Randee, take thee, Jesus, to be my beloved Savior,
> to work together under God's holy ordinance.
> I will love You, worship You, honor You,
> forsaking all others.

But keep You only to myself, I cannot.
I will share Your love with those who need it most,
for Your love would fill many oceans.
In token of the vows I have made before You,
I now take my cross and carry it, rejoicing, knowing that
You will never leave me nor forsake me, knowing that
You will be with me in sickness and in health,
to love and cherish me,
not only till death, but for all eternity."

I don't know what happened to the "chocolate-covered graham cracker" love note Randee handed to me on that rainy day down by the gymnasium. I must have lost it in one of our many moves. But I've read her love note to Him—the other Man in her life—many times. And her devotion to Him is so deep and sincere and loving that I am still in awe of her commitment.

Bernie Knows the Truth

KEN DAVIS
FROM *FIRE UP YOUR LIFE*

In my teens I lived to prove my worth to those around me. Because of this, I often misused the gifts God had given me. Humor is a gift from God, a sword that can pierce through hostility and hardness to reach even the coldest heart with a message of love. But I had turned the other edge of the sword and used this gift to hurt others.

And that is exactly what I did to a boy named Bernie one year at church camp. Bernie was mentally and physically handicapped. He walked with a clumsy gait and talked with a slur. Totally uninhibited and outgoing, Bernie sought the friendship of everyone, but few of us had time for him.

For me, Bernie was merely a source of material. I made jokes about him and would mock his actions behind his back. Because I was living with something to prove, I was willing to step on Bernie in an attempt to lift myself a little higher.

One day on the athletic field, two captains were choosing sides for a softball game, and Bernie and I were the last to be chosen. I was humiliated. In that moment, I breathed a horribly inappropriate prayer: "Please, God, let them choose me next." I *was* chosen next, as it turned out, leaving Bernie standing alone. Bernie's eyes lit up—he didn't care about being chosen last; he only wanted to be chosen, and now that he was the only one left, surely it was his turn. But Bernie's look of anticipation quickly disappeared as the team captains began to argue about who would have to take him.

"You take him," one insisted.

"No, you take him," the other countered.

A counselor quickly stepped in and assigned Bernie to a team. Sadly, I was oblivious to the pain Bernie was probably feeling at that moment. I had avoided the embarrassment of being chosen last, and that was all I cared about; now we could get on with the game.

In fact, I probably wouldn't remember Bernie today if it weren't for what happened at the end of our stay at camp. It was time to go home, and everyone was standing by the buses, waiting to have their luggage loaded. I was with three boys who had become my friends during the week. Friends were a rare luxury for me, and I had compromised in many ways to gain the approval of these boys. As we stood saying our good-byes and promising never to lose contact (I can't even remember their names today), we heard Bernie coming, shouting at the top of his lungs, his voice cracking with excitement. "Good newth!" he cried with his familiar lisp. "Good newth!"

I quickly prepared to make my friends laugh one more time by mocking Bernie's cry, but before I could make that cruel response, Bernie broke into our circle.

His eyes danced with a joy I had not seen before. He gulped, catching his breath. "Good newth!" he breathed in a hoarse whisper. *"Jesuth* lovth me." Then, pointing to his heaving chest, he changed the emphasis. "Jesuth lovth *me!"* Bernie's eyes danced as, with arms outstretched to emphasize his point, he vigorously nodded his head up and down, waiting for us to acknowledge this newly discovered truth.

We stood with our mouths open and our eyes averted in shame. But Bernie wasn't looking for our approval. He didn't need our approval anymore. He only sought a signal that we had heard what he had said. He was simply sharing the good news.

With a squeal of delight, he left us standing there and ran to find another group. I can still hear his voice getting fainter as he made his way to the other end of the camp: "Good newth! Good newth! Jesuth lovth me!"

Bernie knew that he had nothing to prove. Jesus loved him.

Because I care

Because I care

P lease take a moment to read the verses written on the next page. Although there are hundreds of verses in the Bible that tell us about God's love and His gift of salvation, I chose these from the book of Romans in the New Testament.

I care about what happens to you now, but I care even more about where you will spend eternity. If you have never asked Jesus Christ to be your Savior, please consider inviting Him into your life now.

Many years ago I prayed a simple prayer that went something like this...

Dear Jesus,

I believe You are the Son of God and that You gave Your life as a payment for the sins of mankind. I believe You rose from the dead and You are alive today in heaven preparing a place for those who trust in You.

I have not lived my life in a way that honors You. Please forgive me for my sins and come into my life as Savior and Lord. Help me grow in Your knowledge and in obedience to You.

Thank You for forgiving me. Thank You for coming into my life. Thank You for giving me eternal life. Amen.

If you have sincerely asked Jesus Christ to come into your life, He will never leave you or forsake you. Nothing—absolutely nothing—will be able to separate you from His love.

God bless you, dear one. I'll look forward to meeting you one day in heaven.

Alice Gray

For all have sinned and fall short of the glory of God.

ROMANS 3:23

For the wages of sin is death, but the gift of God
is eternal life in Christ Jesus our Lord.

ROMANS 6:23

But God demonstrates his own love for us in this:
While we were still sinners, Christ died for us.

ROMANS 5:8

If you confess with your mouth, "Jesus is Lord,"
and believe in your heart that God
raised him from the dead, you will be saved.
For it is with your heart that you believe and are justified,
and it is with your mouth that you confess and are saved.

ROMANS 10:9–10

"Everyone who calls on the name of the Lord will be saved."

ROMANS 10:13

The Stories for the Heart Series

- *More than 5 million sold in series!*
- *#1-selling Christian Stories series!*

www.storiesfortheheart.com

More Treasures for Teens

Stories for a Teen's Heart, Book 1

Through a blend of humorous and poignant tales, teens will be encouraged in life's journey and reassured that they are not alone on the road to becoming adults.

ISBN 1-57673-646-6

Stories for a Teen's Heart, Book 2

Here are stories of encouragement that celebrate friendship, love, faith, and more in this inspiring collection for teens from the bestselling Stories for the Heart series.

ISBN 1-57673-797-7

Retailers' Choice Award
Winner
Angel Award

A.

B.

Let these pages become a keepsake for the favorite memories of your heart. These companion journals to *Stories for a Teen's Heart* are the perfect place to record inspirational thoughts and celebrate events that add splashes of sunshine to your life. Your writings will tell the story of a very special teenager—you!

A. ISBN 1-57673-705-5

B. ISBN 1-57673-995-3

True Stories of Teens Living Committed Lives for Christ

storiesfor theextreme teen'sheart

Celebrating Teens Who Are Saying Yes to God

Compiled by Alice Gray

Angel Award Winner!

Compiled with the help of teenagers, these inspiring stories show teens like you making a difference in their families, schools, and world. These compelling accounts will encourage you to cultivate a deeper walk with God, while often putting a smile on your face.

ISBN 1-57673-703-9

The Heart of a Teen Speaks...

Popular Novels by Melody Carlson

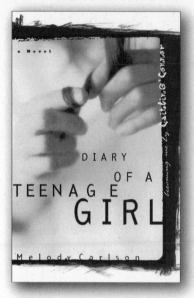

Diary of a Teenage Girl

In this compelling journal, sixteen-year-old Caitlin O'Conner explores the conflicts and joys of growing up, including her adventures with boyfriends, peer loyalty, parental conflicts, and spirituality.

ISBN 1-57673-735-7

Diary of a Teenage Girl:
Teen singing sensation **Rachael Lampa** says, "I had to keep reminding myself that I wasn't reading my own diary! It captures the thoughts and issues of a teenager's struggles to follow God's pathway."

It's My Life

In this sequel to *Diary of a Teenage Girl,* bestselling author Melody Carlson chronicles Caitlin O'Conner's day-to-day dilemmas and fulfillment as a new believer.

ISBN 1-57673-772-1

A New Attitude toward Relationships and Romance

I Kissed Dating Goodbye
by Joshua Harris

Dating. Isn't there a better way? Reorder your romantic life in the light of God's Word and find more fulfillment than a date could ever give—a life of sincere singleness. Singles from 15 to 55 are tired of dating games and are ready for a new attitude toward romance. Whether you're single, dating, or divorced, this practical book can help you understand God's plan for romance in your life.

ISBN 1-57673-036-0

Boy Meets Girl
by Joshua Harris

In this dynamic sequel to *I Kissed Dating Goodbye*, newlyweds Joshua and Shannon Harris deliver an inspiring practical illustration of how this healthy, joyous alternative to recreational dating—biblical courtship—worked for them. *Boy Meets Girl* helps readers understand how to go about pursuing the possibility of marriage with someone they may be serious about. It's the natural follow-up to the author's blockbuster book on teen dating!

ISBN 1-57673-709-8

Searching for True Love video series
by Joshua Harris

The *Searching for True Love* video series builds on the highly popular conference series and bestselling book *I Kissed Dating Goodbye* to give young adults God's direction as they seek lifetime love. Available in a three-pack or separately, the videos explore *Love*, *Purity*, and *Trust* from the Bible's perspective. Forty-five minutes each.

Three-video series	ISBN 1-57673-645-8
Searching for True Love	ISBN 1-57673-634-2
Searching for Trust	ISBN 1-57673-643-1
Searching for Purity	ISBN 1-57673-637-7

ACKNOWLEDGMENTS

Hundreds of books, magazines, and other sources were researched for this collection as well as a review of hundreds of stories sent by friends and readers of the Stories for the Heart collection. A diligent search has been made to trace original ownership, and when necessary, permission to reprint has been obtained. If we have overlooked giving proper credit to anyone, please accept our apologies. If you will contact Multnomah Publishers, Inc., Post Office Box 1720, Sisters, Oregon 97759, corrections will be made prior to additional printings. Please provide detailed information.

Notes and acknowledgments are listed by story title in the order they appear in each section of the book. For permission to reprint any of the stories, please request permission from the original source listed below. Grateful acknowledgment is made to authors, publishers, and agents who granted permission for reprinting these stories.

YEAH, YOU MAKE A DIFFERENCE

"A Portrait of Me" by Lacey Barnhouse. Used by permission. Lacey Barnhouse wrote her poem in January 2001 when she was sixteen. That May she was in a fatal car accident. Lacey believed that the only way she could make a difference in life was to live the faith she felt so deeply. Lacey was involved in choir at school and her church's praise team and puppet ministry. Her future plans had included a mission trip to Morocco and becoming a teacher.

"The Christmas I Got Rich" by Jacob Andrew Shepherd. © 2002. Used by permission. Jacob is thirteen and lives in Central Oregon. He loves playing guitar, snowboarding with Dad, playing with his two-year-old sister, and traveling with Mom to her speaking engagements.

"In an Old, Battered Van" by Katherine Opp. © 2000. Used by permission of the author. Katherine is now a freshman at the University of the Pacific in Stockton, California, studying vocal performance. She hopes to have a career in opera.

"Standing Tall" by Jerry B. Jenkins. © 1996 by Jerry B. Jenkins. This article originally appeared in *Moody* magazine. Used by permission.

"Just Listening" by Sue Rhodes Dodd. © 2002. Used by permission of the author. Sue Rhodes Dodd is president of Amethyst Enterprises, an editorial consulting firm in Tulsa, Oklahoma. She is married, has one daughter, and sings professionally.

"What Is Life?" by David McNally. From *Even Eagles Need a Push* by David McNally, copyright © 1990 by David McNally. Used by permission of Dell Publishing, a division of Random House, Inc.

"Clam Chowder" by Denise Jolly. © 1988. Used by permission of the author.

"Twelve Teens and a Bag of Tricks" by Bruce Wilkinson. From *The Prayer of Jabez for Teens* by Bruce Wilkinson. © 2001. Used by permission of Multnomah Publishers.

"Rookie Driver" by Charles R. Swindoll. From *Improving Your Serve* by Charles R. Swindoll. © 1990, W Publishing Group, Nashville, Tennessee. Used by permission. All rights reserved.

"Goodwill Shopping" by Mary Lou Carney. Reprinted with permission by *Guideposts for Teens*. Copyright © 2000 by *Guideposts*. All rights reserved.

"To Love the Children" by Rachel V. Neet. © 2001. Used by permission of the author.

"Don't Forget to Shine" by Kimberly Shumate. © 2001. Used by permission of the author.

"Meaningful Touch" by John Trent. From *Leaving the Light On* by Gary Smalley and John Trent, Ph.D. © 1994. Used by permission of Multnomah Publishers.

WANNA BE LIKE YOU

"Tribute" by Pamela McGrew. © 2000. Used by permission.

"The Silent Flute" by Felix Mayerhofer. © 2001. Used by permission of the author. Felix Mayerhofer is a former professional trombonist, a retired school band director and coordinator of music, a published author (*Tommy, Sticks and the Big Bass Drum*), and a devoted husband and father.

"You Got Another One, Joey!" by Bob Perks. © 2000. Used by permission of the author. Bob Perks is a speaker and the author of *The Flight of a Lifetime!* Visit Bob's story Web site at www.iwishyouenough.com or contact him by e-mail at bob@bobperks.com.

Acknowledgments

"Two Shirts" was excerpted from *More Random Acts of Kindness* by the editors of Conari Press. © 1994. Used by permission of Conari Press.

"Head of the Class" by Ben Jackson as told to Ginny Williams Dye. © 1996. Used by permission of the author.

"A Promise" by Teena M. Stewart. © 2000. Used by permission of the author. Teena Stewart divides her time between freelance writing, Web design, and spiritual gifts and ministry development via www.ministryinmotion.net. She resides in Benicia, California.

"Danny's Gift" by Sandra P. Klaus. © 1990. Used by permission of the author. A writer for Gospel Missionary Union, Sandra enjoys hosting foreign exchange students. She's been "mom" for teenagers from the Ukraine, Russia, Kazakhstan, Kyrgyzstan, and Brazil.

"Spring in New York" by Charlotte Wechsler. From *Small Miracles* by Yitta Halberstam and Judith Leventhal. © 1997. Used by permission.

"Four Quarters of Love" by Nancy Jo Sullivan. From *Moments of Grace* by Nancy Jo Sullivan. © 2000. Used by permission of Multnomah Publishers.

"The Secret Act" by Donald E. and Vesta W. Mansell. From *Sure as the Dawn* by Donald E. and Vesta W. Mansell. © 1993. Used by permission of the authors.

"Carrying the Torch" by Melissa Marin. © 2001. Used by permission of the author. I would like to thank my teacher, mentor, and editor, Janet McHenry, for all her support; and my mom for all her love.

"When the World Fell Silent" by Philip D. Yancey. Taken from *What's So Amazing about Grace?* by Philip D. Yancey. Copyright © 1997 by Philip D. Yancey. Used by permission of Zondervan Publishing House.

Forever Friends

"The Real Me" by Cynthia M. Hamond, S.F.O. © 2001. Used by permission of the author. Cynthia's stories have been published in magazines and the Chicken Soup for the Soul and Stories for the Heart series, and made for TV. Contact information: P.O. Box 488, Monticello, MN 55362 or candbh@aol.com.

"Scribblings in My Yearbook" by Teresa J. Cleary. © 1990. Used by permission of the author.

"Stray No More" by Jane Kise. © 2001. Used by permission of the author. Jane Kise is a freelance writer from Minnesota. She is a coauthor of the following books: *LifeKeys, Find Your Fit,* and the upcoming *Did You Get What You Prayed For?*

"Chocolate Chip Cookies Taste Better as Dough" by Danae Jacobson. From *Things I've Learned Lately* by Danae Jacobson. © 2001. Used by permission of Multnomah Publishers.

"Sweeter Than Chocolate" by Janet Lynn Mitchell. © 2001. Used by permission of the author. Janet Lynn Mitchell is an inspirational speaker and author of numerous articles and stories in compilations. Janet can be reached at janetlm@prodigy.net or faxed at 714-633-6309.

"Missing the Dance" by Michele Wallace Campanelli. © 1999. Used by permission of the author. Michele Wallace Campanelli is a national best-selling author. Her works include short stories and several novels. Her personal editor is Fontaine Wallace, an instructor at Florida Institute of Technology. To contact Michele, go to www.michelecampanelli.com.

"More Than a Crown" by Anita Higman. © 2001. Used by permission of the author. Anita Higman has twelve books published. Ms. Higman was selected for Houston's Barnes & Noble "Author of the Month," and one of her children's books was #1 on the Houston Barnes & Noble bestseller list.

"New in Hicksville" by Cathy M. Elliott. © 2001. Used by permission of the author.

"Mailbox Friend" by Ashley Blake. © 2001. Used by permission of the author. Ashley can be contacted at sunflowers90@hotmail.com.

YOU KNOW WHAT'S RIGHT

"The Interview" by Michele Wallace Campanelli. © 1999. Used by permission of the author. Michele Wallace Campanelli is a national bestselling author. Her works include short stories and several novels. Her personal editor is Fontaine Wallace, an instructor at Florida Institute of Technology. To contact Michele, go to www.michelecampanelli.com.

"No Turning Back" from *Do You Know What I Like about You?* by Cynthia Tobias. © 1998. Used by permission of the author.

Acknowledgments

"Attacked!" by Greg O'Leary. From *Small Miracles* by Yitta Halberstam and Judith Leventhal. © 1997. Used by permission.

"A Date to Remember" by Lori Salierno. From *Designed for Excellence*. © 1995. Used by permission of the author. Lori Salierno, CEO, Celebrate Life International. Dedicated to Developing Young Leaders of Integrity, 6060-N Lake Acworth Dr., Acworth, GA 30101. www.celebratelife.org.

"The Greatest Reward" by Liezl West. © 2000. Used by permission of the author.

"What Would Jesus Do?" by Katrina Cassel. © 1998. Used by permission of the author. Katrina is the mother of six and lives in southern Georgia. She is the author of *The Junior High Survival Manual* (Concordia Publishing House, 1998), *On the Homefront* (Concordia Publishing House, 1999), *Celebrate Creation* (Shining Star, 1999), and *The Christian Girl's Guide to Success* (Legacy Press, 2002).

"A New Way of Seeing" by Kima Jude. © 2000. Used by permission of the author.

"True to Me" by Sue Rhodes Dodd. © 2002. Used by permission of the author. Sue Rhodes Dodd is the president of Amethyst Enterprises, an editorial consulting firm in Tulsa, Oklahoma. She is married, has one daughter, and sings professionally.

"Goody Two-Shoes" by Debra White Smith. © 1998. Used by permission of the author. Debra White Smith is the author of the popular Seven Sisters series (Harvest House Publishers). Visit www.debrawhitesmith.com to read book excerpts and sign up for her newsletter.

Hang In There

"In the Storm" by Judy Gordon. © 1999. Used by permission of the author.

"Curt's Tears" by Kay Marshall Strom. © 2001. Used by permission of the author.

"Plum Purple City Lights" by Janet Lynn Mitchell. © 2002. Used by permission of the author. Janet Lynn Mitchell is an inspirational speaker and author of numerous articles and stories in compilations. Janet can be reached at janetlm@prodigy.net or faxed at 714-633-6309.

"He's My Brother" by Max Lucado. From *Traveling Light* by Max Lucado, © 2001, W Publishing Group, Nashville, Tennessee. Used by permission. All rights reserved.

"They Want Me for One Reason" by Dave Dravecky. Taken from *When You Can't Come Back* by Dave & Jan Dravecky with Ken Gire. Copyright © 1992 by Dave & Jan Dravecky. Used by permission of Zondervan Publishing House.

"My Favorite Tradition" by Lisa Strom, as told to Kay Marshall Strom. © 2001. Used by permission of the author.

"Beauty Restored" by Kimberly Shumate. © 2001 by Kimberly Shumate. Used by permission of the author. Adapted from *Standing on the Promises* © 2001 by Susan Wales, Multnomah Publishers, Inc.

"Unspeakable Terror" by Laura McDonald as told to Nancy Jo Sullivan. Adapted from *Moments of Grace* by Nancy Jo Sullivan. © 2000. Used by permission of Multnomah Publishers.

"Tornado!" by Tim Heaner as told to Linda Joyce Heaner. © 2001. Used by permission of the author.

"The Road of Life" by Jessica Appleton. © 2001. Used by permission of the author.

"Craig's Story" by Marty Wilkins. © 2001. Used by permission of the author.

"Surprised by God" by Rebecca St. James. From *The Dance of Heaven*, © 2001 by Becky Sowers, Multnomah Publishers, Inc. Used by permission of Rebecca St. James.

"After the Ice Cream Cones" by Amy J. Waddle. © 2001. Used by permission of the author. Amy resides in Clackamas, Oregon. She is currently attending Bethel College in Mishawaka, Indiana.

LOVE'S ALL IN THE FAMILY

"Feeling at Home" by Judy Gordon. © 2001. Used by permission of the author.

"A Father Like That" by Sandra Byrd. © 2001. Used by permission of the author. Sandra Byrd is the bestselling author of books for girls from ages

8–12. Her works include *The Inside-Out Beauty Book,* the Hidden Diary series, *Girl Talk: A Devotional,* and the Secret Sisters series.

"My Mom Understands" by Danae Jacobson. From *Things I've Learned Lately* by Danae Jacobson. © 2001. Used by permission of Multnomah Publishers.

"Happy Father's Day" by Alison Peters. © 2001. Used by permission of the author.

"Sweet Sixteen" by Shelly Teems Johnson as told to Gloria Cassity Stargel. © 1995. Used by permission of the author. Gloria Cassity Stargel, *Guideposts* writer, offers inspiration and encouragement to anyone facing turmoil in *The Healing: One Family's Victorious Struggle with Cancer.* www.brightmorning.com or 1-800-888-9529.

"Momma" by Paige Aich. © 2001. Used by permission of the author. "To my mom who will always be there for me." Paige Aich, age 14.

"Danger: My Mother" by Anne Goodrich. © 2001. Used by permission of the author. Anne Goodrich is a Web site designer in Kalamazoo, Michigan, a mother of three, and the creator of OhAngel!com (www.ohangel.com), an inspirational and angel e-card Web site.

"The Ladder Test" by Heidi Hess Saxton. © 1997. Used by permission of the author. Heidi Saxton has five books to her credit, including *Touched by Kindness.* For more about Heidi, go to www.christianword.com.

"Planting Love" by Nanette Thorsen-Snipes. © 2001. Used by permission of the author. Nanette Thorsen-Snipes has published more than 400 articles, columns, devotions, and reprints in publications and compilation books including: *Woman's World, Home Life, Breakaway, Stories for the Faithful Heart, Stories for the Extreme Teen's Heart, Stories for the Spirit-Filled Woman, God's Abundance,* and others. E-mail: jsnipes212@aol.com.

"Bathrobe Lunch" by Anne Goodrich. © 2002. Used by permission of the author. Anne Goodrich is a Web site designer in Kalamazoo, Michigan, the mother of three beautiful children, and creator of OhAngel!com (www.ohangel.com), an inspirational e-card Web site.

"Trunk of Treasures" by Nancy Jo Sullivan. From *My Sister, My Friend* by Nancy Jo Sullivan. © 2002. Used by permission of Multnomah Publishers.

"Just Like in the Movies" by Amanda Bowers. © 2001. Used by permission of the author.

"Dear Daddy" by Gary Smalley and John Trent, Ph.D. From *The Language of Love* by Gary Smalley and John Trent, Ph.D., a Focus on the Family book published by Tyndale House. Copyright © 1988, 1991 by Gary Smalley and John Trent, Ph.D. All rights reserved. International copyright secured. Used by permission.

WITH YOU ALL THE WAY

"Love Is…" by Danae Jacobson. From *Things I've Learned Lately* by Danae Jacobson. © 2001. Used by permission of Multnomah Publishers.

"The Kid with Green Hair" by Kay Marshall Strom. © 2001. Used by permission of the author.

"Letter to My Daughter" by Anne Goodrich. © 2001. Used by permission of the author. Anne Goodrich is a Web site designer in Kalamazoo, Michigan, the mother of three, and the creator of OhAngel!com (www.ohangel.com), an inspirational e-card Web site.

"The Winner" by John William Smith. From *Hugs to Encourage and Inspire* by John William Smith. © 1997. Used by permission of Howard Publishing.

"You Bring the Groom and I'll Bring the Cake" by Sue Buchanan. From *A Party Begins in the Heart* by Sue Buchanan, © 2001, W Publishing Group, Nashville, Tennessee. Used by permission. All rights reserved.

"A Debt of Hope" by Julie B. Gibson. From *Small Miracles for Women* by Yitta Halberstam and Judith Leventhal. © 2000. Used by permission of Arthur Pine Associates, Inc.

"Mrs. A." by H.S. From *Touched by Kindness* by Kim Boyce and Heidi Hess Saxton. © 2001 by Kim Boyce and Heidi Hess Saxton. Published by Servant Publications, P.O. Box 8617, Ann Arbor, Michigan 48107. Used by permission.

"The Day Cheering Stopped" by John C. Stewart as told to Gloria Cassity Stargel. © 2001. Used by permission. Gloria Cassity Stargel, *Guideposts* writer, offers inspiration and hope to anyone facing change or turmoil in *The Healing, One Family's Victorious Struggle with Cancer.*

Acknowledgments

www.brightmorning.com or 1-800-888-9529.

"The Eco-Challenge" by Rebecca St. James. From *The Dance of Heaven,* © 2001 by Becky Sowers, Multnomah Publishers, Inc. Used by permission of Rebecca St. James.

"Billy's Triumph" by Ern Grover. © 2000. Used by permission of the author. Ern and Anneke Grover are freelance writers who once worked with Corrie ten Boom. They operate a busy clock repair shop in Springvale, Maine. E-mail: erngrover@yahoo.com.

"My Brother's Keeper" by Shannon Kyle Morrow. Shannon Morrow is the sports editor for a weekly newspaper in northeastern California, where he lives with his wife, Traci, and daughter, Hannah. Other than backpacking, Shannon's interests include snowboarding and ultimate disc.

"Chocolate Cake Mystery" by H.S. From *Touched by Kindness* by Kim Boyce and Heidi Hess Saxton. © 2001 by Kim Boyce and Heidi Hess Saxton. Published by Servant Publications, P.O. Box 8617, Ann Arbor, Michigan 48107. Used by permission.

ANOTHER CHANCE

"Rainbow of Hope" by Judy Gordon. © 1999. Used by permission of the author.

"Choices" by Matt Johnson as told to Janet Schreur Cockrum. © 2000. Used by permission. Janet Schreur Cockrum, Ph.D., is a professor at the University of Tennessee at Knoxville in Child and Family Studies and the athletic director at Berean Christian School. She has published articles in *Decision, Aspire,* and *Virtue.* Matt Johnson is a student working toward a business degree. He continues to lead basketball camps for Spirit Express and speak to youth groups.

"Sudden Death" by Wendy Dunham. © 2001. Used by permission of the author. Wendy Dunham is a wife, mom, inspirational writer, and a registered therapist for differently abled children. Contact information: 3148 Lake Road, Brockport, NY 14420. (716) 637–0535.

"A Prisoner of Hope" by Darron Shipe as told to Rick Conner. Used by permission iUniverse. © 2001. Darron Shipe Ministry, P.O. Box 13526,

Richmond, VA 23225.

"My Story" by Olivia. From *Stories That Count,* © 2000 by Youth for Christ. Used by permission. All rights reserved.

"Vacation from God" by Teresa J. Cleary. © 1987. Used by permission of the author.

"The Haunting Smile" by Michael W. Smith. From *It's Time to Be Bold* by Michael W. Smith, © 1997, W Publishing Group, Nashville, Tennessee. Used by permission. All rights reserved.

"The Robber's Return" by Teresa Robotham. © 1999. Used by permission of the author.

"A Treasure Within" by S. J. Barksdale. © 2001. Used by permission of the author.

"Guns 'N' Prayer" by Tom as told to Muriel Larson. © 2001. Used by permission of the author.

"A Christmas Eve to Remember" by T. Suzanne Eller. © 2001. Used by permission of the author. T. Suzanne Eller is a freelance writer, author, and inspirational speaker ministering to teens, churches, and women. She can be reached at tseller@daretobelieve.org or www.daretobelieve.org.

Worth Thinkin' About

"The Future" by Melissa Ann Broeckelman. © 1999. Used by permission of the author.

"The Father's Anguishing Decision" by Carla Muir. © 1999. Used by permission of the author. Carla Muir is a freelance writer.

"Winning the Gold" by David Barnett. © 2000. Used by permission of the author. E-mail: dailyprayers@juno.com.

"The Party" by Lissa Halls Johnson. © 1999. Used by permission of the author. Lissa Halls Johnson is the author of thirteen novels including the bestseller, *Just Like Ice Cream,* and the China Tate series. Upcoming Web site: www.lissahallsjohnson.com.

"The Red Convertible" by Larry Christenson. From *The Renewed Mind* by Larry Christenson. © 1974. Used with permission from Bethany House

Publishers.

"Finding God in Colorado" by Kelly McGuiggan as told to Nancy Jo Sullivan.

"The Man in Your Eyes" by Ross Gunn IV. © 1998. Used by permission of the author. Ross is a graduate of Full Sail Film School and is entering the field of Christian film production.

"A Cross to Wear" by N. Bayless. © 2001. Used by permission of the author. N. Bayless lives in San Diego and is a seasoned writer who has published articles in major Christian magazines.

"Lighten Up!" by Jennifer Knapp. © 2001. Used by permission of the author.

"My Senior Year" by Heather Mezel as told to Robin Jones Gunn. © 1988. Used by permission of the author. Robin Jones Gunn is the bestselling author of over forty-five books, including *Mothering by Heart*, the Glenbrooke series by Multnomah Publishers, and the Christy Miller series.

"Gotcha!" by Steven J. Lawson. From *Absolutely Sure* by Steven J. Lawson. © 1999. Used by permission of Multnomah Publishers.

"No Accident" by Carlin Hertz. From *God Allows U-Turns* by Allison Bottke, © 2001, published by Promise Press, an imprint of Barbour Publishing, Inc., Uhrichsville, OH. Used by permission.

"Teen Santa" by Marjorie Gordon. © 1999. Used by permission of the author. Marjorie Gordon, a Christian author and speaker, lives in Auburn, Washington. Her aim is to glorify God in all her work.

It's a God Thing

"He Is…" by Anne Graham Lotz. From *Just Give Me Jesus* by Anne Graham Lotz, © 2000, W Publishing Group, Nashville, Tennessee. Used by permission. All rights reserved.

"A Father's Love" by Michael T. Powers. © 2001. Used by permission of the author. Michael T. Powers resides in Wisconsin with his wife, Kristi, and their two young boys. He is the author of the new book *Straight from the Heart: A Celebration of Life* and invites you to join the thousands on his daily inspirational e-mail list at www.michaeltpowers.com or e-mail him at michaeltpowers@aol.com.

"Silent Reminder" by Charles R. Swindoll. From *The Tale of the Tardy Oxcart* by Charles Swindoll, © 1998, Word Publishing, Nashville, Tennessee. Used by permission. All rights reserved.

"The Bible Smugglers" by Lindsay Willis. © 2000. Used by permission of the author.

"When I Say, 'I Am a Christian'" by Carol S. Wimmer. Adapted from Carol's poem "When I Say, 'I Am a Christian.'" © 1988. Used by permission of the author.

"The Inscription" by Linda M. Wall. © 2000. Used by permission of the author.

"Freedom Behind Bars" by Neely Arrington as told to Candy Arrington. © 2001. Used by permission. Neely Arrington is a tenth grade honor student. Candy Arrington is a freelance writer and youth discipleship leader. This is their first daughter-mother writing effort. They live in Spartanburg, South Carolina.

"Spray Painting for Jesus" by Ben Bryden as told to Barbara Major Bryden. © 2001. Used by permission of the author. Barbara Bryden has also been published in *More God's Abundance*. She enjoys writing devotionals and inspirational material and lives in Olympia, Washington. E-mail: barbbryden@yahoo.com.

"The Love Note" by Ken Jones. Used by permission of the author.

"Bernie Knows the Truth" by Ken Davis. Taken from *Fire Up Your Life* by Ken Davis. Copyright © 1995 by Ken Davis. Used by permission of Zondervan.